Improving Learni

What's the problem with literacy at college? How might everyday literacy be harnessed for educational ends?

Based on the first major study of literacy practices in colleges in the UK, this book explores the reading and writing associated with learning subjects across the college curriculum. It investigates literacy practices in which students engage outside of college, and teaching and learning strategies through which these can help support the curriculum. With insightful analyses of innovative practices, it considers ways of changing teaching practices to enable students to draw upon their full potential.

Recent research work has challenged the myth of individual student deficit, arguing cogently that people have 'funds of knowledge' from diverse and vibrant cultural roots, and that these have been misguidedly disqualified by the education system. It has claimed that different 'ways with words' can provide valuable resources for learning. However, the empirical exploration of this claim has lagged far behind the theoretical debate. *Improving Learning in College* resolves this by showing the integrity and richness of the literacy practices of a significant population, not previously the focus of such research: those who take vocational and academic courses in colleges. It addresses an issue which has not until now been developed within this research tradition: that of how these practices can not only be valued and validated, but also mobilised and harnessed to enhance learning in educational settings.

This book will interest all teachers, teacher–educators and researchers concerned with post-compulsory education and vocational education in compulsory schooling.

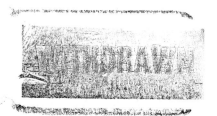

Improving Learning TLRP

Series Editor: Andrew Pollard, Director of the ESRC Teaching and Learning Programme

Improving Learning in College

Rethinking literacies across the curriculum

Roz Ivanič, Richard Edwards,
David Barton, Marilyn Martin-Jones,
Zoe Fowler, Buddug Hughes,
Greg Mannion, Kate Miller,
Candice Satchwell and June Smith

Routledge
Taylor & Francis Group

LONDON AND NEW YORK

First published 2009
by Routledge
2 Park Square, Milton Park, Abingdon, Oxon, OX14 4RN

Simultaneously published in the USA and Canada
by Routledge
29 West 35th Street, New York, NY 10001

Routledge is an imprint of the Taylor & Francis Group, an informa business

© 2009 Roz Ivanič, Richard Edwards, David Barton, Marilyn
Martin-Jones, Zoe Fowler, Buddug Hughes, Greg Mannion,
Kate Miller, Candice Satchwell and June Smith

Typeset in Charter ITC and Stone Sans by
Keystroke, 28 High Street, Tettenhall, Wolverhampton
Printed and bound in Great Britain by
TJ International Ltd, Padstow, Cornwall

British Library Cataloguing in Publication Data
A catalogue record for this book is available from the British Library

Library of Congress Cataloging in Publication Data
Improving learning at college: rethinking literacies across the
curriculum/Roz Ivanic . . . [et al.].
        p. cm.
     Includes bibliographical references.
  1. Developmental studies programs.   2. Underprepared
college students.   3. College students – Rating of.
  4. Literacy.   I. Ivanic, Roz.
  LB2331.2.I55 2009
  378.1′25–dc22   2008038022

ISBN10 0–415–46911–2 (hbk)
ISBN10 0–415–46912–0 (pbk)
ISBN10 0–203–88142–7 (ebk)

ISBN13 978–0–415–46911–1 (hbk)
ISBN13 978–0–415–46912–8 (pbk)
ISBN13 978–0–203–88142–2 (ebk)

Contents

Illustrations

Figures

Boxes

Tables

Authors

Roz Ivanič is Professor Emerita of Linguistics in Education at Lancaster University.

Richard Edwards is Professor of Education and Head of The Stirling Institute of Education at the University of Stirling.

David Barton is Professor of Language and Literacy and Director of the Lancaster Literacy Research Centre at Lancaster University.

Marilyn Martin-Jones is Professor of Languages in Education and Director of the MOSAIC Centre for Research on Multilingualism at the University of Birmingham.

Zoe Fowler is an independent research consultant.

Buddug Hughes is a PhD student at the School of Welsh at Bangor University.

Greg Mannion is a Senior Lecturer at The Stirling Institute of Education at the University of Stirling.

Kate Miller is a Research Fellow at The Stirling Institute of Education at the University of Stirling.

Candice Satchwell is the HE in FE Project Officer at the English Subject Centre of the Higher Education Academy, Research Associate at Lancaster Literacy Research Centre, Lancaster University, and a Senior Lecturer in the School of Academic Studies at Blackpool and the Fylde College.

June Smith is Curriculum Manager for Core Skills at Aberdeen College.

Series editor's preface

The *Improving Learning* series showcases findings from projects within ESRC's Teaching and Learning Research Programme (TLRP) – the UK's largest ever coordinated educational research initiative.

Books in the *Improving Learning* series are explicitly designed to support 'evidence-informed' decisions in educational practice and policy-making. In particular, they combine rigorous social and educational science with high awareness of the significance of the issues being researched.

Working closely with practitioners, organisations and agencies covering all educational sectors, the Programme has supported many of the UK's best researchers to work on the direct improvement of policy and practice to support learning. Over sixty projects have been supported, covering many issues across the lifecourse. We are proud to present the results of this work through books in the *Improving Learning* series.

Each book provides a concise, accessible and definitive *overview* of innovative findings from a TLRP investment. If more advanced information is required, the books may be used as a gateway to academic journals, monographs, websites, etc. On the other hand, shorter summaries and *Research Briefings* on key findings are also available via the Programme's website at www.tlrp.org.

We hope that you will find the analysis and findings presented in this book are helpful to you in your work on improving outcomes for learners.

Andrew Pollard
Director, TLRP
Institute of Education, University of London

Acknowledgements

Research projects of this scale emerge from a lot of work, discussion and goodwill. Our first thanks are to the senior managements, staff and students of the colleges that invited us into their institutions and supported and contributed to the work of the project. In particular, we would like to acknowledge the enormous contribution of the college-based researchers: Roy Anderson, Sharon Aspden, Dave Brown, Angela Brzeski, Jim Carmichael, Beryl Davies, Joyce Gaechter, Ian Gibb, Ronnie Goodman, Janet Gray, David Jarratt, Christine Kendrick, Tracey Kennedy, Joanne Knowles, Margaret Lewis, Sandra Mulligan, Christine Phillipson, Mike Ward, Sarah Wilcock, Anwen Williams, Andrea Wilson and Rosheen Young. They are busy professionals in their own right, but were sufficiently interested in teaching and learning to give time to this research alongside their teaching. They were willing to stand back from their own practices and assumptions, and to ask the sorts of questions which are at the heart of research. Without them, none of what follows would have been possible.

Our research teams at the universities included other members. We would particularly like to mention Daniel Chandler, Margaret Tooey, Marie Ashman and Mary Ashworth, all of whom made major contributions to the projects.

When trying to turn the initial ideas for the Literacies for Learning in Further Education (LfLFE) project into something feasible, advice from Carolyn Davidson, then of the Scottish Further Education Unit, proved invaluable. She brokered meetings with colleges in Scotland and helped to build user support for the project. She continued to support the project throughout as a member of the Advisory Group. We would also like to acknowledge the academic contribution of Mike Breen, who played a leading role in the development of the research project at the University of Stirling, only to retire prior to it beginning. Mike was critical to the initial conceptualising of the research and continued to support it as a member of the Advisory Group.

In Wales, two people played a crucial role in getting the Bilingual Literacies for Learning in Further Education (BiLfLFE) project off the ground. We thank Dr Ian Rees, the Director of Coleg Meirion Dwyfor, for his early commitment to the project, and we are very grateful indeed to Kathryn Jones for her key support at the outset and for her continued input to the project as consultant.

These projects were part of the Teaching and Learning Research Programme in the UK, funded by the Economic and Social Research Council (ESRC), Grants RES–139–25–0117 (LfLFE) and RES–39–25–0171 (BiLfLFE). As such, we gained a lot from engaging with colleagues on other projects funded within the Programme. We would like to acknowledge the support and encouragement we received from the Programme Directorate, in particular, Andrew Pollard, Kathryn Ecclestone and Steve Baron. The Advisory Groups consisted of stakeholders from England, Scotland and Wales from a range of organisations. They provided support and steerage on key issues as the projects progressed.

A special 'thank you' goes to Simon Pardoe of Publicspace. Towards the end of the LfLFE project we decided that a good way of communicating the outcomes of the project was through the production of a DVD for staff development purposes. Simon was commissioned to produce the DVD for us. In particular, the framework presented in Chapter 3 was initially developed by Simon Pardoe in conjunction with Roz Ivanič for use in the DVD. The discipline of communicating through this medium forced us to crystallise the outcomes of the project for those working in colleges. Simon's contribution to helping this shaping cannot be underestimated.

In the time-honoured way, while we would like to acknowledge the contribution of all those above to the outcomes of the project, we, the authors, take the responsibility for this book. We hope we have done justice to ourselves and to the efforts of all those who made the projects possible.

Introduction

The research projects underpinning this book

Two projects inform this book: the Literacies for Learning in Further Education (hereafter LfLFE) and the Bilingual Literacies for Learning (hereafter BiLfLFE) research projects. The projects were funded in the period January 2004 to August 2007 as part of Phase 3 of the United Kingdom's Teaching and Learning Research Programme (TLRP). These projects constitute the first major study of literacy practices in colleges in England, Scotland and Wales, exploring, in particular, the literacy practices associated with learning different subjects, the literacy practices in which students engage in their day-to-day lives outside of college, and the possible teaching and learning strategies through which the latter can help to support the former.

The research focused on the use, refinement and diversification of literacy events and practices to enhance learning across the curriculum. The intention was to achieve a critical understanding of the movement and flows of literacy practices in people's lives: how literacy practices are ordered and re-ordered, networked, traced or folded across domains (home–college, virtual–real, reading–writing), across social roles in students' lives, and what artefacts, processes and practices might mediate such interactions. The projects explored the literacy practices that each participant had accumulated during their life-course to date, the literacy practices required by their course of study and, crucially, different ways of harnessing students' everyday literacy practices to enhance their learning. In short, we explored the potential beneficial interaction between students' everyday literacy practices and the formal literacies required by their college learning. Details of the research design, methods and methodology are provided in the Appendix.

The three-year LfLFE project involved collaboration between two universities – University of Stirling and Lancaster University – and four further education colleges, two in Scotland – Anniesland College in Glasgow and Perth College – and two in England – Lancaster and Morecambe College, and Preston College. Over the three years of the project, the LfLFE

Table 0.1 Curriculum areas and units studied in the research: Scottish colleges

College	Curriculum area and selected units	SCQF level	Lecturer
Anniesland College, Glasgow	*Social Sciences* Higher History: Appeasement and the Road to War	*Level 6*	Jim Carmichael
	Higher History: Income and Wealth	*Level 6*	
	Intermediate with NC: Moral Philosophy	*Level 5*	
	Childcare NC Early Education and Childcare: Care and Feeding of Babies	*Level 4*	Rosheen Young
	HNC Childcare and Education: Assessment Approaches	*Level 7*	
	Accounts NC Business: Understanding Stock Control	*Level 4*	Janet Gray
	HNC Business Administration: Business Accounting	*Level 7*	
	Multi-media NC Higher: Multimedia	*Level 6*	Mike Ward
	HNC: Graded Unit	*Level 7*	

Perth College			Researched by
	Construction SVQ Bricklaying: Erect Masonry Structures	*Level 6*	Roy Anderson
	Scottish Progression Award Intermediate 1: Technology Craft Practices	*Level 4*	
	Childcare NC Early Education and Childcare: The Pre-school Child, Food, Clothing and Play	*Level 4*	Joyce Gaechter
	HNC Childcare and Education: Curriculum Approaches to Development and Learning	*Level 7*	
	Music and Audio HN Music: Creative Industries Infrastructure NQ Int. 2 Sound: Sound In-house Production	*Level 7* *Level 5*	Ronnie Goodman
	Hospitality HNC Professional Cookery + HNC/D Hospitality: Food Hygiene Intermediate	Level 7	Ian Gibb
	NQ Tourism and Hospitality: Food Hygiene Practices	*Level 5*	
	Gleneagles Patisserie Professional Chef Award	*Level 4*	

Key:

▪ Year 1 only; ▪ Years 1 and 2; ☐ Year 2 only

Table 0.2 Curriculum areas and units studied in the research: English colleges

College	Curriculum area and selected units	NQF level	Lecturer
Lancaster and Morecambe College	*Catering and Hospitality* Introduction to Catering and Hospitality	Level 1	Sarah Wilcock
	NVQ 2 Food and Drink Service	Level 2	
	Travel & Tourism NVQ 2 Travel Services: Working Overseas	Level 2	Dave Jarratt/ Sarah Wilcock
	BTEC National Diploma in Travel and Tourism: Visitor Attractions	Level 3	
	Media Studies AS Media Studies: Introduction to Media Studies	Level 3	Patrick Marsh
	Open College A Unit Media Studies	Level 2	
	English AS English Language and Literature: Poetry module	Level 3	Andrea Wilson
	City & Guilds 9483 FENTO Cert. in Adult Literacy: Subject Support	Level 3	
	Childcare Preparation for Employment	Level 3	Christine Phillipson
	Practical Work, Personal Development and Anti-discriminatory Practice	Level 2	

Preston College

Course	Level	Tutor
Business Administration Introductory Diploma units 1 and 2	Level 1	Christine Kendrick
OCR Higher Diploma in Administrative and Secretarial Procedures	Level 4	Angela Brzeski
English AS English Language and Literature: Language Production Module	Level 3	
Childcare CACHE Foundation in Caring for Young Children: Play and Practical Activities	Level 1	Joanne Knowles
BTEC National Diploma in Early Years: Professional Practice	Level 3	
Human Biology BTEC National Diploma in Applied Science: Workplace Practices	Level 3	Sandra Mulligan
A2 Level Human Biology: Genetics, Homeostasis and Ageing	Level 3	
BTEC First Diploma in Environmental Science	Level 2	
Construction National Diploma in Construction: Graphical Detailing	Level 3	Sharon Aspden
Foundation Award in Painting and Decorating	Level 1	Dave Brown
Intermediate Award in Painting and Decorating	Level 2	

Key:

■ Year 1 only; ▢ Years 1 and 2; ▢ Year 2 only

project researched the literacy practices associated with learning on thirty-two units of study in thirteen curriculum areas.

The 27-month BiLfLFE project researched the literacy practices in English and in Welsh of students on six units in three subject areas on two sites of Coleg Meirion Dwyfor in Dolgellau – the leading provider of bilingual and Welsh medium education at college level in Wales. The BiLfLFE project, while starting from the same fundamental premises as the LfLFE project, differed in two respects. First and foremost, its primary focus was on 'bilingual literacies' – that is the reading and writing practices of students who were bilingual in Welsh and English. The texts and practices studied on this project therefore used Welsh, English or a mixture of the two languages. Second, the BiLfLFE project started more than a year later than the LfLFE project, and was able to benefit from the understandings already reached by the LfLFE team, and to extend the work in new ways in a new context.

Scale and scope of the projects

The Literacies for Learning in Further Education project

The LfLFE research was divided between two countries, Scotland and England, with one university and two colleges involved in each country. At each university there were two researchers employed to undertake the research: one full time and one half time. At each college, there were four lecturers recruited to the research, one of whom had an internal co-ordinating role as a College-based Research Co-ordinator (CBRC). There was a Childcare lecturer in each college, and three other lecturers from widely differing areas. We studied two units at different levels from each of four subject areas in each of the four colleges – a unit consisting of a module of study, or a section of teaching over about twelve weeks. So, for example, in Lancaster and Morecambe College in England, we researched units of Media Studies, Catering, Travel and Tourism, and Childcare (the units studied are listed comprehensively in Tables 0.1 and 0.2). Issues over the equivalence of levels of units across the differing Education systems in England and Scotland had to be addressed early in the project in order to enable comparison. In addition, over 100 students were involved in the research, with approximately four from each unit researched. The research team responsible for each unit included the lecturer on the unit, the students taking the course, and a researcher from one of the universities.

Tables 0.1 and 0.2 show at a glance the immense diversity of subject areas, types of pedagogy and student populations encompassed by the project. The curriculum areas ranged from those mainly oriented towards occupational preparation, such as bricklaying, to those mainly oriented towards preparation for university entrance, such as moral philosophy. The types of pedagogy ranged from those based mainly on workplace simulation, such as Childcare: Promoting Play, to those using a more traditional classroom pedagogy, such as Advanced Subsidiary Level English Language and Literature: Poetry Module.

It is notable from Tables 0.1 and 0.2 that many of the units could not be studied across the full two years of the project. This is indicative of the turbulence and discontinuity in the policy context in England and Scotland within which the research was being conducted. The ESRC TLRP project entitled 'The Impact of Policy on Learning and Inclusion in the New Learning and Skills Sector' has documented the massive changes in the policy context over the period of our research, and their impact on teaching staff and pedagogic practice (see, for example, Coffield *et al.* 2005). This turbulence resulted in the college management and at times even the staff seconded to the project finding it very hard to participate as much as had been planned. As a result, in many cases, the lecturers involved in the research found that they were not able to teach the same unit throughout the research period. The effect on the research was, however, that we were able to extend it across an even greater diversity of curriculum areas and units of study, resulting in additional insights with broader inferences.

The Bilingual Literacies for Learning in Further Education project

The BiLfLFE project was smaller scale than LfLFE, in line with its more modest funding. One researcher was employed at the University of Birmingham, and three lecturers participated as college-based researchers in Coleg Meirion Dwyfor in Dolgellau. There were forty-six student participants. The Welsh project contributed data from two units in each of three subject areas: Early Years, Land-based Studies and Welsh. The curriculum areas were chosen both to compare with and to complement those researched on the larger project, and also to represent a wide spread of educational sites for literacies. Further details of this project and the curriculum areas are given in Chapter 7.

Uses of this book

As with other books in the *Improving Learning* series, the main groups of intended readers are people who can put the ideas into practice: college lecturers, providers of teacher education and professional development, managers and policy-makers. This includes not only specialists in language and literacy, but educators in all areas of the curriculum with an interest in improving learning at college, and a recognition of the role literacy plays in learning. The book will be relevant to courses of initial teacher development and continuing professional development in all sectors. In England and Wales it will be of particular use in Cert Ed, PGCE, LLUK Levels 3 and 4, and continuing professional development courses for lecturers in all subjects and vocational areas in post-compulsory education. In Scotland the book will support the teaching of the Teacher Qualification in Further Education, and a range of continuing professional development courses.

The research has implications for six overlapping areas of practice:

- for enhancing students' learning in curriculum subjects by drawing on the characteristics of their everyday literacy practices;
- for the provision of support for literacy development;
- for literacy aspects of the design of college curricula and qualifications;
- for academic research in the fields of literacy studies and education;
- for continuing professional development; and
- for practitioner research.

These implications are the subject of Part III of the book.

The projects were innovative in that designing, implementing and analysing the implications of the findings was built into the research design. In particular, the projects were designed in such a way that college lecturers would be involved in both *research actions for understanding* and *research actions for change*. That is, they were active participants in the initial research, and on the basis of the understandings this research produced, they designed what is usually known as 'action research' – changes in their practice aimed at improving students' learning. This provides a good model for practitioner research, with 'understanding' preceding 'change', and recognising that implications emerge throughout research, not just at the end.

This book makes a major contribution to the development of theory within Literacy Studies, and will be of interest to researchers in this field, and to students on courses focusing on literacy in educational contexts. The book will also provide a useful introduction to the topic of literacies for learning across the curriculum for researchers and research students interested in the broad field of educational research.

While the research was conducted in colleges of further education in the UK, the issues concerning the interface between literacies in different contexts, and the strategic implications of the research are of more general relevance. They are of relevance both to secondary education, with the increasing focus on a broader curriculum for 14–19, and to higher education, where in-service teacher qualifications are now being offered and required. As this book will focus on general principles concerning the nature of literacy practices in vocational and other courses, and the interface between these and students' literacy practices in other domains of their lives, it will be of interest to teachers, teacher–educators and researchers concerned with post-compulsory education, and with vocational education within compulsory schooling in all countries.

The structure of the book

Part I of the book (Chapter 1) introduces the key issues concerning literacies across the curriculum in college education, setting these issues in a policy context, and explaining our approach to literacy.

Part II (Chapters 2–5) presents the outcomes of the *research actions for understanding*, the research undertaken in Phases One and Two of the projects in which the university-based researchers and college lecturers worked together to investigate the literacy practices of the lecturers' own students and courses (for details of the research phases, design, methods and methodology, see Appendix). Chapters 2, 4 and 5 are each grounded in a particular set of research data. Chapter 3 is more overarching in that it presents the theoretical understandings about literacy practices derived from data analysis across all phases of the project, and sets out the analytical framework with which we make sense of the data in the rest of the book.

The four chapters of Part II of the book are sub-divided into two sub-sections, each dealing with one focal aspect of the research.

a) *Students' textually mediated lives (Chapters 2 and 3)*
   These two chapters are about students' everyday literacy practices. Chapter 2 analyses what students use reading and writing for in the different domains of their lives outside college, with detailed examples from the English and Scottish data. Chapter 3 takes these examples as a starting point for presenting the theoretical framework which underpins the rest of the book.
b) *The textual mediation of learning (Chapters 4 and 5)*
   These two chapters are about the literacy practices involved in learning across a range of curriculum areas. Chapter 4 analyses how students use reading and writing in the different aspects of their college lives, taking examples from the thirteen curriculum areas in the English and Scottish colleges. Chapter 5 takes the specific example of Childcare which was studied in common across all five colleges in Scotland, England and Wales, drawing out the similarities and differences in pedagogic practice in this curriculum area.

Part III of the book (Chapters 6–9) draws out implications of the research which was presented in Part II of the book for teaching and learning in a wide range of settings, and for educational theory. Chapter 6 focuses on fine-tuning literacy practices for learning. It describes and discusses a selection of the changes in practice made in the Scottish and English colleges showing how the understandings reached through the *research actions for understanding* (in Chapters 2–5) were translated into implications for practice in the same pedagogic settings. In Chapter 7 we take into account the concern practitioners often express that research is not relevant to them because their context is different. Moving beyond the immediate settings of the research presented in Part II of the book, Chapter 7 extends the analysis to the very different sociolinguistic and educational context in Wales. The chapter focuses particularly on bilingual literacies in students' everyday lives, and on the issue of harnessing these resources for learning on courses in a bilingual educational context. This illustrates how research from one context can be recontextualised into another, and also draws out implications for practitioners wishing to conduct similar research in their own contexts. Chapter 8 takes as its starting point the specific example of the changes in practice which were made in a Sound In-house Production unit, and discusses metaphors for drawing upon literacy practices in students' everyday lives to enhance their learning on their college courses. In so doing, it develops implications for theorising mobility of communicative resources from one context to another. Chapter 9 provides an overview of the research, summarising the findings, exploring inferences arising from them, and suggesting their more far-reaching implications.

Each chapter includes vignettes to help illustrate the points of discussion and pictures taken by researchers and students during the course of the project.

Part I

What are the issues?

Chapter 1

Literacies as a resource for learning in college

Literacy in public discourses: moral panics and crisis narratives

International literacy day: one in five people can't read this!

Young people seen losing the love of reading

Study links drop in test scores to decline in time spent reading

Few advances in adult literacy made in last decade

As these newspaper headlines suggest, we are bombarded almost daily with crisis narratives, the notion that something is not working as it should or could. That there is a problem to be addressed, or that there has been a decline in some shape or form is a constant theme of media discourse. It seems to be endemic to social change that these changes are in some ways seen as marking the decline or end of something. Behind such narratives are a certain fear and often the notion of some golden age in the past against which the present can and should be judged. When the motor car was introduced, it was seen by some as the harbinger of an age of community and religious decline. Mobility would encourage people to change their habits of local and religious commitment. It is true that such changes might have played a role in the evolution of different social habits, but whether they marked a decline is a different question. More recently, the advent of the internet and mobile technologies have similarly been surrounded by crisis narratives as to their negative influence on social practices, in particular people's capacity to communicate 'properly' and to engage in 'appropriate' social interaction.

In education, we are similarly surrounded by such crisis narratives. Almost annually we are confronted with newspaper headlines that standards are falling, education is not producing the results it did, should and so on. 'Literacy' is often singled out as a target for such attacks. There are dire warnings: that young people can no longer write to the standards which are assumed to have existed in some previous period of time; that they engage in non-standard forms of communication, such as texting on mobile phones; that people no longer read literature; that people coming through or returning to education are no longer as able as an earlier generation to read and write and understand as much as would have been the case. Employers constantly complain about the literacy standards of school and college leavers and graduates. The complaints are ubiquitous, the sense of crisis endless.

How as educators do we respond to such crisis narratives? Often we are contributors to them, but should we be? As educators do we not have a responsibility to stand back and consider the situation more dispassionately, to examine the evidence? It does not take much reading of history to realise that crisis narratives have surrounded education since its inception as a publicly funded practice. And perhaps that is unsurprising given the weight that is placed upon education to resolve the ills of society. In this situation, the responsibility is twofold. First, to examine the historical and social scientific evidence of what is claimed in such crisis narratives. Second, where appropriate, where there is robust evidence, to challenge those narratives.

This book draws upon evidence from a study of a specific context – college learning in the UK – to raise questions about such crisis narratives around student literacy, and to put forward ways in which both the debate about educational practices and the practices themselves can be reframed in a more positive way. It seeks to challenge some of the moral panics about literacy and to suggest that the issue is not so much the extent of students' literacy capabilities, but more the sheer abundance of different possibilities for literacy that are being engendered by the changes in society and technology we are experiencing in the developed world. With the advent of new technology, and with the globalised spread of new technoscapes (Appadurai 1990; Kress 2003), we have seen the rapid diversification of artefacts (for example, new software) and of textual resources (for example, new genres such as websites and blogs) for communication within institutional and life-world contexts, and we have seen the opening up of new possibilities for literacy (for both print and screen literacies). Here, rather than a decline in literacy, we are witnessing the multiplication of literacies.

The crisis narratives are often based on simplistic interpretations of standardised and problematic literacy test results, yet there are a wide range of literacy practices at play in most people's everyday lives, of which educators are often unaware. In real life, people do not read and write in a vacuum: they use reading and writing to get things done. Literacy is embedded in the rich and varied activities of people's lives. Indeed, one might argue that the most salient factor in the contemporary communicative landscape is the sheer abundance and diversity of possibilities for literacy, as the range of artefacts and genres grow, diversify and hybridise. Literacies proliferate in response to social change and to the affordances of new technologies. The threat to the educational establishment may not be the individual student's so-called literacy 'deficit', so much as the increasing abundance of text and screen literacies: the rich multimodality of communicative practices, and their ever-increasing hybridisation, wh. precisely cannot be reduced easily, if at all, to a single standard against which all literacy is measured.

As the communicative landscape grows in possibilities, so the artefacts and media are taken up by people in different and diverse ways in order to take and make meaning, communicate and do things through meaningful activity. In other words, there is the opportunity to explore the inherent creativity in the ways in which people use and do literacy, which, rather than be decried as a loss of standards, can be embraced as the achievements of people making meaning and communicating for themselves and others in their lives. Thus texting, for instance, like shorthand, Morse code, semaphore and the writing of telegrams in different contexts, is not necessarily a falling away from a standard of extended prose – the haunting of writing by liberal education – but a creative use of newly available technology through which to communicate and make meaning. The mundane practices through which communication is transformed from one medium into another become sites of communicative creativity.

The moral panics and crises of literacy might then be seen partly as a crisis of an educational and cultural milieu, a powerful minority schooled in particular forms of literacy, who fear for their dominance, insofar as the imposition of certain standards is constantly under challenge. We witness this in relation to debates about high culture and popular entertainment. A similar dynamic is in play around reading and writing, where a norm is established of extended prose as a foundation in reading and writing: a norm drawn from particular forms of culture. Magazines, games, reality television, and other forms of popular culture are by contrast positioned as inherently inferior.

Abundant possibilities for communication – for uses of literacy – are being engendered by wider changes in society. These are made possible by new technologies – screen as well as page – and by the social mobilities and migrations that bring different groups into contact with one another, which necessitate different forms of communication. The crisis is therefore one not of literacy or its lack, but of the very crisis narrative itself. We need to reframe our understanding of the issues if we are to find ways of addressing the future, or we are going to be caught within the dilemmas of the past.

The research projects we write about in this book were borne out of a concern that the ways in which we generally understand literacy do not help educators and that, to some extent, we set up students to fail, because we implicitly or explicitly 'buy into' the crisis narratives that circulate more broadly. These shape our pedagogic practices and lead to self-fulfilling prophecies that students are not capable of appropriate forms of communication. The end result of this is fault finding – with students, with teachers, with lecturers. This is not a productive educative response or position. The situation is far more complex and nuanced. We need to explore the evidence, and its possible implications.

d nature of students' communicative resources is a central
ion generally and more specifically for the research projects
in this book. The book draws on this research in order to
 analyse students' capabilities in terms of literacy practices in
domains of their lives, and the nature of literacies for learning
in a range f curriculum subjects. It then provides examples of changes in
pedagogic practice which are more resonant with students' everyday uses
of literacy, and discusses consequent factors to take into account when
designing learning activities.

The aims of the book are to challenge the widespread assumption that a
simple lack of literacy holds back students, to show the range and sophisti-
cation of their uses of literacy in their everyday lives, and to demonstrate
how these literacy practices may be translated for more effective teaching
and learning. It has often been claimed that different 'ways with words' can
provide valuable translatable capacities for learning, if properly understood
by educators. However, the empirical exploration of this claim has lagged
far behind the theoretical debate. This book will contribute to this line of
research first by showing empirically the integrity and richness of the
literacy practices of a significant student body: those who take up vocational and academic courses in colleges in the UK. More significantly,
however, it will address an issue which has, to date, not been developed
within this research tradition: that of how these practices can be not only
valued and validated, but also folded into the curriculum to enhance
learning in educational settings.

Colleges in the UK: diverse and dynamic educational provision

Colleges are diverse and dynamic environments that play a crucial role in
the lifelong learning and skills agendas of the UK, yet they are 'the poor
relation' in terms of research. While a substantial amount of research has
been devoted to all stages of compulsory schooling and to higher education,
very few researchers have made colleges their research focus. This book
takes a step towards redressing this balance.

Further Education colleges are a core part of the education service in the
UK. Traditionally they provided occupational qualifications for school
leavers and the bulk of their full-time students are still aged 16 to 19.
However, over the years, the scope of what they provide and the profile of
their students has changed significantly. Most UK colleges now provide
educational opportunities from basic education through to higher education, as do community colleges and two-year colleges in Canada and
the USA. They also provide both academic and occupational qualifications.
The age range of students can vary from 14 to the elderly. Many of the
lecturers enter from previous occupations, often moving into teaching of
courses related to the areas in which they previously worked. Not all have

qualifications at degree level and not all are teacher trained on entry, but it is increasingly the norm for all college teaching staff to be trained and to undertake significant professional development during their careers.

The diversity of college education in the UK is also impacted upon by the fact that Further Education colleges sit as institutions within different policy contexts. At the time of the research (2004–07), the education systems in England, Scotland and Wales were different in some respects. In terms of policy and funding they were governed by different governments and funding bodies – the Learning and Skills Council in England, the Scottish Funding Council in Scotland and *Adran Plant, Addysg, Dysgu Gydol Oes a Sgiliau* (the Department of Children, Education and Lifelong Learning and Skills of the Welsh Assembly Government) in Wales. This was also the case to a greater or lesser extent in relation to curriculum and assessment. The Scottish curriculum is governed by one body, the Scottish Qualifications Authority (SQA), which oversees all Scottish qualifications other than those offered by universities. In addition, Scottish colleges can also offer courses governed by English awarding bodies, such as City and Guilds. In England and Wales, the Qualifications and Curriculum Authority (QCA) is a central body responsible for establishing consistent standards, subject criteria and performance descriptions, but there is a vast array of awarding bodies which convert these into programme specifications and qualifications: bodies such as the Business and Technology Education Council (BTEC), and City and Guilds. There are also many awarding bodies devoted to particular curriculum areas such as the Council for Awards in Children's Care and Education (CACHE) that specialises in Childcare programmes of study and awards.

Young people tend to go to college for a variety of reasons:

- They prefer to be in a college environment rather than continue at school.
- They need to re-take exams failed at school.
- They want to augment their existing qualifications for entry into work or university.
- They want to take occupation-related subjects or qualifications not offered at school.

Older people tend to go to college:

- to train or retrain in a different occupation;
- to study in a local setting to increase their qualifications having left school without them;
- to expand their horizons and to enhance the quality of their lives on a personal level.

For these reasons, the students at colleges are widely diverse and of differing ages, backgrounds and abilities. The likelihood is that the students have not opted for an academic course of study in their lives up to this point, although many mature students embark on academic careers through the college route.

Box 1.1   Introduction to Catering and Hospitality: a typical student group

A typical class of students taking an introductory course in hospitality and catering included: a majority of young people straight from school with low-level qualifications; two slightly older students who had taken higher-level qualifications in academic subjects in school, but then switched to a more practical subject area; one mature student from Nigeria who had a degree in Biology; and a mature student from Hong Kong. In terms of literacy, these students had widely varying experiences, expectations and capabilities, but they were all expected to undertake the same course content, using the same teaching materials and the same assessment tools. As with many of the courses we researched, there was a focus on practical work, but there was also a substantial weight given to recording in written form the practical experience gained, and learning – through classroom instruction – about conceptual framings of understanding underpinning the occupation for which they were training.

While the students described in Box 1.1 and the other students in our projects were pursuing their courses in a variety of subject areas and at a variety of levels, they were encountering and using a range of different forms of reading and writing to mediate their learning. These literacy practices were both generic, in relation to studying at college, and specific, in relation to studying a particular curriculum area.

The role of literacies in learning

We view learning as consisting of three components: the cognitive, the practical and the communicative. The commonly used discourse of 'theory and practice' can be said to embrace the cognitive and practical, but we suggest that the communicative element tends to be invisible or marginalised in such discourses. In educational contexts such as a preschool playgroup, a GCSE science classroom, a Painting and Decorating workshop, or an electronics company which takes on apprentices, some learning may take place without any use of language. For example, in a Painting and Decorating workshop, the students may learn to hang wallpaper without a lot of talking or use of written instructions. However, an observer does not have to look far to see spoken conversations, explanations and instructions, or written guidelines, books, printed sheets and computer screens, all using language as a resource for the development of capabilities, knowledge and understanding. People performing the roles of teacher, lecturer, trainer or instructor almost certainly do so through language. They may be physically present, and/or embodied in documents, materials or computer programmes. In such settings, spoken and written language are often the major vehicles through which teaching and learning take place.

This research focuses particularly on *written* language. The starting point for the research is that the majority of learning is textually mediated, where text is taken to include anything which carries meaning through written language (usually in combination with other semiotic modes), for example, books, websites, whiteboards, notes, handouts, assignments. The list is as long as the possibilities for literacy allow. A fundamental principle underlying the research is that communication, including literacy, is integral to the learning and teaching of all subjects, and not a discrete set of skills to be learnt alone. It is therefore the responsibility of all educators to consider the communicative aspects of pedagogic practices. This is at the heart of the discussion within this book.

Following Lee (1996) we view literacy as a 'resource' for learning across the curriculum. This is in the tradition of work on the role of language in learning (Vygotsky 1934; Britton 1970), and on writing across the curriculum (Russell 1991). We were researching the literacy practices in which students participate in order to be successful in learning the content (however broadly conceived that content may be in terms of knowledge, understanding and capabilities) of their occupational, academic or leisure courses, and, where necessary, in demonstrating that learning in order to gain qualifications through assessment tasks.

Although learning across the curriculum can provide purposeful contexts for literacy learning, this was not our focus. Our focus was on the other direction in the equation: the ways in which reading and writing act as resources for the learning of content; that is, what have been termed by some (e.g., Wyatt-Smith and Cumming 2003) as 'curriculum literacies'. Inevitably, this brought into focus questions of what counts as literacy and the differential values placed upon different literacy practices.

Conceptualising 'literacy'

A range of initiatives in the UK have focused on the induction of people of all ages into at least 'functional', 'basic', 'core' or 'key' literacy and numeracy, and on 'essential' communication skills, computer literacy and literacy-dependent so-called 'transferable skills'. Our research projects sought to complement and inform practice and policies in relation to such initiatives. However, our work started from a critique of the policy discourse, which is based on a traditional view of literacy. Traditionally, the term 'literacy' has been used in the singular, referring to people's ability to read and write particular forms of texts. Literacy has been taken to mean

and writing formal paper-based texts using predetermined rules
ing the use of a national language. This view treats literacy as an
autonomous value-free attribute lying within the individual – a set of
singular and transferable cognitive technical skills which can be taught,
measured and tested at a level of competence against pre-specified standards. This way of viewing literacy is situated within a view of learning as
the acquisition of knowledge and skills through direct instruction, rather
than learning through participation.

We saw policy to be privileging certain forms of reading and writing,
which were established as the correct ones to be taught within the contexts
of education. These are often associated with more extended uses of
reading and writing and particular genres – for example, essays – and are
embedded in standards against which individuals are assessed. This
approach arises from the assumption and leads to an idea that literacy can
be taught, learnt and demonstrated independent of a context of use, and
to attempts to measure 'how much' literacy each individual has. This then
becomes a driver for the perceived success or failure of the education
system and individual teachers. (For further discussion see Smith 2005a;
Miller and Satchwell 2006.)

This view has been challenged by researchers of the everyday, certain
branches of cultural studies and those developing literacy studies. It is the
latter that has informed the work of our projects. The literacy studies
approach offers an alternative view of literacies as multiple, emergent and
situated in particular social contexts (Barton *et al.* 2000; Barton 2001,
2007; Baynham 1995; Gee 2000, 2003; Barton and Hamilton 1998). In this
view, the term 'literacies' is used in the plural to indicate that there are
many different ways of reading and writing for different purposes and
within different cultural values and practices. The focus is on what is read
and what is written, where, how, by whom, why and under what conditions. This meshes with the tradition of locating learning within sociocultural practices of participation that has become increasingly influential
in education (e.g., Lave and Wenger 1991; Wenger 1998). It is an approach
that encourages us to talk differently about how documents get read and
written as embedded in the everyday and often mundane purposes and
activities of life, including education. In this view, literacy practices are
naturalised within the contexts of their use. In other words, they become
taken for granted and, as we shall see, often not viewed as literacy as such.

The key concepts in this view of literacy are 'literacy event' and 'literacy
practice'. The term 'literacy events' was first used by Shirley Brice Heath
(1983) to describe observable actions or groups of actions in which text
plays a role. In our research, our starting point was to note the wide range
of literacy events which go to make up college life. Walking along the
corridor in one college, we saw a group of students eagerly studying a
noticeboard. They were students on a Stage Production course, needing to
find out the rehearsal schedule and when they would be 'called'. In another

area, we saw a group of students smoking at a table. Nearby was a notice-board which had on it, among other things, a notice saying 'No smoking permitted in this area', yet there was no area designated where they would be able to smoke. In the classrooms and other learning spaces around the college, we saw a teacher making a spidergram with many coloured pens on a whiteboard, a student working at a computer screen and consulting two books and her A4 pad at the same time. All of these were 'literacy events': individual instances of the use of reading and writing which we were able to use as data to build an understanding of literacies for learning in college.

The use of the term 'practices' extends this idea to refer to regularly occurring ways of doing things with texts. This leads to a focus on differences in literacy practices from one context to another, and on the purposes, values, knowledge, expectations and relations of power which are inscribed in them. So, for example, we noted that reading practices, such as responses to public notices, depend not on how well the readers are able to process the text, but on context, purpose and relevance. We will elaborate on the distinction and relationship between literacy events and literacy practices in Chapter 3.

Literacy studies embraces the forms of reading and writing associated with screen technologies as well as those of the page. The increasing use of information and communication technologies brings with it both challenges and possibilities of combining icons/pictures with words and representing them in different ways, often combining different modes of communication. Thus digital literacy, multimodality (Kress 2003) and multiliteracies (New London Group 1996; Cope and Kalantzis 2000) have emerged as important concepts in understanding new forms of literacy. Similarly, Lemke's work (1998) on the post-compulsory curriculum in science suggests that students must learn to co-ordinate and use multiple literacies in an integrated manner across different genres and across diverse semiotic modes (verbal, visual and written), even when not using digital technology. We therefore see a far more complex semiotic landscape than that framed in discourses of functional literacy, one which points to hybridity and multiplicity. This is part of the abundance to which we have already referred.

Rather than working with those crisis narratives and the moral panics about literacy, then, we are interested in the pluralisation of literacy practices and the possibilities they have for pedagogic practice. For educators, the issue becomes not a lack of literacy among students and potential students, but the relationships that can be built between their everyday literacy practices and those of the formal curriculum. Here we have to be careful of course in our use of terminology. 'Everyday' does not only embrace what goes on outside of colleges, but can encompass the more informal practices in which students engage in colleges as part of their learning of the subject. For many students, their learning is folded into and entwined in their everyday lives. Similarly 'formal' does not only relate to the curriculum. Students regularly engage with other institutions as part of their everyday activities – for example, banks, local government – about which there can also be degrees of formality. The concepts we use therefore are working concepts and as such are slippery.

Drawing on data from the projects, we point to the ways in which viewing literacy as sets of socially situated practices rather than as skills can open up possibilities for pedagogy that challenge some of the central assumptions of dominant policy and media discourses. We challenge the individual skills discourse and the deficit discourse of blame, developing a socially situated approach to literacy.

Drawing on vernacular practices to enhance learning

Literacy studies, as indicated above and further elaborated in Chapter 3, views literacy practices as socially situated. It is part of a wider body of work that over the years has sought to explore the diversity of literacy practices in which children, young people and adults engage (e.g., Keddie 1970; Gonzalez *et al.* 2004; Hull and Schultz 2002; Pahl and Rowsell 2005; Mahiri 2004). This work has not only demonstrated the rich variety of literacy practices in which people of all ages engage as part of their daily lives, but also that these are not always mobilised as resources within education provision.

Research has shown that, for many students, entering further or higher education involves a renegotiation of identity, that the education system privileges certain literacy practices over others, and that studying seems to have little in common with the vernacular ways of knowing, valuing and communicating which students bring with them from other domains of their lives. This lack of relation raises an important theoretical issue for literacy studies: if literacy practices are socioculturally situated, to what extent are the boundaries between one context and another impermeable?

The task of the LfLFE project was not only to examine curriculum and students' vernacular literacy practices, but also to develop and research the impact of changes in practice that seek to mobilise what we termed 'border literacies'. By 'border literacies' we meant those reading and writing practices in other domains of students' lives – home, work, community – that are, or have the potential to be, situated also in the educational domain, and may therefore be mobilised to support student learning, as represented in Figure 1.1.

The LfLFE project built on a pilot study which found that most college students engaged in a sophisticated and complex variety of literacy practices outside the college which were not mobilised into college-related literacy events (Smith 2004). It was this study that led us to conceive our task initially to uncover the creativity in people's everyday semiotic practices, to identify *'border literacy practices'* (see Figure 1.1), and to support the *'border crossing'* of literacy practices from the everyday to

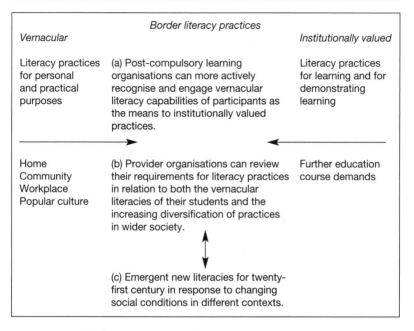

Figure 1.1 Border literacy practices: drawing on vernacular literacy practices to enhance educational opportunities

college. This was in order that these literacy practices can become resources for learning in the teaching and assessment associated with attainment of qualifications. Thus our interest in concepts of mobility and situatedness, and the potential contradiction between them, within this project.

These concerns also raise the issue of the ways in which 'context', 'domain', 'site' and 'setting' are conceptualised. Concepts such as 'context' are often thought of in a container-like and bounded sense, but this is not productive for theorising the interface between informal and formal practices. It is more useful to think in terms of an arena of activity with fluid boundaries, in which context does not pre-exist practice but co-emerges through and with it. The issue of how to theorise this fluidity was central to the research.

Our interest in these conceptual issues is part of wider debates in and around what have become termed social theories of learning (e.g., Tuomi-Gröhn and Engeström 2003), and around notions of the formal and vernacular. Metaphors of boundaries and borders, and of boundary zones, boundary objects and border-crossing abound in our project, as they do elsewhere in the social sciences and humanities (Edwards and Fowler 2007). A lot of this discussion and the concepts associated with it have been generated by addressing questions of context and how to develop a relational rather than contained understanding of learning (Chaiklin and

Lave 1996, Edwards *et al.* 2009). Our immediate concern in the LfLFE project ties in with these wider debates elsewhere.

Conclusion

To summarise, we view literacy practices as socially situated, which places a focus on context and forms of participation for learning. This raises the issue of how, if literacy practices are situated or contextualised, they can also be mobilised across contexts to be resources for learning. Theoretically, this challenges our understanding of concepts such as 'mobility', 'context', 'border', 'border-crossing', 'situatedness' and 'practice'. Empirically, this raises questions about the adequacy of the formulation that students do or could mobilise their literacy practices from their everyday lives as resources for learning within their college courses. These issues are at the heart of this research, and will be the main focus of Chapter 8.

Part II

What does the research tell us?

Chapter 2

What students do with reading and writing in their everyday lives

We worked closely with students to explore the types of reading and writing that they did other than college work. This chapter offers an overview of the range and diversity of these students' literacy practices. Overall, this chapter illustrates the wide range of reading and writing that students generally participate in as part of their everyday lives and strongly challenges certain over-generalised portrayals of college students as lacking in literacy. We show how everyday uses of literacy are not to be dismissed, but are complex practices comprising capabilities which are often invisible in college. (For further detail about this aspect of the research, see Smith 2005b, 2006; Smith and Edwards 2004.)

Box 2.1 Researching students' everyday literacy practices: the lecturers' perspective

Before I did the project I wouldn't have said to them 'what do you read at home?' or 'what do you read in your job?'. . . but having asked them, I realise that they do a lot of reading, even though they say that they don't read at all. When you start actually talking to them, all of a sudden they've got all this literacy going on and I thought, well, other students must do similar things too.

Sandra Mulligan, Science teacher at Preston College

Like many lecturers, I think I would have approached my students with a view that they were individuals that perhaps didn't read very much, that had a limited range of skills in terms of literacy, but the reality has been that we've discovered that students' literacy practices are far more complex, interesting and different than perhaps we might have assumed.

Jim Carmichael, Social Sciences lecturer
at Anniesland College, Glasgow

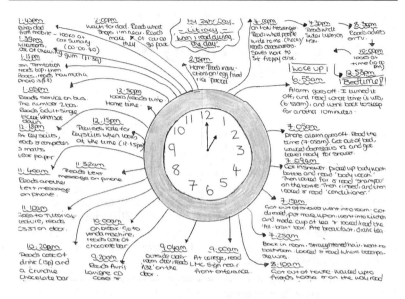

Figure 2.1 An example of a 'clock-face' completed by a student showing the reading and writing she did in her everyday life

Reading and writing can serve many different purposes in different settings. Students were often surprised when we identified the different kinds of reading and writing that they did as 'literacy', and this reflected how some literacy practices are validated as such by institutions such as schools and colleges whereas other kinds of reading and writing are not. Aaron Bassett, a student participant studying at Anniesland College, said: 'What the literacies project really has helped me to realise is that it's not just in essays and it's not just in novels where you use literacy, it's really in my day-to-day life.'

Literacy practices are set within the context of the lived experiences of students across different domains of their lives, draw upon many different technologies and are used for many purposes. The data were coded drawing upon the six areas of everyday life which were identified by Barton and Hamilton (1998) for categorising vernacular literacies: personal communication, private leisure, organising life, documenting life, sense-making and social participation. For the purposes of presenting the data in this chapter we have made a further distinction between domains of students' lives and uses of literacy, since both ways of cross-cutting the data provided revealing insights about the diversity of practices. Figure 2.2 provides an overview of the matrix we use in the rest of this chapter to delineate the dimensions of that diversity: five domains of life outside college, and six uses of literacy in everyday life. While these categories provide a useful way of organising the data, a single literacy practice might fit within a number of categories and

Uses of reading and writing	Domains of everyday life				
	Family	Leisure	Work	Religion	Peer-group and community
Communication					
Organising life and getting things done					
Documenting					
Finding things out and taking part					
Learning and sense-making					
Pleasure					

Figure 2.2 Dimensions of diversity in everyday literacy practices

the categories themselves are overlapping. In some cases, a use of literacy may be more or less specific to a domain. For example, 'reading and writing for pleasure' is associated mainly with the 'Leisure' domain of everyday life. However, this is not a simple one-to-one relationship, since the pleasure of, for example, reading to children, is part of the 'Family' domain too. In the figure, dotted lines indicate that the categories are not watertight, but that a literacy practice might serve purposes in more than one domain, and/or might combine two or more uses of reading and writing.

Literacy practices in different domains of students' lives

People's engagement with literacy depends on the patterning of their lives. In this section we focus on the ways in which literacy practices are shaped by the domains of social life.

Family

Many literacy practices are associated with being part of a family. For some of the younger students, being part of a family meant that they did not have to take responsibility for dealing with the bureaucracies of household bills, bank accounts and so forth. Older students and those living alone often talked about the systems that they had developed for dealing with these bureaucracies. These literacy practices often involved attending to two or more texts at the same time, and complex integration of reading and writing as documents were read and responded to according to personal circumstances.

Being part of a family also related to private leisure activities. Some students read aloud to children. Peter read Harry Potter novels aloud to his six-year-old brother. Katy read to her son and took pride in his enthusiasm for this practice: she described her son as 'absolutely obsessed by books'. Eve shared books with her young son, although many of these were picture books rather than containing a written narrative. Paul talked about 'doing a lot of reading with the kids'. He was surprised by how much reading he did with the children and he did not always find this easy: 'I can read, I can read quite well but when you're reading to the kids it's reading out loud and the two of them are listening – it's quite hard work.' He thought that 'trying to do voices' while reading aloud made the reading more difficult.

Leisure

Although students often asserted that they were not readers and did not read books, the majority of students gradually revealed a wealth of reading that they did as part of their leisure activities. Students read fiction and non-fiction books, magazines, newspapers, encyclopaedia, Ceefax and Sky, digital TV menus, the internet, and games during their leisure time. Often the students had not previously thought about these practices as reading. However, students who wrote as part of their leisure were more likely to associate this activity with literacy. Students had a wide range of enthusiasms including football, cars, horoscopes, family history, computer gaming, all types of music, dog breeding, to name but a few (see Box 2.2 for an example). A range of literacy practices mediated their engagement in their leisure activities, often involving both reading and writing, and purposeful shifting of attention between texts, or from screen to text. The purposes for reading and writing for leisure include not only enjoyment, but also all the other uses of literacy exemplified in the next section.

Box 2.2   Carol: reading and writing across different domains of her life

Carol was a Painting and Decorating student. She was active in her local Christian church and she had become involved in a local history project it was running. She decided to do this collaboratively with her sister and cousin. Every Wednesday afternoon, the three young women spent time researching their family tree and the history of the house that they lived in. They went to the local records office to consult registers of births, marriages and deaths. They had loaded a program on family trees onto their family computer and they worked together inputting details from an old copy of their family tree, photocopies they had made of relevant documents, and information they had jotted down in the records office: 'one of us sat at the computer, one of us looking at the family tree and one of us jotting things down – there's quite a lot of work involved in it'.

Carol's sister had bought a wardrobe which Carol found easy to put up following instructions – she realised that her sister would not be able to do this. She read through all the instructions, checked that she had all the pieces, and then did it step by step. This was a practical activity which Carol felt confident with. Carol also had to follow instructions on how to fill in her passport. She found these instructions difficult to follow: 'It's a big form, I just get put off. Because there's so many different sections and none of it normally makes sense.'

Carol's reading of books was episodic: 'I've read loads recently, but I do tend to go through phases of not reading anything for months and months.' She was easily distracted so liked to read in a quiet space, 'which is sometimes quite difficult' in her busy family home.

She discussed the relative value of different modes of communication: 'If she emails, then I email back; if she writes then I write back. . . . I quite like writing letters . . . it makes a change, it's nice'. She thinks that she writes 'more properly' if she writes letters. 'Email's not very personal, I think.' She saved email for more impersonal purposes, for example keeping track of internet orders. She handwrote her letters, proofread them and if she was not happy she ripped them up and started again: 'I think it's a good kind of old-fashioned way of keeping in touch with people instead of the phone.'

Work

Work provided another textually mediated domain of life for these students. The majority of college students are involved in some kind of paid work outside their college studies (Fowler *et al.* 2002). The students involved in this research project worked in jobs as various as administration, bar work, call centres and DJ-ing. All examples of paid work involved some kinds of reading and writing, whether this was integral to being able to complete the work content, as was the case in particularly literacy-rich jobs such as NHS administration, or more peripheral, such as completing timesheets and tallying stock, as was the case for the hotel chambermaid. Even the latter literacy practices were not straightforward or self-evident, often involving careful reading and a thorough understanding of the uses which would be made of what was written.

Sometimes there was overlap between students' college and work domains: many of the Catering students also had paid jobs in kitchens or hotels; higher level Childcare students often earned money in childcare settings alongside their course; and the Level 4 Business Administration students needed to provide evidence for their paid work as part of the criteria of their qualification. Other students worked in completely different areas from those which they were studying. While students sometimes talked about the difficulties of fitting in their paid work with their college work, no students talked about having difficulties in negotiating the literacy demands of their work.

Religion

A scattering of students talked in interviews about the role of religion in their lives. Some students, such as Megan and Carol (see Box 2.2), were active within their church communities. Through her church, Megan helped with playgroups, sang in the choir, organised group activities and participated in bible study. Some students attended mosque school each evening or on Friday evenings. Religious literacies varied from reading the bible or hymns as part of the processes of religious participation, to very close analysis of the religious texts. For example, as a devout and practising Muslim, Malik read the Qur'an in Arabic but he found this difficult so he read a version that had an Urdu translation sitting alongside the Arabic text. He only read a few pages at a time because he wanted to reflect on its meaning and understand it and not just memorise it. Within his mosque, Madhur voluntarily worked as the secretary of a charity group. The students took reading and writing associated with these church activities for granted, and lecturers often did not know about them. Yet they can involve substantial amounts of engagement with text, comprehension and discussion of meanings, inquiry, internet use, personal communication and reading and writing for record-keeping.

Peer group and community

Belonging to a peer group was an important part of students' lives and underpinned many of their literacy practices. A large amount of students' writing was motivated by their wanting to keep in touch with their friends, as described in 'Communication' in the following section. While students were not asked specifically about community activities, several mentioned involvement in the wider community as part of their everyday lives. Joe and Jason were both members of the Territorial Army and Jason taught younger cadets. Jack was a member of the St John's Ambulance. Jemma had recently started training to be a cub leader. Some students helped at local youth groups, and those who lived in smaller villages often took active roles in village life through staffing stalls at village fêtes and regularly reading village noticeboards. Each of these activities had its own unique texts which needed to be read and acted upon, or produced: purpose-driven reading and writing which is embedded in getting something done.

Uses of literacy in students' everyday lives

The domains discussed in the previous section clearly support different kinds of literacy practice. However, practices are not determined by domain alone: uses of literacy often cross domains, and intersect with them in interesting ways, as represented in Figure 2.2.

Communication

Most students are prolific and sophisticated communicators for personal reasons. They were rarely seen without mobile phones; some college libraries struggled to police the amount of personal emails written and sent during college time, and MSN messenger was banned from some college computers. Students also wrote letters and notes as ongoing communications with family and friends.

Texting: 'it's shorter and it's quicker'

Gina is typical of many of the students when she observes: 'I use my phone a lot – I text people, they text me – it's a lot of reading. Well, if you can call it that, it's not really writing or reading is it, abbreviations and everything – but, yeah, I use it a lot.' Students often did not consider their use of the mobile phone to be reading and writing, but this textual communication is a ubiquitous literacy practice. Students exchanged text messages with family members, lovers, friends and employers. They wrote to let parents know where they were or how long they would be, sent trivial messages to their boy/girl friends to show that they cared, gave tasters of gossip so that friends would telephone them, co-ordinated their social lives, organised working shifts with employers, and confirmed practice sessions with band members. The practices differed subtly according to the domain within which they were being used, according to the purpose to which they were put and, perhaps most significantly, according to the addressee.

The literacy practices of reading and writing text messages are complex and demonstrate sophisticated uses of technology and sensitivity to audience needs. Students sent text messages to different audiences for different purposes and their choice of style and language was often deliberate, and not an incidental consequence of the technology. Kate, like many students, used full English when writing text messages to her family because she thought that they would be unable to understand the abbreviated 'text language' that she used to communicate with friends.

Some students took pride in being competent at using abbreviated text language. Arfan, for example, spoke about how he found texting 'easy' – 'cos you can write in slang . . . just make it short'. But not all students valued their expertise in this area and several students were critical of their uses of abbreviated language, seeing this as a bad habit, particularly when, as Childcare student Helen observed from her own practices, it leaked into other kinds of writing that she might do. Some students always tried to write in full sentences and words when sending text messages, possibly influenced by the value judgements about 'proper writing' which they had encountered in the education system. Even those students who felt competent using text language and who were aware of the need to communicate differently to different audiences, sometimes found the idiosyncratic style of other people's messages difficult to read; for example, Alison used text language but her younger cousin sent her messages she could not understand.

Texting made it easy for people to edit what they had written. Unlike writing with a pen and paper, the appearance and content of the message could be edited and altered prior to completion without the need to rewrite the whole message. Some students identified the value of being able to check a text message before sending it, suggesting that for some editing is an integral part of the writing process when the message is destined for a person who matters to them – something which did not seem so apparent to them when writing college assignments.

While a small minority of students were excluded from texting because they could not afford a mobile phone, the practices of many more students are restricted by the financial costs of sending text messages. Some students anticipate the financial restrictions of the practice and shape their behaviour accordingly, figuring out how to send a message with the minimum number of characters, as in the telegrams which were still a part of the English curriculum in the 1950s.

Email and MSN messenger: 'it depends on what I'm talking about'

Although the use of email and MSN messenger was not as widespread as texting across the students, more differences emerged in students' reading and writing using these media.

MSN is a real-time online instant messaging medium. The use of MSN was frequently described as 'talk' or 'chat' by the students who used it: although the students are typing on a keyboard, this is not described as writing. MSN is a medium which enables a range of flexible modes of communication – smiley faces, emoticons and vibrating text abound. Increasingly, messaging can be accompanied by live video link-ups. This real-time aspect to the practice of using MSN creates a synchronous flow of communication, whereas email is asynchronous and more fragmented over time. As with texting, MSN often serves a predominantly social purpose. Melanie, a Travel and Tourism student who frequently used MSN, explained: 'There's not anything in particular you talk about – just pointless chit-chat with anyone or everyone who comes on line.' She did it 'whenever I've got nothing better to do'.

Email was often related to work or to college with some students using their college email account to email assignments to their home computers. Although not all students chose to do this, some students particularly valued the opportunity to edit and redraft emails prior to sending them. Patricia commented: 'I don't like to send rushed emails because I might look at it later and find that I've spelt something wrong.' Most students who used both identified different purposes for the different media. Related to the need to communicate was the students' frequent sensitivity to the kinds of language that they wrote. As with texting on mobile phones, many students switched between conventional usage and abbreviated language, depending upon the intended reader's familiarity with it.

Letters, greetings cards, and notes: 'a good old-fashioned way of keeping in touch'

Several students felt that communicating via digital technologies was less personal than handwriting letters. For example, Logan, a catering student, felt that if he had to write an apology letter he would do this by hand, whereas if it was 'just to inform someone about something' he would do it by computer. Box 2.3 presents the case of Nadine, who also used different means of personal communication for different purposes.

Leaving notes to family members was an established practice in some families. In some cases the notes were brief scribbles on the back of an envelope, in other cases the notes could be more detailed. Location is important in leaving notes around the house to communicate with family members because the note needs to attract the attention of the intended audience. Emily took paper from the computer printer and left the note on the landing in front of the door; Bryn scribbled on the back of the nearest piece of paper and stuck this where he thought his parents might notice.

Box 2.3   Nadine: writing for a wide range of purposes

Eighteen-year-old Nadine's text language had developed through communicating with her family: she sent texts to her boyfriend and her friends, her mum and her dad, and her grandma. She used text language: 'Instead of writing full words, like abbreviate them just to little ones. Like two – number 2 and stuff like that . . . Like hello, do you know hello? I put it l.o. – I got that off me dad.'

Nadine also wrote letters regularly: 'I write letters to this – it might sound stupid – but there's a lad that I know that's in prison and I've known him since I was a kid so I write to him.' She had been writing letters to him for three years.

> We just talk about what's been going on – he tells me what goes on in there, I tell him what goes on out here and that 'cos I'm really close with his mum as well and his sisters and that. So we just talk about all sorts. He rings me and that – we're just good mates.

Nadine wrote a letter to him every two or three days: 'Every time I get one, I send one and he gets it next day, but it takes two days to get from him to me.' She thought that she would carry on writing letters when he was released from prison: 'We don't really talk – we just write letters. It's how we get along.'

Nadine also kept a personal diary: 'I keep a book and if like I'm down or anything – I've got a red book – I put the day, the time, and what's gone wrong and things like that.' She had kept this diary for about two years and frequently read back through it. For Nadine the value was partly aesthetic and the appearance of her writing was important to her. Although no one else read this text, she valued its appearance purely for herself: 'It's got to look smart and I always put at the top as well who I'm loving at the moment, like you know when you like someone, I put who I like at the top.' Nadine reflected upon her writing and sought to improve it: 'I used to be really bad with my spelling and that but it started getting better and I can see like the changes and things in it.'

She was also in the process of developing systems of organising her life: 'I just keep my wage slips together so that I know how much I've got.' She kept her wage slips and other documents in a shoebox under her bed, a system of organisation copied from her father.

Organising life and getting things done

Students organised different aspects of their lives in diverse ways using a range of technologies. They talked about developing systems for organising not only their household affairs but also their CD or record collections, their magazines and materials related to their leisure interests. Some students were resistant to the idea of any kind of rigorous organisation while others had learnt by experience that they needed to develop organising practices. They also talked about reading and, to a lesser extent, writing involved in the practicalities of everyday life. For example, some students talked about literacy practices relating to shopping: making lists, buying on-line or from catalogues, and reading the packaging on products to make sure that they matched their intentions. These types of reading and writing were highly purposeful, driven by the need to get things done and increase efficiency.

Household paperwork: she 'does the money'

Mature Childcare student Georgia was responsible for all the home finances – she and her husband had a filing cabinet with bills, warranties, bank statements and so forth. She kept an Excel spreadsheet of money coming in and going out. She did not deal with bills as they came through the letterbox, but waited until her husband got paid. She kept a home diary which organised all the bills until this time.

Richard, who was in his fifties, had also evolved a system of organising his domestic finances over time:

> Because I was paid monthly we got to the point where, instead of suddenly having bills dropping on the mat at certain times of the year, we put them into a direct debit system so then we knew exactly how much money we had left at the end of each month.

He used the internet to keep track of bills and payments. He had used internet sites to make comparisons between the costs of different utility suppliers. Richard also used computer software on his PC to track finances. Commenting on his use of the computer to organise things, he said that it had become 'another chore less' using these methods.

Gina had recently got her first car and was sorting out insurance, road tax and MOTs. Insuring her car had created the need for her to engage in many new practices: 'I went on all the websites, filled in the questions, put in all my details, and it just comes up with a quote.' This small example illustrates graphically how complex everyday literacy practices are: Gina did not just need decoding and spelling ability, but a sophisticated understanding of what the questions were asking, how her replies related to her own circumstances, what would be the consequences of how she chose to complete each box, as well as ability to navigate the website and switch her attention between the website on screen and the various other documents relating to her car which she needed to consult.

Older students tended to have more encounters with bureaucratic texts (as was the case for the postgraduate students in Fawns and Ivanič 2001).

Younger students' lives, generally, were less subject to these texts – for example, because many lived with their parents they did not have mortgages or rental agreements. Many of the younger students were beginning to encounter official texts for the first time, as will be shown in more detail in Chapter 5, where we present the case of Eve, a Level 1 Childcare student who had her own child to care for. Some students had a high level of dependency upon their family and this often became apparent when talking about dealing with bureaucracy. For example, Emily received a notification of jury service through the post. She 'wrote saying I was at college', although the letter was scribed by her father. She read through her bank statements and then her father kept these in a file in the garage, which was also used as office space. Similarly, while Leticia kept college letters in her room, her parents kept material such as bank statements, bills and birth certificates. In some cases, the family involvement in organising life helped the students to develop their own practices in this area.

Being organised in one area of life does not necessarily migrate to other areas but, similarly, apparent disorganisation in some practices is not necessarily representative of the student's life as a whole. Although Alison considered that she was organised at work, she did not see herself as being very well organised at home and suggested that she needed to improve this: 'I just like leave letters lying around and stuff, I need to sort myself out, get some files up.'

Organising time: 'I like to plan ahead, like write things down, but that's just so that I know what's going on'

Many students photographed their diaries or calendars when we asked them to photograph reading or writing that they did in their everyday lives. Organising time emerged as an important use of literacy which was integral to all domains of their lives. However, students differed considerably in their practices in this respect. One student had a handheld palm-pilot with which she rigorously organised every aspect of her life. Other students had diaries and wall calendars. Some students wrote memos into their mobile phones to record dates and often set a function on the phone to audibly remind them of these. A small number of students explained that they did not like being 'constrained' by a diary.

For Nancy the diary acted as a centrepiece for the different activities in her family's lives. She made most of the entries but her husband occasionally read the diary too. The range of appointments and reminders included her children's football and her assignments for college. She thought she would be 'totally lost without it'. She made notes during the day and transferred these into the diary later. Other students struggled to keep diaries, even if they recognised the value of this practice.

Documenting

Some students had developed ways of documenting their lives using texts. Several students archived text messages and emails so that they could revisit them, or saved, catalogued and archived photographs. Students who wrote diaries recognised that they might revisit these texts, so they, in effect, documented their lives. However, literacy practices relating to documenting life were not widespread. The following examples offer descriptions of practices entered into by a few students.

Documenting the self: 'there's quite a lot of work involved in it'

Madhur spoke at length about the literacy practices relating to documenting her life – something that was clearly important to her. She kept all her birthday cards and notes from friends when she was at primary school and reread them to remind herself of them. She kept all her certificates and liked to show them to her sister and wanted to keep them to show her children. Her father kept all her important documents in case she lost them. Similarly Angela kept texts that charted different parts of her life. Her passion was dancing and she kept a large number of dance certificates, dancing programmes and tickets. She rarely looked at them but brought them out to show members of the family.

Several other students explained that they had previously kept diaries but had stopped because someone else, often siblings, had read them. Jackie's reason for handwriting her diary rather than writing things on computer was that the computer was less secure, increasing the risk that someone might read what she had written. The need for privacy also impacts upon the location of this practice – these students wrote at home in the privacy of their own rooms.

Documenting others: 'I don't really understand it'

Textual demands seemed to proliferate if the student had children or pets. Eve had the 'red book' that all parents must keep to record their baby's growth and development. She also had to keep records during her pregnancy in a booklet she was given by her doctors. Katy had to negotiate a plethora of paperwork when her son started nursery. Katy had also recently bought a pedigree puppy and had to fill out a lot of texts relating to the dog's registration.

Finding things out and taking part

Although these two uses of reading and writing could in principle be dealt with separately, in the data they were often interdependent. People wanted to find things out in order to take part in a leisure activity or to participate in a religious or community group; finding things out enabled taking part; and being engaged in particular activities often entailed finding out other information.

Reading associated with leisure interests: 'everything going on in the world'

Alison was a football enthusiast. Since her father moved to Ireland she had not attended so many football matches but 'I go on the internet quite a bit to look at what's going on.' She also bought programmes when she went to matches and 'read through them'. She watched any football matches that were shown on the terrestrial channels. She used TV magazines and an internet site to find out about which matches were showing. She used teletext to find out about matches that she had missed – 'it's quick to find out'. Alison was a Level 4 Business Administration student but her literacy practices in this area were similar to those engaged in by Imran, a Level 1 Business Administration student. Football was important to Imran and he supported Manchester United. He bought a lot of football magazines. He first looked at the contents pages of these magazines to find sections on Manchester United. He used Ceefax to find out football results – he thought that this was quicker than doing it on the computer. Imran and Alison both had the same driving passion, but they pursued it through different literacy practices, using different media and different text types to a common purpose.

Much of the students' engagement with the world was mediated through various technologies. Students navigated digital television with complex handheld controls, shifting their attention between the live coverage, the running text and the TV guide with programme listings. Some students had active gaming lives – either participating in online gaming communities or playing on media such as Playstation. Talking about online gaming revealed a diversity of literacy practices which are required to play the games successfully, as shown in Box 2.4.

Box 2.4   Bryn: the literacy practices involved in playing computer games

Bryn played computer games for about two to three hours each evening and most of the day on a Saturday. Most of the games that he played are online – he used his home PC to go on the internet. He researched different online games through using review sites on the internet and through reading computer gaming magazines. When searching for review sites he used the sites that he had bookmarked on his favourites, used a search engine, or followed hyperlinks from other sites he visited.

He played extensively on one international computer game: 'I go on a role playing game. It is all reading.' To play the game he needed to follow detailed written instructions on the screen and then type into the site what his character did. Playing the game required a great deal of writing. He had created an alter-ego character called Reverend Pink Mullet for this game, keeping extensive handwritten notes on this character and compiling some of the things that the Reverend Pink Mullet had done into a book 'inside his head'. He had not written out this book because he could not decide the genre in which he would write it.

The game had a 'village board' where everyone could post messages: 'Sometimes I just read through every message to see what's there, or if I see someone I recognise I'll just go and see what they're saying.' There were associated sites which he sometimes chose to look at, and instructions which he needed to understand and follow to be able to develop his avatar's involvement in the game. There were email addresses to contact people individually. Through the chat room and email, Bryn had 'got into a number of arguments with people'.

For Bryn, the different literacy practices were all part of the same activity, and he found it quite difficult to disentangle all the separate kinds of reading and writing that he did as part of playing the game. Diverse and complex literacy practices were part and parcel of being highly adept at computer-gaming, and he had learnt them through participation in the games and in the gaming world with which he identified.

Learning and sense-making

Learning and sense-making literacy practices can accompany a wide range of activities in all domains of life. For example, students who regularly used the gym often read instructions to learn how to use the machinery; students who had domestic responsibilities needed to make sense of leaflets and advertisements relevant to the home and family. Writing can be used to make sense of things too: to sort out ideas or thoughts. Some students saw such practices as an ordeal but others embraced them.

Cooking: 'I just nicked it and wrote it down'

Different students favoured different practices even when these took place within similar contexts; for example in relation to cookery and cookbooks. For some students, following the instructions in a recipe book was a means to an end. Once the student had learnt to cook that particular dish, the instructions did not need to be followed any more. The literacy practice was a temporary intermediate practice. For example, Hazel had 'quite a few' vegetarian cookbooks, but she did not use them as much as she used to 'now I've got used to it'. Nancy adapted and personalised recipes. Similarly, Joseph used a combination of reading the instructions on a packet and improvising with some of his own ideas. While the reading of magazines for leisure appeared generally to be gendered, the pursuit of recipes seemed to mean that students read magazines that they might not have otherwise. Paul explained:

> I've got quite a few cookbooks that my dad's given me when he was moving house but I do a lot of the recipes out of the back of the *Daily Mail* or the girlfriend gets the girly magazines and some of them have recipes in and they're quite good, you just make them bigger for her and me and the kids.

Learning to drive: 'it were really easy to learn on the computer'

Many of the students were of the age that they were learning to drive and several spoke about the practices that they were developing to acquire the knowledge necessary to pass the theory part of the test. Most popular in these practices was the use of the CD-ROM which simulated the theory test. Eve explained:

> It's like a disk, you get a disk with it, put it on, and it like tells you like – you can go through them and try them yourself or you can go on something else I'm not sure and it shows you the answers and you can go through them.

She found this disk easy to use: 'I go on the computer a lot but I don't usually use disks and stuff.' Brian, who had passed his theory test, found the CD-ROM similarly easy to use. He related this to the fact that the CD-ROM 'gives you' many of the questions that are in the actual exam. He felt that the book had too many questions so you would not know which ones to revise. Gina felt that the CD-ROM was particularly effective because it used the same format as the actual test:

> That's just basically like a theory test – it's the same conditions, it has the hazard on and everything, it's just the same really so you actually get like practice at actually doing the test, not just reading it from a book because it's a different situation isn't it? So it was good that.

Paul, who tended to develop practices involving other people, did not have his own computer and he was using a book from which to revise. The book had the questions on one side and the answers on the other – 'so you just get a piece of paper and cover one up; you read through it'. His girlfriend was helping him to learn: 'she's took it [the book] off me a couple of times and tested me'. The CD-ROM meant that students were able to revise by themselves, whereas the use of the book seemed to require the involvement of other people.

Learning how to use technology: 'forget it, I'm playing'

A new mobile phone requires familiarisation with its functions, and students reported three very different practices for achieving this familiarisation. First, Paul had just got a new phone at the time of his first interview and he was keen to show this off. He reflected that 'there's quite a lot of reading that I've had to work out for this'. While many of the functions were similar to his previous phone, he had needed to read up on additional functions. Second, by contrast, Will would avoid looking at instructions when working out new functions: 'I'd never look at the instructions – too much information to read.' Third, rather than learning by herself, Chelsea was shown how to use her phone by her mother.

Reading and writing for pleasure

In the five categories discussed so far in this section, reading and writing are means of achieving something else, and are often relatively peripheral to the main activity. This category is slightly different, as it is concerned more with reading and writing for their own sake. The reading and writing are constitutive of the activity: they are centre stage.

Fiction and non-fiction: 'maybe I should read more'

Amongst the students that read fiction, popular genres were science fiction and horror, particularly Stephen King novels and the Harry Potter books. Some students preferred to read non-fiction, and many students spoke about reading true-life stories of difficult childhood and child abuse. The amount that students read for leisure often seemed dependent upon other aspects of their lives at that time. Alison identified herself as a keen reader of fiction but felt that between working full time and studying, she currently had little time to read: 'I do read books, but since I've been on our course I've not been reading that much [laughter], you feel guilty!'

Most students considered reading fiction to be a highly valued cultural practice and value statements were often made in relation to the books being read. This contrasts with many other literacy practices where there was no association with a value discourse. Many students were disparaging about the value of what they read, or about their own lack of ability or commitment to reading. Students who expressed an initial aversion to reading books or reading in general often revealed a variety of texts in their lives. For example, 21-year-old Emily stated that 'I don't do reading.' Initially she amended this by allowing that her friend recently bought her a big book on *Friends*, her favourite TV programme. She then revealed that she also had a book from her childhood, *My Naughty Little Sister*, in her bedroom. Emily had apparently discounted these books because they were 'children's books': she had not treated them as having the same value as 'books' (she was presumably meaning adult fiction). This marginalisation of children's literature recurred across several interviews – students who claimed not to read, gradually revealed that they read what are classified as children's books.

Newspapers and magazines: 'it is just skimming over'

The reading of newspapers and magazines spans reading for pleasure and reading to find things out. Some students referred to buying newspapers ranging from the *Sun* to *The Financial Times*. Other students read newspapers which were bought by their families or which they picked up around college or in the workplace. In the larger cities, students might skim read free newspapers during their journey to college. Different students took different routes through the same newspapers – some flicked through for celebrity news, some stayed abreast of current affairs, some turned straight to the sports pages. And different students had different purposes in reading these media – some read for knowledge, some read opportunistically as a way of passing time during their journey or their lunch break. Most students elected which sections to read according to their interests. A notable contrast to this was Stasia, a young Russian student, who described reading the newspaper from cover to cover. Here her purpose was more related to her determination to improve her English language than other interests.

Much reading of magazines and newspapers had an observable social element. Many students talked about sharing the newspaper with family members. The social role of a magazine seems to contribute to the meaning that a reader will take from it and the reading of magazines often has a social purpose.

Different students valued different magazines and newspapers, and often this value system related to the identity of the student. For example, Hilary said that she did not read magazines, dismissing them as too frivolous and a waste of time, but then went on to say that she did read *Record Collector* (a specialist collector's magazine). She had not automatically associated this with being a magazine; she thought of this publication as something more adult and of a more serious nature.

Some students invested significant amounts of money in buying magazines. For example, Joe regularly spent around £10 a month on magazines which he called 'guys' mags' – magazines that have stories in them about gadgets, football, cars, jokes and 'male stuff'. He also bought a monthly car magazine. And, while some students shared magazines as a way of increasing their value and meaning, Joe found that his practice was disrupted when his sisters looked at these magazines: they focused on different aspects of the magazine than he did.

Writing for pleasure: 'I wouldn't show it to no one'

A small minority of students wrote for their own pleasure. Siobhan described the process behind writing a recent song:

> I was on the bus on the way home and the sun was setting and it was a really red sky and I thought 'that would be really nice to put in a song'. So I got home and, like, did all my college work and then sat down and relaxed and I remembered the inspiration of the sky and I just thought of things that would go with it and somehow I wrote it . . . I wrote it on paper, I don't like typing things unless I am copying them down.

She associated her writing with enjoyment and relaxation, but later associated it with more therapeutic functions:

> You don't want to read one of my poems, they're really depressing . . . I like to write down how I feel because I don't really talk that often . . . I can't express my feelings in words very well so I write things down, I always have done as well.

In such cases, writing is partly for pleasure and partly for 'sense-making', as described in the previous section. This merging of the creative with the therapeutic in personal writing recurred across several student interviews. Janet was a student who had had a challenging life. She thought that she would have taken her own life if she had not had the release of writing in her journal. For her, writing was a way of giving vent to her emotions and she saw this writing process as a dialogue between her and God: she would never say the things she wrote to another person and she always kept the journal locked away. The journal was a way of recording hopes, fears and despair.

Each of these students wrote as a solitary activity and their intended audience was themselves. These practices of writing for private leisure and sense-making provided examples of writing that is deliberate, self-generated and which is an end in itself rather than being incidental to another end.

From data to conceptual framing

It is clear that college students mostly do engage in a wide range of literacy practices in their everyday lives, many of them what might be called 'vernacular literacies' in the sense that they spring from the students' own

passions. Another significant set of practices arise when they
tact with the various bureaucracies that govern important
veryday. It is also the case that the overwhelming majority
either do not identify what they do in their everyday lives as
literacy or do not value it in the same way as 'schooled' literacy practices.

The examples in this chapter have all been drawn from domains of
students' lives other than education – from family, leisure, work, religion,
peer group and community, the five domains which structured the first
section of the chapter. The discussion in the second part of the chapter has
shown how reading and writing serves many purposes which cross-cut the
five domains: literacy practices are tools for communication, for organising
life and getting things done, for documenting, for finding things out and
taking part, for learning and sense-making, and for pleasure. It is a small
yet crucial step to recognise that these uses of literacy are highly relevant
to educational settings too. Reading and writing in educational settings are
also for communication, for organising life and getting things done, for
documenting, for finding things out and taking part, for learning and sense-
making and for pleasure, just as they are in other domains of everyday life.

From our analysis of the data, we have identified a number of common
characteristics of the literacy practices which students use across the
different domains of their everyday lives, and across the different uses of
literacy outlined. These practices tend to be:

- purposeful to the student;
- oriented to a clear audience;
- shared, that is, interactive, participatory and collaborative;
- learnt through participation;
- in tune with students' values and identities;
- agentic, that is, with the students having control;
- non-linear, that is, with varied reading paths;
- specific to times and places;
- multimodal, that is, combining symbols, pictures, colour, music;
- multimedia, that is, combining paper and electronic media;
- varied, not repetitive;
- generative, that is, involving meaning-making, creativity and getting things done;
- self-determined in terms of activity, time and place.

It is these characteristics that help us to identify practices from the
everyday that might be drawn upon within the learning of college courses,
and provide the starting-point for the conceptual framing which is the focus
of Chapter 3.

Chapter 3

Ways of understanding literacy practices

In Chapter 1 we explained what we mean by a situated view of literacy. Here we develop this conceptual framing, drawing on the examples in the previous chapter. We first revisit the key concepts which we introduced in Chapter 1. We then present a framework for understanding more about literacy practices, explaining each element in detail. This provides the foundation first for comparing students' everyday literacy practices with those on college courses (in Chapters 4 and 5), and second for analysing the changes lecturers made in the reading and writing on their courses (in Chapters 6 and 7). The framework is not only a useful research tool, but can also enable teachers to understand more about their students' literacy practices.

A social view of literacy

The idea that literacy is practice-based has come into being in the past twenty years. It is a broad approach to the study of reading and writing which starts out from what people do in their lives. It starts by noting that in carrying out many activities in life people use texts. A useful concept for understanding and, especially, for researching this aspect of social life is the idea of 'literacy events'. Put simply, literacy events are activities where literacy has a role. Many literacy events in life are regular, repeated activities, such as paying bills, sending text messages, reading bedtime stories. In fact the original idea of a literacy event was the bedtime story event (see Heath 1983) in which a parent and a child sit down and share a book between them, and the term has spread from this to cover all activities involving texts. Identifying such activities has been a useful starting point for practical research into literacy in many different settings. Some events are linked into routine sequences and these may be part of the formal procedures and expectations of social institutions such as workplaces, schools and welfare agencies. Some events are structured by the more informal expectations and pressures of the home or peer group. Events are observable episodes and the notion of events stresses the situated nature of literacy: that it always exists in a particular context and gets part of its meaning and value from that context.

Texts may be a focal point of the event, as with the bedtime story example, or they may exist in the background. When the text is relatively central to the literacy event, there may be talk around the text. Texts include rapidly scribbled notes, calendars, books, web pages, text messages, signs, instruction leaflets. There is a seemingly limitless list of possible types of text which make an action into a literacy event. In whatever form they appear and however they are used, texts are a crucial part of literacy events and often they provide some stability to activities and across different settings. How such texts are produced and used is a central part of the study of literacy as a social practice; this is a very different focus from measuring people's 'literacy skills'. The way into this research has been to start in a concrete way with eliciting accounts of literacy events in students' lives and observing literacy events going on in colleges.

As literacy researchers, our aim is to see regularities and patterns in the multiplicity of literacy events about which we accumulate data: to make the analytical move from studying literacy events to identifying 'literacy practices'. Literacy practices are the general cultural ways of utilising written language which people draw upon in their lives. The concept of literacy practices operates at a greater degree of generality and abstraction than the concept of literacy events. In the simplest sense, literacy practices are what people regularly or habitually do with literacy, whereas a literacy event is just one instantiation of a practice. Literacy practices also represent recurring patterns in the values, attitudes, feelings and social relationships which are associated with the use of written language in a particular context. Attention to literacy practices requires the researcher to take account of people's awareness, framings and discourses of literacy, demonstrated in how people talk about and make sense of it. Practices are the processes which connect people with one another, and they include shared cognitions and artefacts represented in ideologies, rituals and identities. This offers a powerful way of conceptualising the link between the activities of reading and writing and the social structures in which they are embedded and which they help to shape. Practices are shaped by rules which regulate the use and distribution of texts, prescribing who may produce and have access to them.

In any situation we see a range of literacies, that is, configurations of literacy practices, acting together. In particular domains of activity, such as home, or education, or employment, we see common patterns of activity and we can often contrast the ways literacies are used in these different domains. Starting from particular domains is a useful way for then seeing how different domains interact and overlap and how there is much hybridity, folding and fusion. The boundaries, transitions and the spaces between domains are then very salient: they are significant, for instance, in understanding links between students' home lives and college lives or the differences between educational practices and workplace practices.

People talk of academic literacies, or everyday literacies, or workplace literacies to emphasise the different practices in these various domains but we need to be more specific than this. Looking in detail at people's practices, the framework which we present in this chapter enables us to identify the distinctive characteristics of literacies within educational contexts, and to compare them with the students' literacy practices in other domains of their lives. Students are learning the reading and writing demands of the occupations for which they are training, such as catering or construction or hairdressing, which are the literacies of particular workplaces. At the same time there are particular ways of reading and writing which help students in their learning, and these literacies for learning are the central focus of this study. These literacies for work and literacies for learning also exist alongside other distinct forms of reading and writing associated with assessment and, increasingly, with accountability, as in the record-keeping students and teachers have to do.

A conceptual framework for understanding literacy practices

The thorough study of students' reading and writing outside college led us to recognise that literacy events and practices are made up of a number of elements, each of which can be configured in many ways. As we pursued our research aim of identifying how students' everyday practices might be used as resources for their learning on college courses, we developed a working set of aspects of literacy events and practices which allowed us to talk about them in fine detail. In this section we present the framework which emerged from iterative analyses of data throughout the research. The framework provides a point of reference for the rest of the book, and provides both researchers and practitioners with a useful way of describing and comparing literacy practices in their own work.

The idea that a literacy event or practice can be analysed using a set of constituents is implicit in literacy studies: it is integral to the literacy studies research paradigm to ask the fundamental sociolinguistic questions, 'Who is doing what? with whom? to/for whom? where? when? how? why? and under what conditions?' (Hymes 1962; Green and Bloome 1997). Within literacy studies, Hamilton (2000) identified the key elements of a literacy practice as participants, settings, artefacts and activities and Barton (2000) refers to texts, practices, activities and artefacts. More recently Street and Lefstein (2007: 193–9) have identified what they refer to as eight dimensions of events and practices which can act as a starting point when researching literacy. These are: settings, participants, texts and other objects, actions and sequencing, rules, interpretation, contexts, and pulling it all together. They have a set of questions to be posed in relation to each dimension and they work through a detailed example of ordering a meal in a restaurant.

These are useful starting points and serve the different aims of different research. Here we needed a more detailed framework, and we have extended and reconfigured these lists for our own purposes, drawing on a broader range of work which provides accounts of the constituents of a practice, including van Leeuwen (1993) in semiotics, Gee (1992) in discourse analysis, and Russell (2009) in relation to Activity Theory. We integrated these approaches with categories emerging from our data. On this basis we have developed a set of nine aspects of a literacy event or practice in the form of a two-dimensional framework. This is shown in Figure 3.1 and it provides an analytical tool for interrogating data, and for talking explicitly about the aspects of literacy practices. The framework integrates five key questions about literacy events and practices with the nine aspects in a way which provides a conceptual framing for understanding the social nature of literacy and a language of description for literacy events and practices.

This framework was initially developed for use in the project DVD to frame the analysis and discussion of pedagogic literacy practices (Pardoe

	What?	*Why?*	*Who?*
	Aspects of a literacy event or practice		
	content	purposes	audiences
Under what conditions?	languages, genres, styles and designs	flexibility and constraints	roles, identities and values
How?	modes and technologies	actions and processes	participation

Figure 3.1 Aspects of a literacy event or practice

and Ivanič 2007). We have simplified or extended the list of aspects represented in the framework in different ways for different purposes (see, for example, Ivanič *et al.* 2007; Ivanič and Satchwell 2007; Satchwell and Ivanič 2009; Ivanič forthcoming). The exact elements and number of elements on the list are not so important as the principle that there are a finite set of elements which constitute literacy events and literacy practices, each of which can be configured in an infinite number of ways.

Some of the elements in the framework are common to all practices, and might be used to describe an activity which does not have a significant communicative dimension to it; for example, playing football. *Purpose(s), identities, roles and values, participation, activities and processes*, and *flexibility and constraints* are aspects of any practice. Other elements in the framework are specific to communicative practices and literacy practices. The aspects in column 2 of the framework – *content, languages, genres, styles and designs, modes and technologies* – are specific to literacy practices, and *audience* is a specific aspect of the 'Who' in literacy practices. Although technologies are becoming increasingly pervasive in all aspects of life, in this study we are paying particular attention to information and communication technologies, so we are treating this aspect as literacy-specific. Even the more general elements in the framework have particular characteristics in a communicative practice. For example, in a communicative practice, the *actions and processes* include both physical and mental ways of engaging with or composing text – actions which would not be significant in practices which do not involve textual mediation.

The framework allows the user to start from one of the questions, and then to use the elements in the same line to expand on that to which the question might refer. So, for example, in asking *what* is involved in a literacy practice, this question can cover at least the following three more detailed questions:

- What is the *content* of the texts? – what topics and issues are being written and/or read about, what is the meaning or the message?
- What *language* (or *languages*, in a multilingual text) and script(s), what *genres*, what conventions of *style* and *design* (for example, conventions of layout, font and colour) are being drawn upon?
- What semiotic *modes* (spoken language, written language, visual, material and/or animation) are employed, in what ways, using what *technologies* and associated media, tools, materials and physical resources such as computers, notebooks, glitter pens, textbooks?

In a complex literacy event or practice which combines the reading and writing of more than one text, there may be several answers to each of these questions. The nine aspects each instigate a line of inquiry about a literacy practice, but they are not hermetically sealed from one another. For example, a discussion of conventions of style and design will overlap with the identification of modes and technologies. Each of the elements in the middle and bottom rows of the framework combines responses to two questions. For example, *flexibility and constraints* is concerned with 'Why' the practice is the way it is, and 'Under what conditions' the other aspects of the practice are operating. The questions provide the 'way in', and the nine aspects in the framework work in concert with the questions to provide a rich description of a literacy event or practice, or to provide a basis for comparison among practices.

Each of the elements in the framework can be understood on at least two levels. They can be seen first as factors which are amenable to observation and to the collection of concrete evidence from specific literacy events. For example, the *participation* aspect invites attention to details of who is involved and how they are interacting with one another. However, we can also move beyond the immediate, descriptive detail of literacy events to engage in deeper probing through participant accounts, interpretation, processes of abstraction and making connections between the local and the institutional context in which the literacy events are located. This constitutes a move to the analysis of literacy practices. At this more abstract level, the *participation* aspect invites attention to participants' under-standings of their rights and responsibilities as participants in the practice, to 'rules of engagement', issues of prestige and status, power relations and habitual structures of participation in the practice.

The nine aspects can also be used as a starting point for developing sub-categories for more fine-grained description. For example, in thinking about the *roles, identities and values* of the people involved in a literacy practice, it is possible to expand this category to cover also the participants' feelings and priorities, or to sub-divide 'values' into values associated with literacy, and values associated with the content of the text. In this way, the framework can be used at greater or lesser degrees of delicacy to reveal what is going on in any practice which involves the use of written texts. (For further explanation, see Pardoe and Ivanič 2007.)

Each of these constituents of a literacy practice can be configured in many ways, and change in any one of them changes the nature of the practice. We ended Chapter 2 by summarising the tendencies we observed in the students' everyday literacy practices. The characteristics we listed there constitute particular configurations for many of the elements in the framework. So, for example, the *participation* in their literacy practices tended to be collaborative and interactive; the *purposes* and the *audiences* of the students' literacy practices tended to be clear to the students. In many of the literacy practices in which the students engaged, the reading and writing *processes* were non-linear: moving from one part of a text to another and reading, or writing, at variable speeds according to the part of the text. In the reading and writing they were expected to do on their courses, however, there was an assumption that the text would be read or written sequentially. It is these characteristics, compared to those of the pedagogic literacy practices on the students' college courses, that helped us to identify aspects of practices from the everyday that might be drawn upon to enhance learning opportunities.

In the rest of this section we discuss each of the elements in the framework in more detail. We start with the *purposes* element, which has a special status as it both involves and, to a large extent, shapes the other aspects of literacy practices. We then go clockwise round the other categories on the outer edge of the framework, ending with the central element in the framework: *flexibility and constraints* which, like *purposes*, affect all other aspects of literacy practices. We make links with key findings about students' everyday literacy practices in shaded boxes.

Purposes

Why are the participants in the practice reading or writing? What are they aiming to achieve?

The purpose may be partly the students' own, but it may also be institutional (see Clark and Ivanič 1997, Chapter 4). Talking about purpose can be very useful in leading to talking about the other aspects of literacy practices.

A practice-based approach to literacy does not assume that purpose is intrinsic to the text. Rather, the purpose depends on the activity in which the text is situated. Sometimes purpose is anticipated by the text (for example, purposes are implied by the genre of texts such as novels, recipes); sometimes purpose relates to the activity within which the text has a role: the individual has a purpose that they are trying to achieve and the literacy practice acts as a tool towards this. Bryn talked about his literacy practice of reading Stephen King novels. Here his purpose was to engage with the text: there was not a wider activity or set of purposes towards which his reading played a part. Examples where the purposes of the literacy practice related directly to the textual engagement, rather than as part of a wider activity, were most often found in the domain of private leisure. We found that it was these activities that students most closely associated with 'literacy'. Students read novels because they wanted to read stories; most often this was an end in itself. But these literacy practices were a minority and most reading and writing was incidental to a wider activity, enabling some other purpose whether this was to build a wardrobe successfully, to catch up with current affairs, to learn a new recipe, or to know which new player Manchester United Football Club had bought.

Purpose is located in an individual's engagement with and utilisation of a text. For example, while the implied purpose of a recipe book is to provide instructions on cooking, individuals might utilise this same text for different purposes: while Logan read recipe books for his professional development, Emma read them for private leisure (and confessed to not having enough time to actually cook anything), and Gina read them to balance the nutritional demands of her vegan diet. Individuals can appropriate texts for purposes different from those which appear to be explicit in the text's intended function.

> Literacy practices that individuals engage with in their everyday lives tend to be purposeful.

We found that most students were purposeful in their reading and writing, but there was a variety in the degree and focus of purpose. Some students' reading was casual, accidental, circumstantial: some students talked about reading everything that they could find – the backs of cereal boxes, free newspapers, magazines, notices and flyers. The purposes here were to pass the time, to alleviate boredom, or purely to read something because it was there: an opportunistic practice. At the other end of the spectrum, students engaged in clearly purposeful reading activities as in the examples above.

Purpose is a complex aspect of literacy practices. As Barton and Hamilton (2005: 6) point out, 'individual and social purposes might be conflicting or confused'. Students engaged not only in vernacular literacy practices, that is, those which arose from their own interests and concerns, but also in a wide range of formal literacy practices which were demanded by the practicalities of their lives; for example, work-related literacies, bureaucratic literacies, literacies for learning to drive. Most of the students were working part time and were drawing on a range of literacies as part of their jobs.

Understanding purpose in a literacy practice is pedagogically important. Where students have a clear purpose they become able to engage with texts which they might otherwise consider to be inaccessible. Arfan provides a good example of this. In class, he was a student who most often failed to complete any reading during lesson time and who associated himself with being a non-reader – in interview, he referred to books as 'scary' and 'boring'. Arfan had an interest in cars and, to further his knowledge in this area, he read the *Autotrader* magazine, with its tiny text type, and Haynes car manuals, which do not show any particular attention to readability. These texts became accessible because Arfan's engagement with them was driven by a clear, self-generated sense of purpose.

Audiences and participation

Who is the text being written for? Or who was it written for? Who are the focal participants reading and writing with, and how? For example, are they discussing it as they write? Are they writing parts of it, for someone else to check or finish? How are they using information that others have written?

There are social aspects to students' everyday literacy practices in terms of both the people they are communicating with through their literacy practices, and the other people who are involved in the practices. *Audiences* and *participation* constitute two separate elements in the framework, since it is often useful to pay separate attention to both the receivers and the producers of messages. In particular, in writing practices, it is important to be aware of who is being written to, as well as who the writers are. It is often useful to examine the text(s) which are being read, and consider who their intended readers are, that is, their implied audience.

> Literacy practices that students engage with in their everyday lives tend to have a clear sense of audience.

However, these social aspects of literacy practices were often intertwined in the students' everyday literacy practices, and *audience* becomes indistinguishable from *participation*. For example, while Logan might text someone to communicate with them, he might then read out this text message to his friends for the sake of entertainment. The participants in this literacy practice are reading, writing and talking around text in a complex pattern of participation during which they shift frequently between reading and writing. We came across examples of people who read the newspaper aloud within their social group at lunchtimes, sharing stories and snippets of information. We also talked with people who read the newspaper alone but with the intention of then having something to talk about later that day with their friends in the pub. The social aspect of literacy practices exists in the real sense of people sharing a text (reading out text messages, handing around copies of a magazine), in an anticipated sense (reading newspaper stories to share with friends later that day, looking up information on paint so that joint decision making over what to buy could be better informed), or in shared virtual space (for example, students who joined games forums, chatrooms, and so forth).

> Literacy practices that students engage with in their everyday lives tend to be shared, interactive and collaborative.

The majority of students' everyday reading and writing had a strong social element. Students were keen to communicate with one another through texting, emailing, instant messaging, and letters and notes. They shared magazines and newspapers. A minority of practices tended towards being more solitary. Students' reading of fiction and non-fiction tended to take place when the student was alone – typically students talked about reading in bed. Students who wrote for private leisure were particularly protective of their privacy. Interestingly, these more solitary activities were those which students associated most readily as being literacy even though they did substantially less of these than other literacy practices. For example, if students did not often read fiction on their own they did not initially think of themselves as readers. The more participative and interactive the communicative activities, the less they were considered to be literacy or reading and writing.

> Literacy practices that students choose to engage with in their everyday lives tend to be learned through participation.

Barton and Hamilton (1998) argued that many vernacular practices are learnt informally through participation in the practice with others, and our research data supports that claim. Students' routes towards learning new literacy practices within their everyday lives tended to be shaped more by their experiences of doing than by an authoritative guide to how something should be done. For example, Bryn learnt new practices through participating in online gaming communities and through his role in the family. These forms of learning are not systematised by an outside authority and, therefore, the roles of novice or learner and expert or teacher are not fixed and shift from context to context.

Roles, identities and values

Who is the text written or read by, and in what role(s) are they writing and/or reading? What values and priorities do they bring to it? How does the text position them, as readers or as writers?

People's multi-faceted identities affect, and are affected by, engagement in literacy practices. This element is concerned with the social positioning of participants, the possibilities for selfhood which are available to participants in a practice, the values they bring to the practice, and the values associated with participation in it. These issues are further developed in Ivanič (2006), and Satchwell and Ivanič (forthcoming).

From a practice-based perspective, the people involved in any practice are themselves situated and we encountered significant differences across the student body. Eve recognised that she took on multiple roles in her life:

as a daughter, a mother, an adult partner, a Childcare student, a chamber maid and a teenager. Both Bryn and Megan identified themselves as people who could not read properly because of negative experiences during their compulsory schooling.

> Most of the literacy practices that students engage with in their everyday lives tend to be in tune with students' values and identities.

An individual might engage with different literacy practices according to different roles in their lives, which might provide them with routes to texts that they would not otherwise encounter. For example, Brian took responsibility for cooking the main meal for his girlfriend and her children. While he was an experienced cook, he did not have access to many cookery books at her house and would, instead, find recipes from his girlfriend's magazines. His identity as care-giver/food provider meant that he engaged with texts (women's magazines) that he would not otherwise have read.

The project data suggest that people's sense of identity (that is, their sense of who they are and who they want to become) affects, to a degree, which practices they become involved with and the purposes they aim to meet, the meaning they take from texts and the values which become attached to those texts and practices. For example, Elena had the real world identities of being a science and business student, as well as her other identities working in PR, competing on her horse and being the daughter of an affluent family. Her aspirational identity was to be a successful career woman in the business world. There were strong links between her current identities and her aspirational identity. She was working in a job which was providing valuable work experience in a business context, she read *The Financial Times* at home and tracked her shares on the stock market. In contrast, Siobhan, who was studying on the same course as Elena, identified herself as a punk rocker, a rebel and an outsider. Her aspirational identity was to be a science graduate. Gee (2003) refers to 'repair work' needing to be done in cases such as Siobhan where no bridges seem immediately possible between these two identities. To be a successful learner, Gee argues, requires identity commitments because successful learning requires aspirations and goals which are coherent with the purposes of the practice. In Elena's case this seems self-evident and her everyday literacy practices match or complement the requirements of her course of study; for Siobhan the relationships are more complex and suggest greater conflict.

Identities can be explicitly created through literacy practices (for example, Bryn's creation of fictional selves in online computer games), literacy practices can be used as a route towards aspirational identities (for example, Elena's reading of *The Financial Times* was part of her envisaged identity as a business woman), and the artefacts associated with literacy can symbolise the user's identity (for example, a key part of Rebecca's identity was represented through her choice and personalisation of her mobile phone). Emily's tutor observed how she had modelled participation in a literacy practice – pretending to read the instructions on a game during a Childcare lesson – as a step towards constructing her classroom identity. Similarly, another Childcare student spoke about how she pretended to send text messages on her mobile phone while she was waiting alone at a bus stop so that people would not think that she was 'sad'.

Regardless of who they are, who they think they are, or who they aspire to be, all students are likely to encounter some texts which position them in the same way: as consumers, as citizens, as candidates – obvious examples of this relate to the textual demands of bank accounts and wage statements or the driving theory test. The need to engage with these texts is externally imposed. Within this there might be some space to personalise the practices; for example, developing organisation systems to keep track of bank statements or deciding to use the CD-Rom to revise for the driving test because other people have found this successful. However, there is less space here for the articulation of individuality than in other areas of the students' lives.

Differences among students affected the ways that they valued particular practices and texts. For example, we encountered a broad spectrum of opinions on text messaging, ranging from students who took pride in their ability to use abbreviated and specialist vocabulary through to students who were critical of any move away from standard English spelling and punctuation when using text on a mobile phone. Many students seemed to accept public discourses around the value of kinds of reading and writing. Abbreviated text language was seen to be 'bad' or 'lazy'; students considered that they did not read enough literature or good enough literature. College practices tended to be described as both more difficult and more valuable than students' everyday practices. One student contrasted how he read magazines with the kinds of reading that they had to do at college:

> It is just skimming over. You don't really need to bother cos it is nothing important. Whereas reading something out of a (text)book or a paragraph you really need to take it in what you are reading because it will be relevant to what you are doing in class.

He did not value his ability to skim read a large amount of text to find content that interested him. Other students provided examples of parodying texts, thereby challenging existing genres and value systems. For example, Megan described reading to her aunt the health and safety text that she had been given as part of her induction to her workplace, deliberately parodying what she saw to be the ridiculousness of the text.

The interplay of roles, identities and values in students' everyday literacy practices indicates a complexity that is not embraced in notions of individual deficit. The latter may be at some level easier to hold on to and it is one to which students may themselves subscribe or ascribe to themselves. Our data indicates much more is at stake in the practices in which people engage.

Actions and processes

What is the reading or writing part of? What is the wider action in this case? What are the processes (or the stages) by which this reading or writing is achieved? What sorts of meaning-making and design-work does it involve? Is the (intended) reading linear or non-linear?

Reading and writing are about getting something done, or achieving something we value or enjoy, such as fixing the car or planning a project or reading a novel. This element is in the 'Why?' column of the framework because, as we explained in the *purposes* section above, reading and writing is shaped by the broader action or activity of which it is a part. So, for example, Carol described how she had read the instructions attached to her sister's wardrobe as a tool towards understanding how to put together the furniture. In this example, the literacy practice was embedded within the broader actions involved in building the wardrobe. Reading and writing of this sort, which is subordinate to some other activity in everyday life, is unlikely to be continuous, and more likely to be taken up and put down as necessary, reading different parts of the available text as the need arises.

> Literacy practices that students engage with in their everyday lives tend to be non-linear; for example, with varied reading paths.

This aspect of literacy practices also encompasses the more detailed processes involved in acts of reading and writing themselves, as represented by literacy-related verbs. In relation to reading this includes skimming, scanning, looking-up, leafing-through, glancing, reading over and over. In relation to writing it includes composing, planning, drafting, noting, scribbling, editing, re-reading, checking. Many students who said they 'didn't do any writing' were nevertheless involved in processes which they described as 'design work' or 'publicity'. This aspect of literacy practices also includes descriptions of how these actions are done: intensively, speedily, slowly, sporadically, with great attention to detail, and of the times and timing, places and uses of space.

> Many of the literacy practices that students choose to engage with in their everyday lives involve design work and getting things done.

The actions and processes of some literacy practices are characterised by certain times and places. For example, many students read books at night in bed but not at other times of the day, newspapers might be encountered over the breakfast table or shared in the student canteen at lunch time, letters might be written at desks in the evening. But literacy practices involving new technologies tended to be compartmentalised less according to time slots throughout the day. Students' uses of mobile phones are characterised more by their timelessness. Texting is quick and an activity that students take part in throughout the day rather than being restricted to certain times. Matters of time conversely shape and restrict the literacy practice of texting: texting is a way of spending time and of saving time. Many of the students we worked with text opportunistically as a means of spending time when they are not otherwise entertained – on long bus journeys, during breaks (and boring lessons) in college, etc. But the practice of texting can also be seen as a form of communication that saves time: Travel and Tourism student Sally explained how texts are more convenient than a letter and cheaper than a call, Childcare student Angela preferred to keep in touch with people by text because it was quick and because people tended to respond immediately. Those students who used abbreviated text language tended to justify this in terms of saving time.

> Students' literacy practices have specific characteristics of time and timing, of place and space, depending on their purposes.

In previous sections we have discussed how students particularly value shared or collaborative practices. Practices might be shared through taking place in a shared physical space (for example, Logan and the Catering students read out and shared text messages during their breaks in the college café). Here the participants are together in real physical terms. Similarly, practices might be shared through taking place in a shared virtual space, although the participants might be physically separate (for example, Bryn regularly communicated with people who shared his online gaming environment but who were in the United States).

At the start of the research process we sought to understand students' literacy practices by proposing three interlinking contexts of home, college and work. But these domains proved troublesome in the light of the student data. Many literacy practices were not related to either work or college, even though they took place on these sites with the use of mobile phones, computers, or the sharing of magazines during breaks. Similarly, college literacy demands might be met through the student working on a home or work computer, or working with pen, paper or textbooks in locations other than college. There are not boundaries between the identified domains, nor inevitable border crossings from one location to another – for example Gina said that she was organised at home but not at college.

Also, participation in international virtual communities challenges the idea that vernacular literacies tend to have their roots in people's homes and in their upbringings, in the local and particular. The students developed vernacular literacies through being involved in technological practices such as texting, MSN messenger, and online gaming communities. Whether students physically took part in these activities at home, college or work, was secondary to their virtual location in a particular virtual space.

Modes and technologies

Is it multimodal – including images and/or sound as well as text? What technologies are used to achieve this communication?

Modes refers to the range of semiotic resources which can be employed to make meaning: spoken language, written language, visual, material and/or animation. *Technologies* includes not only electronic media but also the material media and resources of 'old technologies' such as books, newspapers, magazines, pens, chalk and different types of paper.

Students encounter a wide range of literacy-related artefacts in their everyday lives: students talked about mobile phones, TV, laptops, magazines and so forth. These media enable a broad range of multi-modal communication. Beavis (2002: 49) describes how digital popular culture inducts young people into a multimodal literacy world, leading him to recommend that 'we need an expanded set of understandings of texts and literacy, and to recognise the literacy skills many children bring with them to school and develop in their out-of-school worlds'. Low (2005) notes how models of literacy are challenged to keep up with lived practices because of this proliferation of new media and ICT. The icon mapping exercises carried out with the students in this research showed that they particularly valued a broad diversity of technological artefacts, including computers, mobile phones and other handheld devices.

In their everyday lives, students tend to prefer literacy practices which draw upon a range of media and multi-modal forms of communication.

For many students, the computer is a normalised part of their lives. As Georgia, a mature Painting and Decorating student, explained: 'I guess you start to take it for granted now . . . the computer just automatically comes as part of your day really.' Some students did not have a computer at home, or the home computer was located somewhere where they could not use it (several students were unable to use home computers because they were in their brothers' bedrooms), or they did not have the freedom to spend substantial amounts of time online because of the costs of internet providers. This causes a divide to emerge between those students who were able to use MSN and other real-time packages which required the user to be online, and those who were not. While the students who regularly used instant messaging were almost evangelical about its use, not all students even knew what it was. This provides a timely reminder that we cannot assume that all students are technologically competent – although many regularly use email, this is not representative of all students and cannot be assumed of any group of students.

Some students cannot conceive of their identity without a mobile phone. Leticia referred to her phone as 'my baby. I love my phone. It is my new toy' and described herself as a 'gadget girl'. A mobile phone enables the user to take part in many different practices: students send and receive text messages; they organise their lives using the diary function and the alarm clock wakes them up in the morning; they access the internet, send emails and download music; they take photos, watch video clips and play games. The mobile phone straddles many functions and domains: personal communication, organising life, documenting life, work and so forth. Unlike the significant divide which emerges between students who do and who do not have access to a home computer, the vast majority have their own mobile phones. Only a very small minority of students did not have mobile phones.

Changing television technologies meant that many students talked about surfing channels through reading and operating handheld remote controls. Although this technology was new at the time of the research, students spoke confidently about their ability to navigate this televisual technology and none reported any problems. These practices were often complex and multimodal, but had clear purposes such as finding out what programmes were on different channels, and setting up the technology to record programmes.

Languages, genres, styles and designs

What language (or languages, in a multilingual text) and script(s) are being used? What writing styles are used? What is the design and flow of information? What conventions of genre, style and design does the reader or writer need to know?

In a skills-based approach to literacy, 'language' is the sole object of attention. Accuracy and correctness of language use, and, in some more recent teaching methods, appropriacy to the genre in question are all that concern the teacher (for further discussion, see Ivanič 2004). While issues of language, genre, style and design remain an indispensable aspect of literacy as a social practice, the crucial difference is that here this is just one element in a framework which also draws attention to eight other aspects of literacy. In a social practice view of literacy, not only are language, genre, style and design inseparable from the other elements in the framework, but also the questions we ask about them are different: we are concerned not with accuracy and correctness as a reified ideal, but with the relationship between the language and the purposes for which it is being used.

The first focus of investigation for this aspect of a literacy practice is the texts which are in use in any instantiation of the practice: making an inventory of the texts involved in the practice, noting the language(s) and script(s) used, and analysing the linguistic, visual and material features of each text. The researchers on the projects studied the texts which mediated one key activity on each of the selected units they were teaching (as exemplified in the next two chapters). Many of the photographs taken by students of their everyday literacy practices also featured the texts with which they engaged, which were notable for how they contrasted with pedagogic texts. Crucially, they were extremely varied, and shaped by the purposes they served. They ranged from the extremely colourful magazines they chose to read, which used a vast range of graphic and linguistic attention-grabbing techniques, through relatively visually and linguistically homogeneous electronic messages, to dense, linguistically and visually impenetrable bureaucratic forms and documents.

This element of the framework had particular significance in the Welsh data, since it was highly significant which languages were being used in a literacy practice, and whether any texts were bi- or multi-lingual, mixing Welsh and English within the same text. This had considerable consequences for other aspects of the practice. There were also students in Scotland and England who were literate in two or more languages, often even two or more scripts; for example through the texts they encountered in mosque school, and when communicating with family members in countries other than the UK.

> Literacy practices that students choose to engage with in their everyday lives tend to be varied; not repetitive.

The *languages, genres, styles and designs* element in the framework also invites us to go beyond the linguistic and visual features of the actual texts which are part of a practice, and to pay attention to the linguistic, generic and discoursal resources that are being drawn upon. This requires us to extrapolate from several instances of the texts in use to identify patterns and regularities among them. In the research, we found more regularity in the genres used in the pedagogic domain and more variety in the genres students engaged with in other domains of their lives.

Content

What are the participants in the practice reading and writing about? What are the topics and issues with which they are engaging? What is the meaning or the message?

This element of the framework concerns the content, or subject matter of the texts which are being read or written. Almost any text is not only 'about something', but also provides food for thought through the way in which each topic is addressed. Topics are represented in different ways, which are often institutional and controversial. Perhaps one of the most pervasive misconceptions about written text is that its content is just 'information' whereas most texts also embody socio-political positions and social relations.

This aspect of a literacy practice is perhaps the principal one which distinguishes communicative practices from other practices. The distinctive capacity of semiotic resources is to recontextualise one practice within another, that is, to represent some (other) aspect of reality within the representing context (for further discussion, see van Leeuwen 1993, 1995, 1996). Thus, when people are reading and writing, they are reading and writing *about* something, and that 'something' is represented from a particular point of view. In this respect the *content* element in the framework interacts with the *languages and genres* element, since the different ways of representing reality are carried by the representational resources of genres and discourses.

The students in the research read and wrote about a vast range of topics and issues, ranging from dog breeding through military equipment to every type of music and fashion. Their reading and writing was driven by interest and the desire for engagement in the topics and issues. However, the content was not always the most important aspect of a literacy practice. Many students observed that their text messages and instant messages were often more concerned with maintaining and developing relationships than with sharing information or ideas.

Many of the literacy practices that students choose to engage with in their everyday lives involve meaning-making and creativity.

It is not co-incidental that the *content* aspect of literacy practices is next to the *purposes* aspect in the framework. The purpose of a literacy event or practice is often meaning-gaining or meaning-making. People often want to read because of their interest in the content of the text – the story, or the topic. People often want to write because they care about the message they are conveying. In many literacy practices, therefore, *purpose* is inextricably bound up with *content*.

Flexibility and constraints

Why now? Why here? Why like this? Who has the power to decide the characteristics of this literacy practice?

The *flexibility and constraints* aspect of a literacy practice is concerned both with material conditions of time and space, and with institutional and sociocultural conditions within which the practice is operating. There are always constraints of time, space and resources, but also areas of flexibility and opportunity. These need to be discussed explicitly so that students can understand the constraints, but also so that they know where they can make choices and decisions. There are also value systems imposed by institutional and social structures which shape what can, cannot and must be read and written, and how. Power relations establish what counts as literacy in a particular context, but such prescriptions and proscriptions can be challenged and changed. People find ways of working 'between the cracks' of institutional imperatives, and subverting them.

> Literacy practices that students choose to engage with in their everyday lives tend to be self-determined in terms of activity, time and place.

In their everyday lives students experienced a good deal of flexibility as regards the literacy practices in which to engage, and how they would engage in them. For example, the majority of students talked about searching the internet. Many of them had the flexibility to do this when it suited them, at a pace that suited them, searching sites of their own interest and interacting with them according to their own preferences. Some students exerted a higher degree of agency, evaluating different search engines and talking articulately about which they preferred and why. Flexibility was also evident in what students told us about the way they wrote letters and notes, where the artefacts were often quite different, and space and place were often related to the purpose of the practice. For example, Emily would take paper from the computer tray in order to write notes for her family whereas Bryn would write on the backs of envelopes and bank statements.

Some literacy practices are generated by the necessary response to imposed textual demands. For example, the literacy practices of filling in an application for a bank loan or registering for council tax might be seen as predetermined and inflexible. However, there is still some flexibility within the apparent constraints of dealing with bureaucracy. In their responses to external textual demands, people develop their own individualised ways of engaging with the textual activity. For example, Eve had personalised the process of completing her online loan application to the bank by using her home computer in her bedroom. She was seeking her own route through the process, drawing upon her existing repertoire of practices (including her ability to use the computer and her previous experiences of filling in forms) to meet the requirements of this activity. When Georgia moved house, she built an Excel spreadsheet of her utilities' providers, banks and other formal organisations, and then mail merged a standard letter to each of them to inform them of her new address. Patricia kept different coloured ring binders for different areas of her household bureaucracy. Russell used a computer program to organise his household finances. This suggests that there is a degree of flexibility in the way formal, externally imposed textual demands might be met through individualised literacy practices.

Data for this project included examples where students appeared to have freedom to choose to engage or not engage with texts, to develop some literacy practices and ignore others. Barton and Hamilton (1998) suggest that vernacular practices give the possibility of more voices and a range of different voices – but the students also provide evidence that they are restricted by the identities that they have or which they want to form. For example, the Childcare students shared their copies of women's magazines but, alongside this sharing, assumed that each other would have read the same magazines and gained the same content, imposing literacy practices upon members of the group through these interactions. Hilary ignored the celebrity and girly magazines that were read by her contemporaries and chose, instead, to read the *Record Collector*. However, she would not read the *Record Collector* at college in case she was mocked by the other students. The dichotomy between the vernacular and the formal, externally imposed literacy practice collapses from both ends of the spectrum. Hilary, as most of the students, felt under some pressure to adhere to the status quo, in this case the magazines that her contemporaries would think were acceptable to read. Although Barton and Hamilton (1998: 253) recognise that 'vernacular literacies are still subject to the social pressures of the family and other social groups and they are regulated by them', we would want to make this claim much stronger in relation to these students.

Students exert a degree of agency over the literacy practices in which they engage in their everyday lives, through making value judgements and choices.

Access to multimedia would seem to imply a greater range of available practices, and therefore a greater degree of individual agency in selecting which practices to use to satisfy different purposes. However, the opposite may well be true. As Burbules (2002: 76) explains:

> While there seems to be a high degree of choice in how and where users move within the Web space, the pragmatics of limited time and resources, of inexperience, or of minimising inconvenience and complexity can all conspire to encourage more passive navigational strategies, and, as such, susceptibility to a higher degree of semantic manipulation.

An example of a practice which is constrained through the relatively limited affordances of the technology is text messaging. There was a degree of similarity in the ways that students received and wrote mobile phone text messages, using similar artefacts, similar language, and with a general ubiquity of space and time. Although the students did not always see the content as particularly creative or interesting (and some students remarked on the banality of their text messages), they experienced the practice as having a clear audience and purpose, agentic, self-determined and multimodal. They also identified with the practice as something that they and their friends 'own' as a preferred means of communication, and they shared the values associated with sending and receiving text messages. This means that these students are most likely to be amongst those creating new registers using the affordances and constraints of the technology, as described for example by Greenfield and Subrahmanyam (2003) in relation to chat-room discourse.

Conclusion

The framework we have outlined provides the basis for understanding the literacy practices in which students participate and provides a language of description through which to frame them. By deconstructing literacy into a set of aspects, we have generated a tool for making explicit their particular configurations and the assumptions that frame them. When referring to literacy therefore, it is necessary to think of it as 'a literacy' which is particular to its context, and to specify how the various aspects are configured. Each configuration could be thought of as a 'micro-practice', the possibilities for which are countless. The characteristics of students' preferred literacy practices have been identified in shaded boxes through-out this chapter, and are summarised here in Box 3.1.

Literacy therefore is not something that we can take for granted as a monolithic category, which we all understand. We have started to see that literacy is not a thing in its own right but an effect of certain arrangements of people, purposes, artefacts and activities. We have explored this in relation to students' everyday literacy practices. We now turn to the literacy practices which mediate learning in college.

Box 3.1   Characteristics of students' preferred literacy practices

1   Literacy practices that individuals engage with in their everyday lives tend to be *purposeful.*

2   Literacy practices that students engage with in their everyday lives tend to have a *clear sense of audience.*

3   Literacy practices that students engage with in their everyday lives tend to be *shared, interactive and collaborative.*

4   Literacy practices that students choose to engage with in their everyday lives tend to be *learned through participation.*

5   Most of the literacy practices that students engage with in their everyday lives tend to be *in tune with students' values and identities.*

6   Literacy practices that students engage with in their everyday lives tend to be *non-linear;* for example, with varied reading paths.

7   Students' literacy practices have specific characteristics of *time and timing, of place and space,* depending on their purposes.

8   In their everyday lives, students tend to prefer literacy practices which draw upon *a range of media and multi-modal forms of communication.*

9   Literacy practices that students choose to engage with in their everyday lives tend to be *varied, not repetitive.*

10   Many of the literacy practices that students choose to engage with in their everyday lives involve *meaning-making, design work, creativity and getting things done.*

11   Literacy practices that students choose to engage with in their everyday lives tend to be *self-determined in terms of activity, time and place.*

12   Students exert *a degree of agency* over the literacy practices in which they engage in their everyday lives, through making value judge-ments and choices.

Literacies across the college curriculum

Having shown the richness and diversity of students' everyday literacy practices, and having presented a framework for analysing literacy practices, we now discuss how the college curriculum is textually mediated in the wide variety of subject areas which we studied (see Tables 0.1 and 0.2).

New college students, whether straight from school or after some experience out of education, will often be embarking on curriculum areas they have had little experience of before. Some academic subjects such as Forensic Science, Philosophy or Media Studies are likely to be new areas involving not only new content, but also new literacy practices. Occupational courses also involve students getting to grips with many and varied literacy practices which they may never have encountered before. For students returning to education after a break, literacy practices associated with an educational setting may have changed. For example, students are often expected to read and possibly produce PowerPoint presentations, and some assessment tasks are now carried out online. Adult students in Construction, for example, needed to negotiate not only the questions for their Health and Safety certificate, but also the technology for inputting their answers. Some mature students may have 'forgotten' how to write essays or reports, while others may feel they have never known. These phenomena are well documented in analyses of academic literacies (e.g., Ivanič 1998; Lillis 2001; Lea and Nicoll 2002).

This chapter examines the literacy practices utilised by lecturers to support learning and those expected of college students. At the early stages of the project, lecturing staff were interviewed about their teaching and the literacy practices they used in their teaching. A number of the college-based researchers, mirroring the students' perspectives on the lack of literacy in their everyday lives, indicated that there was little literacy in their teaching and in what was expected from their students. For example, a Business Administration foundation course unit in Scotland called 'Understanding stock control' was described by its tutor as having no literacy attached to it because it was 'all about numbers'. Closer inspection revealed that the course involved literacy in many different forms. Similarly, Graphical Detailing, a Level 3 unit in Construction in England, is not 'just drawing' as originally depicted by its students. Both courses involved students making notes, filling in forms, reading overheads (OHTs) and handouts, using a PC, and writing reports. The research projects clothe in detail the powerful insight that we live in a 'textually mediated world' (Smith 1990; Barton 2001), and show how it plays out in the context of college education.

For subject lecturers, literacy was often positioned as something that specialist staff dealt with and it was not therefore part of their considera-tion when teaching. This was despite an overwhelming commitment on behalf of the staff to their students and the desire to support the students to achieve as much as possible (for further discussion, see Miller and Satchwell 2006). When teaching was observed, however, and as the college-based researchers became more involved with the project, two things emerged. First, there was a recognition in even the most 'practical' of courses that literacy practices constantly mediate teaching and learning. Here the traditional discourses of viewing courses in terms of theory and practice were seen in a sense to hide the communicative practices that mediate learning. In some subjects, lecturers recognised that literacy prac-tices were an essential part of the 'theory' units on their courses, but not of the 'practical' units. The projects highlighted that such distinctions were misplaced. Second, we noted, as has been the case elsewhere (Bloomer 1997), a disjunction between the espoused curriculum, that is, that which is reported as going on in learning sites, and the enacted curriculum, that is, that which is observed to go on. While all lecturing staff espoused student-centredness, in many learning sites the practices were far more mixed, with teacher-centred and assessment-centred practices often play-ing a significant role in teaching and learning.

The research 'actions for understanding' of pedagogic literacy practices included observation, interviews, the collection of literacy-related artefacts and an in-depth study of pivotal texts used in teaching specific units. The research highlighted the wide and diverse range of literacy practices used by lecturers and expected of students in learning different curriculum subjects. For the college-based researchers it also threw into question the often generalised assumptions about the nature of students doing their course. (For further examples and detailed discussion from this data set see Edwards and Smith 2005; Ivanič et al. 2007; Miller et al. 2007; Edwards 2007; Satchwell and Ivanič 2007, 2009.)

Box 4.1 Mike Ward: lecturer in Multimedia and member of the research team

At the research's inception Mike was 43 and had been teaching for six years. He had left school at 16 with few qualifications. Mike did not volunteer to be a participant in the research project. He began as a willing conscript: he joined at the suggestion of his head of department who wanted to replace a member of staff who had been promoted within the college.

Prior to teaching at Anniesland, Mike had worked as a wedding and promotional video maker. He started studying as a part-time student gaining his NC and HNC in Media Studies. Then he completed his degree, a BSc in Media Technology, in 1998. He gained his teaching qualification (TQFE) in 2002 whilst working part time at Anniesland. For Mike, his practical experience prior to being a teacher in FE was very important. He drew on it when working with students in the classroom. He preferred to teach through the use of practical assignments rather than using a theoretical approach. Indeed, he felt his TQFE training had been too reliant on theory and not enough on practice.

At the outset of the project, Mike was a temporary lecturer in the Multimedia section working in the School of Communications and Languages. By the end of the project he had been made full time and permanent and had been moved to the School of Computing. Throughout most of the first eighteen months of the project, he was concerned about his employment status. In addition to this anxiety, the team he worked with was moved from one teaching section to another. This move caused Mike, and the small team he worked with, some anxiety because with it came a change of leadership style and focus. Mike found himself teaching new subjects to a very different student group. It was important for the wider research team to acknowledge these anxieties and understand their impact on Mike's contribution.

Mike had not been involved with research until this project. He felt that research would be an academic activity and he was concerned that he may not be capable of it. Lack of time for the research was an ongoing problem for Mike. But as the research progressed he became more confident and felt that the experience helped him to understand his students on a level he had not previously been able to achieve. He said he understood the importance of listening to them and not assigning motivations to their behaviours. Rather, he would ask them more 'Why?' questions. Another important long-term impact for Mike was that he changed from asking students to undertake tasks in a step-by-step style to encouraging them to find their own routes through the problem set. However, he felt reluctant to change too many aspects of his teaching practices because he felt an ongoing pressure to meet the criteria required by the assessments. Despite all these constraints, he felt that the whole experience had made him a more reflective practitioner. He particularly blossomed when asked to do something which fitted in with his existing skill set and so volunteered to video our whole team meetings. However, after the research was over, he felt he would probably not engage in research again.

In this chapter, we first raise some important issues relating to 'common-sense' assumptions about teaching and learning, and the role of reading and writing within them. We then describe some of the range and diversity of literacy practices across a wide variety of curriculum areas using a four-point categorisation. We then use the framework outlined in Chapter 3 to analyse a sample of these data in detail. This provides an illustration of how 'noticing' (Mason 2002) through 'actions for understanding' can provide the basis upon which to develop 'actions for change'.

Questioning assumptions about literacies for learning

Through the research we have come to question some widely held assumptions about literacy in the curriculum. First, the research challenges the assumptions inherent in the common distinction between 'vocational' and 'academic' subjects. Our research indicates that the dichotomy between academic and vocational might be re-thought according to the literacy practices required on different courses, which can be seen to relate not only to the subject area, but also to the level at which it is studied, the associated modes of pedagogy and assessment, and the future – imagined or real – of the participants. The dichotomy suggested by vocational subjects being directly related to the world of work, and academic subjects being undertaken for their intrinsic content and value is not so straightforward. Indeed, we now believe the debate needs to be reframed to explore the occupational and academic aspects of any course in colleges and that the concept of vocation needs a complete re-evaluation.

We can illustrate the redundancy of the vocational/academic divide in education from our data. For example, some of the students on a Painting and Decorating NVQ course were retired or pursuing the course purely out of interest in the subject rather than preparing for a working environment; whereas some of those studying Travel and Tourism had no real imagined future in the world of work in the area, but foresaw themselves pursuing further study. Science might be classed as an academic subject, but a BTEC course in Forensic Science is described as having a clear occupational focus; Box 4.2 provides an instance which works in the opposite direction. These examples suggest that it is not the subject area that deems how academic or occupational a course is, so much as the design of the course, the way in which it is taught and assessed, the level at which it is studied, or even the place in which it is studied and the motivations of the students. Each of these factors carries values and priorities which can affect the literacy practices involved.

> **Box 4.2   The interplay between 'occupational' and 'academic' aspects of a course: the case of Multimedia**
>
> Multimedia might be considered an occupational course, but on the units which we researched at the HNC Level many of the practices were more academic, especially with regard to assessment. For example, one unit required students to produce a CD, yet the most important aspect of the unit was to produce a complex planning document which explained what the students were going to do, why, when, how, with whom, changes they implemented and why. Finally, they had to write a critique of what they did. Ultimately, although this was a Multimedia course, it was the writing about the task which was more important for gaining a high mark rather than the making of the CD. In educational contexts, reading and writing *about* something is often more highly valued than doing that something.

There is often the assumption that more academic and higher level subjects require higher order literacy skills. This project indicates that students on an academic track are encultured into a fairly narrow range of literacy practices, and they receive a consistent message that what is expected are forms of extended reading and writing. The literacy practices required for academic studies tended to be more similar to one another, and more continuous with those at school, than in traditionally occupational subjects. In other words, the literacy careers of students on academic courses are clearly mapped. By comparison, occupational and lower level courses often required a diversity of literacy practices from students, resulting in inconsistent messages about the literacy practices required of them. In occupational subjects, the literacy demands are many and varied, and, crucially, frequently include literacy practices which are more commonly associated with academic subjects. While the value of literacy practices associated with academic subjects may be higher in cultural terms, the literacy practices associated with occupational subjects may in some respects be more demanding, complex and confusing.

Literacies in colleges

We found four broad groupings for the reading and writing involved in studying at college. Each category has literacy practices which are specific to it and characteristics which distinguish it from the others. While these categories are derived from the study of colleges, we believe they have wider interpretive power, applying to other forms of educational provision too.

A   *Literacy practices involved in becoming and being a college student*
Examples include filling in registration forms, claiming a travel pass, reading noticeboards, using a college diary.

B   *Literacy practices for learning content*
Examples include reading and making notes from a textbook; researching using the internet.

C   *Literacy practices for assessment*
Examples include producing an essay or a report; demonstrating key/core skills; and providing evidence such as a logbook or portfolio.

D   *Literacy practices relating to an imagined future*
Examples include writing food orders; reading menus; creating advertising materials, academic referencing conventions.

In what follows we illustrate and discuss each category, with a particular focus on C, since these are such high-stakes literacy practices.

Literacy practices for becoming and being a college student

When students first decide to go to college, there are procedures they are required to go through, many of which are mediated by texts. They may first read prospectuses in hard copy or online. They have to apply for courses. They have to navigate the spaces of the college, often by following signs to specific buildings and rooms. Students enrol by completing multiple forms relating to their personal details, their qualifications and the courses they wish to take. The registration process is becoming more electronically based to varying degrees in different colleges, but still requires the completion of paper-based forms.

During induction they are given enormous quantities of paper-based texts relating to the college facilities, health and safety, travel arrangements, college policy, timetables, maps, details of their courses. Noticeboards are often overloaded with texts and are often contested spaces for staff and students. Students are required to undertake personal learning plans, given study planners, provided with leaflets from various organisations, literature on funding, and evaluation forms on the induction process. Interviews with students indicated that the sheer quantity of paperwork meant that many of these texts were stowed in bags and remained unread. Interviews with staff suggested there was no expectation that these documents would be read but that they needed to be produced as part of the culture of accountability.

Students from families on low income in England also need to negotiate the paperwork associated with Education Maintenance Allowance (EMA), which itself requires students to have their own bank accounts, while those with children may also need to complete forms to secure places in the college crèche. All of this is before the students even begin their chosen courses.

Figure 4.1 The textual mediation of enrolment

Once the course starts, tutors frequently begin classes with ice-breaking activities, designed to allow the students to get to know one another and to form relationships within the group. Often these activities will involve students in reading scenarios or tasks and some form of writing. For example, students in Childcare were asked to write down information about themselves including their likes, dislikes and imagined futures. In addition, students may develop means of communication amongst themselves as friends and peers, including sharing phone numbers and email addresses, and joining chat-rooms.

Throughout their time at college, students will also be interacting with texts which relate to their ongoing involvement with the college as well as their actual courses. Hence, they will read student diaries, newsletters, poster boards, displays, signs, menus, brochures, leaflets, college and university prospectuses. In addition they will deal with texts which are not specific to college life itself, such as bank accounts, telephone accounts, health forms, childcare forms, and job and university applications. In this way, becoming a student is not simply about the relationship with the college, but can also entail encounters with other bureaucracies as well. The research showed that these were not always handled on an individual basis, but were supported and negotiated with parents, staff and peers. (For further discussion of students' engagement in such literacy practices, see Fowler 2008.)

Literacy practices for learning content

Ubiquity and diversity of literacies for learning

The course content is established largely by the interpretations of unit descriptor texts produced by the awarding bodies, and specifications are provided for tutors to follow. This means that curriculum and pedagogy depend on an interaction between predetermined specifications, organisational context and culture, and approaches favoured by individual tutors. We found considerable variation in the methods employed, which depended in part on tutors' own preferred literacy practices, beliefs about teaching and learning, their status within their department, and their consequent feelings of confidence and autonomy. Many of the lecturing staff felt they had less autonomy to decide content and pedagogy than in principle they do have.

The repertoire of literacy practices in teaching and learning exhibited far less variety than the literacy practices in students' everyday lives. There were many similarities in texts and practices across contexts: reading college-produced handouts and booklets, reading from textbooks, providing written answers to written questions, copying from whiteboards, reading from PowerPoint presentations produced by tutors, researching on the internet, producing diagrams on flip chart paper, making notes from

Figure 4.2 Learning technical terms in Painting and Decorating

books, websites and lectures. Literacy practices for learning tended to be teacher-directed: there were relatively few instances of students taking their own initiative as to how to use reading or writing for learning. What was in common across all the courses and units studied was the prevalence of literacy as a tool for learning. Even on courses where the tutors had thought that there was little reading involved, they were amazed to discover just how much their students had to read and write in order to learn. In lower level and more occupational courses, there was often an even greater diversity of text types and artefacts drawn upon in teaching and learning, for example, definition cards used for learning technical terms in Painting and Decorating, as shown in Figure 4.2. The evidence shows that there is a textual dimension to nearly all learning, in addition to cognitive, social, practical and affective dimensions.

On many courses the students were reading and writing a wide variety of genres. In English Language and Literature AS Level, for example, the students would ultimately be assessed by an externally set exam. During the term, a great deal of their time was taken up with formative assessment tasks set by the teacher to monitor their learning. These took the form of written assignments, practising the literacy practice which would be required in the exam, although importantly using the technology of the keyboard rather than the pen. However, the students also engaged in more creative writing tasks, imitating various genres, such as teenage magazine articles, children's stories, newspaper articles and biographies. Students were therefore required to read examples of these genres and to practise writing in different styles. This diversity was also to be found in occupational courses, where, for instance, Level 1 Childcare students had to design and produce a leaflet for parents, using text and images. Although ostensibly a low level course, the design principles required to produce such an artefact are high level.

Academic literacy practices on higher level courses

At higher levels there was more emphasis on students researching for their own information. In other words, there was often less reading and writing for regurgitation and more activity which in principle was intended to establish the student's own understanding. Students were given particular topics to 'research'. However, intention and reality did not always match up. Sending students to 'The Learning Centre' to use the internet to research a topic often did not, according to the librarians involved, lead to learning and understanding. Students needed guidance on the evaluative reading practices associated with the information gathering aspect of research, on establishing the credibility of different sources of information and on how to make use of them. For example, when some Childcare students were asked to find out about autism, some did not recognise the difference between personal accounts of the condition and more general clinical information. This is despite the fact that they have no difficulty with selecting and evaluating internet sites related to their own interests.

The inclusion of more academic elements in courses seemed to be associated with the level of the course: the higher the level, the more academic literacy practices were required. The students appeared to be being prepared for further study at university rather than for a specific occupation. The higher level courses (BTECs) in Childcare, Forensic Science, and Travel and Tourism had characteristics of academic study, such as the requirement that assignments need to be thoroughly researched and include references, bibliographies and appendices. Hence, although these curriculum areas are ones which are considered to be occupational, at higher levels the literacy practices become more academic. Given that the students on, for example, the Level 3 BTEC in Travel and Tourism course were, like the Level 2 students, interested in travel and working abroad, and were similarly described as lively, outgoing and practical people, these academic literacy practices did not seem relevant to the future they saw for themselves.

Students moving from unit to unit and from course to course could often get different and confusing messages. This was most noticeable in relation to the common practice of asking students to write 'an essay'. In some subjects, an essay was expected to be an argued case, as in the more tradi- tional definition of the genre. However, observation of the artefacts being produced as essays showed that in other subjects, short question-and- answer assignments were viewed by tutors as essays, while in others, management-style reports were expected. The definition of 'essay' seemed to be subject-specific, and varied considerably from course to course.

Literacy practices for reflecting on learning

A subset of literacy practices for learning content was identified later on in the research which we termed 'reflective literacy practices for learning'. On some courses, students were being asked to use writing to reflect on their learning processes. For example, in Construction a tutor who believed it was important for his students to view their work with a critical eye, and to develop a quality control strategy for themselves, asked them to produce a reflective log containing photographs of their construction work. Towards the end of the year, they created from this a group PowerPoint presentation about the year and presented this to the rest of the class, leading to discussions and critiques of their techniques.

Some tutors used what they called logbooks on an informal basis, where they were more like reflective diaries, for example in Business Admini- stration, where they were used to record the students' learning. As with essays, the 'logbook' genre, normally associated with providing evidence for external assessment (see below), could be used for different purposes, thereby reshaping the nature of the literacy practice.

One Business Administration tutor asked students to keep a record of all their work as a diary. However, some students did not appear to value this practice and made only minimal entries in their diaries. Because there was no time regularly set aside for this activity, the students found themselves trying to fill in several weeks at a time, which they found repetitive and boring. This not only points to the importance of students understanding the purpose of the literacy practices in which they are asked to engage, but also poses questions about assumptions made that specific forms of writing come naturally to people. To write a reflective diary is a specific genre of writing that itself has to be learnt.

Literacy practices for assessment

Assessment is a significant part of all courses in college and indeed it has been argued that learning and teaching in colleges has become assessment driven, a view endorsed by the findings of this research. Many of the texts and practices observed were focused on preparing students for assessment tasks and scaffolding them to be able to do the tasks set successfully. In particular, we noticed that on many courses the main role for writing was in demonstrating knowledge and understanding, rather than as a resource for learning itself; to put it another way, writing was being treated as a product, rather than a process. Many of the literacy practices described in the previous section, where they resulted in a written product, were also used as part of coursework portfolios which would ultimately be assessed.

The literacy dependence of summative assessment

There were disjunctions between the literacy practices for learning and those for assessment and also between the assessment tasks and the sorts of workplace literacy practices for which students were being prepared. The students often appeared to be being assessed on criteria drawn from anti-cipated further study at university rather than from a specific occupation. For instance, in the Level 3 BTEC Travel and Tourism course, for assess-ment the students were required to find and record information relating to three tourist destinations. The literacy practices relating to the content of the course included searching on the internet, reading textbooks and mak-ing notes. Providing their work in the form of an assessment, however, required writing up in coherent sentences and paragraphs, using their own words instead of those in the source text, and supplying references, bibliog-raphies and appendices. These are academic literacy practices which in themselves do not contribute to the students' knowledge of their subject area and have little bearing on a future world of work, which was the prime goal of the students. This raises questions about the authenticity and synergies in the reading and particularly the writing for assessment.

Figure 4.3 The excessive textuality of assessment on college courses

However, not all literacy for assessment was focused on traditional academic genres. For instance, in Travel and Tourism Level 2, assessment included writing a report about customer service, with headings provided, and demonstrating an understanding of relevant legislation by writing which laws have been breached in a set of twelve different scenarios, provided in a workbook.

Evidence-providing literacy practices

Evidence of learning is also often assessed in vocational courses through the completion of a portfolio or log book. In Business Administration Level 4, students were required to bring evidence from their working lives to college to enter into a portfolio against the specific criteria set by the awarding body. In Painting and Decorating Levels 1 and 2 students assembled portfolios including captioned photographs of their work in and out of the college workshop, coursework and other evidence such as letters and certificates.

In Catering and Hospitality, filling in the logbook is a means of providing evidence of students' practical work. The means of communicating this evidence is through writing, by hand, in a format which requires the student to read carefully the instructions and surrounding information. There are also 'Underpinning Knowledge' questions to provide evidence of the students' understanding. Figure 4.4 shows Catering and Hospitality students completing their logbooks in their waiters' uniforms, in between busy periods in the training restaurant. Many students find the literacy practices for providing evidence more onerous and problematic than carrying out the practices themselves. There is an irony in the fact that recording the practice is more difficult than doing it.

Unlike reading or writing a menu, or taking a food order, which have a clear practical application and purpose, filling in a logbook is an example of a literacy practice imposed as an additional requirement for the completion of the course. Although the logbook states that questions may be administered orally, in practice this does not take place. Further, while the students may produce elaborate posters or PowerPoint presentations advertising the restaurant, they are not accredited for these literacy-rich activities. The literacy artefact which counts in the NVQ qualification is the completed logbook – arguably requiring a literacy practice which is found nowhere other than in an educational setting.

Literacy practices to mediate assessment requirements

On several courses we noticed what could be called 'intermediate documentation', designed to explain or simplify the assessment requirements and to alleviate the difficulties lecturers expected students to face. During

Figure 4.4 Students completing their logbooks in the training restaurant

the course of the research, the Catering and Hospitality tutors also produced a restaurant journal which was intended to accompany the logbook
to provide evidence as required by the awarding body. The intention
behind these documents was to help the students to negotiate more
complex texts and to act as a bridge for the students before they commit to
the final documentation. They go some way towards addressing the
difficulties voiced by students such as:

> I used to just write in the box what I'd done and hope it'd be okay . . .
> Cos you don't want to go up like five times in a row and go like 'I just
> don't get it. It's not making any sense'.

In some ways the completion of these documents means 'doing the same
thing twice', but in other ways is perceived, by both tutors and students, as
crucial to the accurate completion of official documents. By using colour,
pictures, larger fonts and accessible language, tutors are scaffolding and
modelling the way into more formal literacy practices with which the
students would not immediately identify, and which could potentially
intimidate and stultify students' progress. As one tutor explained, it would
be almost impossible to fill in a logbook without help, as she herself could
do it only after 'years of practice'.

Fulfilling key/core skills requirements

An important aspect of assessment was that of key/core skills. In England,
students under the age of 19 were required to take key skills qualifications
in Communications, Application of Number and Information Technology.
The work undertaken for these qualifications was sometimes integrated into
the teaching of the subject, and sometimes taught in separate classes, with
or without specialist teachers. Many tutors attempted to relate the content
to the curriculum area being studied. For example, for key skills Communications, Level 2 students were required to read and produce a summary of
two documents and write two different kinds of texts. During the research
the Hospitality key skills tutor introduced the theme of a 'fantasy restaurant'
and students produced a variety of texts relating to this, including posters,
menus, advertising materials, floor plans, reports and so on. On this course
key skills sessions were additional to the classes devoted to the qualification.
The literacy practices for key skills assessment significantly included values
associated with academic literacy, and the key skills guidance information
referred to the need for correct spelling, punctuation and sentence construction. In key skills work students were assessed according to these
criteria. The imaginative tutor in this case encouraged the students to use
their interest in catering to inspire their choices of texts, but for the NVQ
itself, the production of these literacy artefacts was extrinsic and additional
to the requirements of the qualification.

For college students taking academic A Levels, the achievement of key skills qualifications was considered to be less demanding than for occupational students, simply because the literacy practices required are extensions or replications of those that are required of them already. Students could even use the same piece of work twice if it fulfilled the requirements that they 'make a formal presentation; read and synthesise information from at least two extended documents; and write two types of document giving different information about complex subjects' (QCA 2004). By 2010, however, 'key skills' are to be replaced by 'functional skills', and the balance of criteria may change.

Literacy practices relating to the imagined future for students on the course

In more academic and higher level courses, students are often rehearsing the literacy practices that will be required for them to progress to higher level study, including such things as referencing conventions, reading extended texts and so on. For occupational courses, the situation is more complex. Educational progression is usually only one outcome of such courses. Preparation for the occupation is another. As we have indicated, there can be an implicit tension in the literacy practices required for the purposes of progression and for entering the occupation (for further discussion, see Edwards and Miller 2008). This is played out particularly in those courses that either have work placements or simulate the workplace. Here students are often required to do double literacy, that is, that required for operating in the workplace and that required for the purposes of their study. The literacy practices of these (simulated) workplaces are often overlooked by both tutors and students, as the focus is on the practical without recognition of the communicative.

Figure 4.5 shows four examples of students reading and writing in workplace settings. Photos a, b and c show students on Catering and Hospitality courses at work in a real work environment (RWE): the college training restaurant. These are the same students as the ones who appear in Figure 4.4: the photographs were taken within about an hour of each other. In all the photos the students are dressed in their restaurant service uniforms. Just a glance at the photos illustrates graphically the vast differences between literacy practices for assessment and literacy practices for doing the job. In the literacy practices for assessment, the students are subject to pedagogic power relations, satisfying the requirements to gain their qualifications and are supervised by a tutor. They have heads down, working in identical blue folders to complete grids of information about their learning. In the college restaurant, the students are also waiters, waitresses and restaurant managers, reading and writing orders to get the job done: the paperwork is integrated into the activities of serving customers, getting them seated, taking their orders, communicating their orders to the chefs,

Figure 4.5 Literacy practices in real work environments, placements and
learning through practical experience on vocational courses

keeping track of their bills. The students are learning through doing. Even
though photos a, b and c in Figure 4.5 are taken within a college building,
not only the texts involved, but also the literacy practices surrounding them
are shaped by real-life action, rather than pedagogic imperatives.

Photo d is from the Painting and Decorating workshop, in which the
teaching and learning is based around the types of task that the students
will need to do in their future work. Compared to RWEs such as the training
restaurant, and placements such as the Childcare Centres discussed in the
next chapter, these are simulated work experiences. However, the reading
and writing is still 'for real' as it is part of getting the job done.

Literacy practices in Catering and Hospitality:
an extended example

In this section we present an extended example of the literacy practices
associated with learning in one session of one course (see Box 4.3). We
then use the framework introduced in Chapter 3 to analyse in detail some
of the similarities and differences among the literacy practices represented
in the example. (See also Ivanič 2006; Satchwell and Ivanič 2007 and 2009
for further discussion of the literacy practices on Catering and Hospitality
courses.)

Box 4.3   Literacy practices in a day in a training restaurant

Students on a Catering and Hospitality course at Lancaster and Morecambe College spent one full day a week in classes and the rest of their week in a Real Work Environment (RWE). There were four RWEs at the college: Coulsons, the college silver-service restaurant, where members of the public could come for a meal; the Bistro, which was the college canteen serving students and staff; the Main Production Kitchen which prepared food for both the Bistro and the Restaurant; and the Pastry Kitchen. Students spent two long days – 9.00am to 9.30pm – or three shorter days – 9.00am to 4.00pm – in a RWE. Although the LfLFE project focused its research on one unit at Level 1 (Introduction to Catering and Hospitality) and one at Level 2 (NVQ2 Food and Drink Service), the students at Levels 1, 2 and 3 worked together as a team in their RWE. This meant that the literacy practices implicit in the tasks carried out by students were not necessarily differentiated according to the level of the qualification being taken.

The following list describes the literacy events occurring during a typical session in the Coulsons restaurant between 3.00pm to 9.00pm. The students were in their restaurant worker uniforms throughout.

1 A student used the computer in the kitchen to complete a PowerPoint presentation to be used on the TV screens in and around the restaurant to promote special offers in the restaurant for Christmas.
2 A student read and completed a 'Stillroom Duties' checklist. This involved reading the sheet, which was a double-sided standard text used in all restaurant sessions, designed to help the students remember what they needed to do as well as set standards for how things should be conducted. When they had completed each duty, the student ticked a box, and then a member of staff signed next to it once it has been checked.
3 Stillroom duties included putting in requisitions for food items. This involved using a small commercially produced ('Challenge') dupli-cate pad. The student checked the stock already in the stillroom and then wrote an order in the book for the items needed. They worked with reference to the stillroom checklist, which had a recommended stock list and the amounts needed.
4 A student read names and covers from the bookings diary in order to create a table plan. This was usually done by Level 3 students but could be Level 2 students on occasion.
5 The students practise taking drinks orders in teams. The texts pro-duced are handwritten in biro on scraps of thick yellow paper and

continued

include the table number, the order and the student's initials. These texts needed to be understood by the person working behind the bar making up the drinks.

6 The students laid up the tables, including setting out menus, comment cards, wine cards and indemnity cards.

7 A student created an arrivals and courses sheet based on the bookings in the diary. This involved filling in names on a template, which was headed 'Daily Restaurant List'. This list was later updated by a student on the hotplate as courses were served – the sheet had columns by each name for each course.

8 Students read through the menu as a group and checked that they knew what each dish consisted of. This involved each student having a copy of the menu, and a tutor or the head waiter (a student) explaining the contents and answering questions. The menu was likely to contain words and phrases from other languages, particularly French.

9 Students were informed of what the canapés are (by other students working in the kitchen) and they wrote this down on a scrap of paper for themselves to inform customers.

10 Students took food and drinks orders from customers. This could involve explaining dishes to customers, dealing with questions and writing orders.

11 Students read food orders for changing cutlery appropriately.

12 Students working on the bar needed to read drinks orders, the bar till and the wine list. They inputted information into the till, printed off receipts and sent them to the customers or reception to contribute to making up the bills.

13 The wine waiter read the wine list, advised customers and wrote wine orders. The wine list contained elaborate descriptive language and words and phrases from various European languages.

14 The head waiter recorded the number of portions available and the desserts list. The desserts list, relating to the sweet trolley, was written on the whiteboard in the kitchen and students read and memorised this for customer information.

15 A student on reception completed the arrivals list and read all the drinks and food orders to complete the customer bills and the cash summary sheet. The bills were completed on the computer and printed out for customers. The cash summary sheet was printed out and one section was completed by hand, filling in figures in boxes.

16 Students collected and read all comment cards (double-sided) completed by the customers.

17 At points during the session the students entered information into their logbooks. This involved the student reading the performance

criteria (although students said in interview that they did not necessarily read these), filling in the date and writing in the activity carried out. The tutor would then tick the box according to what has been done to the correct standard for each performance criterion.

18 The students were also provided with information booklets relating to each unit. For example unit 2FDS5 'Provide a Silver Service' had an accompanying information booklet containing five double-sided pages of information. It was divided into two sections headed '5.1 Silver Serve Food' and '5.2 Clear Finished Courses'. At the end of each section was a heading 'What have you learnt?' with three questions and space for the answers. This was designed by a tutor at the college as a way of introducing the Underpinning Knowledge information which eventually needed to be entered into the logbook.

19 There was also a tutor-produced booklet of three double-sided pages relating to 5.1 and 5.2 headed 'Underpinning Knowledge Questions'. This contained questions which were taken from the logbook, but which were expanded and/or reworded. The intention was for students to complete the questions in the booklets for each unit instead of in the logbook because the logbook was perceived to be complicated and daunting to students. The booklet appeared much more reader friendly than the logbook. For example it contained pictures, tables, the pronoun 'we' rather than 'you', 'simpler' language and a self-explanatory layout.

The majority of the literacy practices in the vignette relate to the students' present and imagined workplace. Most of the literacy practices will be replicated in the students' futures if they pursue a career in catering and hospitality – although some may vary subtly; for example, some restaurants will have different conventions for producing menus or writing food orders. However, because the Catering and Hospitality students are working in a 'real' work environment, involving real food and real people, some activities have multiple dimensions involving literacy practices which fall into more than one category. For example, the completion of the order book (Item 3 in Box 4.3) is, like many of the tasks, needed in a practical sense, in this case to maintain the stock levels in the stillroom. A copy is also needed for the supplier as evidence of what has been taken from the stock. The intention behind the activity is for students to learn to order food and equipment internally and to understand the importance of keeping records. The text is similar to one which would be used in the students' future careers, and completing the form is therefore a literacy practice related to the workplace, but in this context the activity has pedagogic functions too: the text itself is also required as evidence for assessment.

From our observations of students at work in the training restaurant, the literacy practices which are intrinsic to 'getting the job done', despite being multiple and diverse, pose few problems to the students. As part of carrying out a job which represents a future with which they identify, reading and writing become unremarkable as such. In the same way that a student talking about playing a computer game does not focus on how much reading is involved (on screen and in the instruction booklet), a dedicated chef or waiter does not complain about writing or reading a menu. It is in the doubling of the literacy practices to also provide evidence for assessment in more conventional educational ways that the challenges are faced. Here the scale of the students' learning is not only assessed on their capacity to participate and contribute successfully to the workplace alone, but also on the reification of their practices through particular forms of reading and writing that are scaled in more traditional ways.

The framework of aspects of a literacy practice helps us to understand literacies in educational contexts, to compare and contrast them with each other, and with practices in other domains of life, and to identify aspects of them which might be amenable to change. We can see that the literacy practices involved in the session in the training restaurant are different from one another in a variety of ways. The clearest distinction during observations was between those practices that students engaged with as part of serving in the restaurant and those that they found more difficult to engage with, such as completing the logbooks. If we look at these in terms of the framework, we can see that they differ in significant ways.

The reading and writing involved in running the restaurant and serving customers has a clear and identifiable *purpose* and *audience* which could be perceived by different individuals as simply getting the job done, or as 'making people happy' as one student described it. While engaging in the literacy practices described in the restaurant, the students take on *roles, identities and values* of waiters and restaurant managers: people who have a unique position in social life, some of them resenting their duties and their subservience to the orders of the restaurant manager, some taking pride in the service they offer and taking pleasure in a job well done, including the textual aspects of it. If the students identify with a future in the catering industry, they are likely to share the values associated with it and this will strengthen their identification with the roles and subject positions held out by these practices. Their *participation* in these practices involves interaction, collaboration and direct communication among people, with other workers (students) or customers or both. Explaining a menu to a customer and writing down her order involves not only the *actions and processes* of speech, gesture and movement but also reading and writing. The reading includes scanning the menu for the details of particular items, and linking these to recently acquired knowledge about the characteristics of these dishes. The writing has to be fast, perhaps having to change what is written several times on a small piece of paper, in a way which will be understood by the cooks in the kitchen (see Figure 4.5, picture a) as well as by the restaurant manager responsible for the bill (see Figure 4.5, picture b) – all this simultaneously with holding a pleasant conversation with the customers.

The literacy practices associated with different jobs in the restaurant involve a wide range of *modes and technologies*, and draw on a wide variety of *genres, styles and designs*. For example, the PowerPoint presentation to promote the Christmas menu and booking details (Item 1 in Box 4.3) uses a desktop computer, linked to plasma screens in the restaurant. By contrast, the technology for the stillroom requisitions is a pre-printed pad to be completed in pen or pencil (Items 2 and 3 in Box 4.3), and the texts on the table settings are created by computer, but distributed on different types of card (Item 6 in Box 4.3). The *modes* of communication integrate spoken and written language with visual modalities, particularly pictures (on the PowerPoint), graphics (on the menus), features of font (on the texts placed on the tables), tabular layout (the stillroom checklists) and freehand graphics (the table plan). In contrast to this diversity, the *language* of all texts is English and the *content* of these texts is limited to food, drink and customer satisfaction. Some aspects of these literacy practices have a degree of *flexibility* as to how they are realised; for example, the content, modalities and conventions of style and design for the customer information about special offers for Christmas (Item 1 in Box 4.3) are open to the students' choice and creativity, and there are few constraints of time, space and participation structures on how this information is produced. However, other practices (Items 9–15) are subject to quite rigid *constraints* regarding what is read and written, and how, when and where this is done, imposed by the immediate needs of serving customers, and by the norms for doing this imposed by the restaurant management.

In contrast, *purpose* and *audience* are less clear once we include the secondary purposes of learning through experience, and acquiring evidence to contribute to a qualification through compiling a logbook (Items 17, 18 and 19 in Box 4.3). This has a non-immediate and unspecified *audience*, such as the tutor, the external verifier, the awarding body, or all of these. Hence the *purpose* – beyond fulfilling a requirement of the course – is not immediately clear. In terms of patterns of *participation*, the completion of the logbook is an activity which requires working individually, under the supervision of the tutor. The students are working individually, and yet they are all doing the same thing, unlike many of the activities 'on the job' where individuals undertake different tasks which contribute to the running of the restaurant, as in real life (Items 1, 2, 3, 4, 7, 13, 14 and 15 in Box 4.3). While the students may aspire to work in the catering industry, they are less likely to identify with the *roles, identities and values* of a literacy practice which has the sole purpose of providing evidence of events already carried out. One student valued his logbook as a record of his achievements and was keen for it to be presented as neatly and comprehensively as possible. Other students thought that the logbook would not be used to differentiate between potential employees, but was simply a requirement for gaining a qualification which all potential employees would be expected to have. The logbook itself is a *genre* which uses conventions of *style and design* which are unlikely to be encountered anywhere else, and, while broadly having the same subject-matter as the other reading and writing in the restaurant, deals with this *content* in a 'pedagogised' way, making it seem unfamiliar and divorced from reality. While there is some *flexibility* regarding when, where and how the logbook is completed – in this case, it is done in between sittings in the restaurant – there are also severe *constraints* regarding what is considered appropriate *content*, and regarding the conventions of *language* use and *style* which are required for successful completion of the task.

The analysis of literacy practices involved in the Catering and Hospitality unit illustrates the number and variety of literacy practices related to the workplace which are hardly recognised as relating to literacy at all. One of the reasons for them appearing to be insignificant is, we suggest, that they are shaped by purpose, and are experienced as meaningful. Hence they do not pose difficulties for the students – they simply 'get on with them' as part of 'getting the job done'. A reason for this might be that, according to our analyses in relation to the framework, work-based literacy practices have more in common with everyday literacy practices (having many of the characteristics identified in Box 3.1 at the end of Chapter 3) than with those associated with formal curriculum and pedagogy.

Literacy practices in colleges: issues arising

Colleges are textually mediated communicative spaces. From the descriptions above, we can see that students are required to learn new literacy practices as they pursue their courses: learning to be a college student, learning the course content, completing assessments and preparing for the future. There are specific literacy practices which might be required in the students' futures, for example, writing food or drink orders in catering, reading building specifications in Painting and Decorating, handwriting on posters or displays in Childcare. If the students' futures are perceived as more academic, then new literacy practices might include writing bibliographies or extended essays, but, as we have argued, these are more like continuations of academic literacy practices experienced in school. In some courses, the completion of the course itself involves learning a specific literacy practice, such as filling in the logbook or portfolio required to gain the qualification.

The above has been illustrative and illuminating of the amount, diversity and often hiddenness of literacy practices in colleges. At one level, we found a greater similarity of literacies for learning across curriculum areas than we had envisioned. PowerPoint presentations, handouts, formatted assessment tasks are all illustrations of artefacts produced across a range of curriculum areas. However, within this similarity, there are nonetheless important differences, which we were able to identify and which then provided the basis for the development of a more explicitly literacy-informed pedagogy.

Literacy practices which are required for the completion of college courses often had very different characteristics from those of literacy practices in everyday life, which we identified at the end of Chapter 2 and recapitulated in Box 3.1. For example, the writing of an assignment for a Travel and Tourism Level 3 course in England requires students to work alone (*participation*), producing text in a linear format (*process*), and the *activity* involves reformulating and presenting information previously provided, using the conventions of academic *genres* such as referencing and bibliographies. The reader(s) for the activity are ambiguous, as different students may perceive different readers, such as the tutor, the external verifier, or the awarding body. Students may view these *audiences* positively (for example they may like their tutor) or negatively (they may see the external verifier as critical and demanding). Crucially, the students are unlikely to be absolutely clear about what their reader wants. The *purpose* may be perceived as equally ambiguous: it has a referential rather than communicative function, but the information is already known by the reader(s). Therefore it has the quality of a test, designed to establish whether the writer knows what the reader knows, but also requiring the writer to produce the information in a standard format in a specified number of words (*language, genres, styles and designs*). The writing of the assignment may be carried out either at college or at home, but college sessions are often also devoted to the task, and a deadline is specified (*flexibility and constraints*).

The differences identified here may partly be attributed to the preoccupation within educational institutions with assessment and accreditation. Many of the literacy practices we observed, and among these the majority of the writing practices, were focused exclusively on the demonstration of knowledge, understanding and competence, or on the completion of logbooks to provide evidence of what had been learnt. Whatever the reasons for these differences, the research showed that many students were disaffected by the reading and writing required of them, and were not identifying with their purposes, content or any other aspects of these practices. When asked to consider how the findings of the research might inform changes in practice to address these issues, there was a feeling amongst some of the lecturers involved in the research that they are constrained by factors beyond their control. These include the timetable, the availability of resources in the classroom, the examining body's assessment criteria, the format of the logbook, the demands on tutors' time, the lack of desk space in a staffroom and so on. All of these are legitimate and well-founded concerns within many colleges, and a by-product of our research is that it indicates the frequency, extent and impact of some of these constraints.

Being a college student, learning and demonstrating competence are all textually mediated activities and processes, all requiring an array of reading and writing which constitute and contribute to many different literacy practices. These are not simply sets of skills, but are complex combinations of aspects or dimensions of literacy, some of which students might value and identify with, and some of which they will not. It is clear that the communicative aspects of the curriculum are often hidden from both tutors and students and that some of the assumptions made about literacy need to be rethought in order that learning is supported *through* literacy rather than being constrained by the assumptions made *about* literacy by lecturers and students, as well as by the wider communities. We will now pursue some of these issues in a bit more depth in the specific context of the Childcare curriculum.

Chapter 5

Comparisons across contexts

The textual mediation of learning on Childcare courses

Part of the rationale for the research was to compare and contrast literacies for learning between the Scottish, English and Welsh colleges, given the different policy and curriculum contexts. In order to do this, it was decided that one of the curriculum areas studied within each of the colleges would be Childcare. This area was of particular interest for this research because language and literacy not only mediate the students' learning, but are also subjects to be learnt about, since children's language and literacy development are part of the content of Childcare courses.

Box 5.1 Joanne Knowles: lecturer in Childcare and member of the research team

Joanne Knowles worked as a nursery nurse for six years before becoming a nursery manager for two and a half years. She then went into teaching in college, which she saw as 'a natural progression'. She worked as a full-time lecturer in the large Academy of Health, Social Care and Early Years at Preston College. At the time of the research she was the BTEC placement co-ordinator at the college, supporting and encouraging the students in the workplace as well as teaching them in college. She loved teaching and thoroughly enjoyed her work.

She took on the role of college-based researcher for the project, for which she had two hours remission from teaching a week. She researched one of the units she taught from each of two courses: 'Play and Practical Activities' from the Level 1 Foundation Childcare Award, and 'Human Growth and Development' from the Level 3 Edexcel BTEC National Certification in Early Years.

She said that after she had been involved in the research for a year, ideas from the project started to manifest themselves in her teaching. She described how her understanding about students' literacy practices 'travelled' to the rest of her teaching. For example, it emerged from the research that students did not understand the meanings of some words

---

continued

which might be critical to their understanding of the course. She also found out that the students often used the internet to find things out in their everyday lives. So the following year, when she introduced a new topic on the Level 3 course, 'Equality, Diversity and Rights', she took dictionaries and laptops to the first session of the topic, offering the students a choice of how to look up the new terms. She said that the students immediately took ownership of the task, one saying to another 'Look on dictionary.com'. Her work is featured on the LfLFE project DVD (Pardoe and Ivanič 2007).

Childcare as a subject raises interesting questions which are relevant to vocational subjects more generally, since it seeks to enable both academic progression and progression into the workplace. Yet the literacy practices, types of texts and types of engagement with texts required vary according to the destination of the student. In examining Childcare, therefore, we were able to explore how, if the dual purpose of the curriculum is to prepare the student both for the occupation and for educational progression, these two purposes should be balanced and integrated. To what extent is the purpose of the programme to extend education, and to what extent to fit occupational context? Each has implications for the literacy practices in which people participate, both students and tutors. Literacy practices therefore provide a lens through which to explore other important educational questions, such as progression (Edwards and Miller 2008) and for this reason Childcare offered a telling case.

Our study of Childcare courses also helped us to explore issues around the mobilisation of literacy practices from one domain to another in a telling way, as working with children entailed work placements as well as college learning, in addition to interfacing with the literacy practices of the students' everyday lives. To this end, we start the chapter with a case study of a single Childcare student, Eve. This case addresses the issue of how far practices in one domain can transfer into others, and throws into question the assumption that literacy practices per se are transferable. The capacity to mobilise practices across domains is also linked to aspects of the framework we presented in Chapter 3. We then pull back to the wider comparison of the different policy contexts of England, Scotland and Wales, in order to explore similarities and differences in Childcare provision using the lens of literacy as a way of focusing our understanding. Most of the examples come from the Scottish and English data, with one section devoted to specific aspects of the teaching of Childcare in Wales. Here, despite the different policy contexts, we find more similarities than differences in terms of the enacted curriculum. The learning and teaching of Childcare is a textually mediated hybrid space in which practices from different domains intermingle on a regular basis.

The interface between everyday literacies and literacies for learning: the case of Eve

Eve was an 18-year-old woman studying on the Level 1 Childcare course taught by Joanne Knowles (featured in Box 5.1). Eve had given birth to her son, Alex, a few months prior to taking her GCSEs at high school and she felt that this had had a negative impact upon her grades. Dressed in sporty clothes with the occasional designer label, Eve was bright and chatty. She had a good relationship with the other eight students taking her course and interacted well with her tutor.

To get to her Childcare classes in a morning required Eve to make a complex journey and the points along her journey represent some of the main contexts of her life. She would get up at her boyfriend Ben's house, where she and Alex lived. Although the recently bought house was in Ben's name, Eve had taken responsibility for paying some of the household bills. Together, Ben would drive them to Eve's mother's house in the neighbouring town where, until recently, Eve lived with her parents. While Ben departed to his paid job, Eve's mother would drive Eve and Alex to the community nursery, which she managed. Alex attended this nursery and Eve elected to do her Childcare placement there. On college days, Eve would then say goodbye to her mother and Alex and catch two buses to college. Given the complexity of navigating these multiple places, one should not perhaps be too surprised that Eve sometimes struggled to arrive promptly at college for the 9.30 start to lessons. At weekends and one day a week, Eve also worked as a chambermaid at a local hotel.

Table 5.1 summarises some of the textual encounters in the mass of data collected about Eve's life structured according to their *purpose(s), modes and technologies, participation, audiences, and roles, identities and values.* The textual encounters have been organised broadly according to how difficult Eve perceived these to be when she was talking about them. This provides insight into Eve's sense of her identity and confidence within each of these literacy practices.

Space, place and movement were recurring themes in the different literacy practices with which Eve engaged. At home with Ben, she dealt with the household bureaucracy of utilities bills and council tax, kept local food outlet flyers for future reference, played on her computer and hoarded stacks of popular magazines under her bed. At her mother's address, Eve received paperwork associated with Alex including Child Tax Credit, which her mother claimed on her behalf. At college, Eve worked on her course and spent her spare time flicking through celebrity magazines which the students shared and gossiped about. At work, Eve developed a new diary system to record her working hours more accurately and navigated easily the literacy requirements of her job.

But while these literacy practices can broadly be seen to be situated by place and space, these contexts were fluid and practices sometimes migrated

Table 5.1 Eve's literacy practices

Eve's ranking according to difficulty	Practice	Aspects of each literacy practice			
		Purpose(s)	Modes and technologies	Participation and audiences	Eve's roles and identities
Very difficult	Taking the Genesis test	To progress onto a work-based NVQ rather than studying on a college course	Paper-based test written by external organisation help her with this	Eve on her own: she does not know anyone who could	Applicant
Very difficult	Doing Child Trust Fund paperwork	Received paperwork relating to the child trust fund that has been awarded to Alex	Paper forms, leaflets	Eve was going to ask her mum to help her make sense of this	Mother
Very difficult	Completing child health record book	To record her son's development	Small red book containing information and spaces for parent to complete	Doctor, health visitor	Mother
Quite difficult	Applying for welfare benefits	To receive child tax credit	Paper-based form, accompanying leaflet	Currently sent to her mum's address – Eve intends to change this	Daughter moving to young adult
Quite difficult	Sorting out paperwork associated with house	When they recently bought a house, Eve and her boyfriend needed to sort out a mortgage, paperwork relating to the house, utility bills, council tax etc.	Assorted paper-based forms	Boyfriend knows how to do this because he used to own a house before. Eve phoned up for form from council tax office	Adult in cohabiting relationship
Quite difficult	Receiving healthcare	Intended to inform Eve about her pregnancy,	Did not read books after	Books given to Eve by her midwife	Mother/ daughter

	books relating to pregnancy	impending birth, and care of her child	childbirth because asked her mum for advice instead		
Quite easy	Recording laundry and room numbers	'You have to write all the room numbers down and then what needs doing . . . I have to write what I take out of the rooms'	Form devised by hotel, completed by pen	Eve on her own – system devised by hotel management	Worker
Quite easy	Recording working hours in diary	'I've just like write it all down in case I don't get paid'	Diary format devised by Eve	Eve on her own	Young adult/worker
Quite easy	Learning driving test theory	Preparing for driving theory test	CD-Rom	Eve on her own	Young adult
Quite easy	Junk mail and takeaway menus posted through letterbox	Sometimes keeps the takeaway menus so that she and her boyfriend can order food	Paper-based texts	Eve sometimes with her boyfriend	Adult in cohabiting relationship
Quite easy	Reading children's books	Enjoyment and leisure	Books	Eve with her young son	Mother
Quite easy	Texting	Personal communication with family and friends	Mobile phone	Eve, friends, boyfriend, mum	Young adult – taught her mum how to use phone
Quite easy	Reading magazines	Enjoyment and leisure	Magazines	Eve does this alone or with friends on her course	Young adult (talks about having grown out of teenage mags)

from one place to another. An extreme example of this migration is provided through Eve's use of her mobile phone. Each night she would text her mother from home to tell her that she loved her; throughout the day she texted her boyfriend whether she was in college, at work, at home or travelling between these places. She also texted her friends and, sometimes, her course tutor.

Similarly college work was not chained to the physical space of college. While Eve completed most of her work at college, sometimes she preferred to take work home to type it up on her home computer. The information-gathering that she was doing around home decoration on her home computer was also carried out in the Learning Resource Centre at college where she had internet access. These examples suggest that agency within the practice is not only attached to the involvement of different people with different power positions: literacy practices are partially contextualised through the *technologies* they employed – mobile phones, computers, port-folios of college work. The situatedness of the practices cannot be framed simply in terms of home, work and college.

Two issues arise from the case of Eve. First, although as educators we focus on matters associated with learning the course as if they were central to the lives of students, for students themselves, whether full or part time, their learning practices are only a small proportion of those they participate in. Learning may not be central to students' lives in the way educators may assume or desire. Second, identifying specific literacy practices with specific domains is problematic, as there is greater fluidity than we might assume. Aspects of literacy practices leak from one situation into another. (For further discussion, see Fowler and Edwards 2005.) We return to this theme at the end of the chapter. First, however, we turn to the wider comparison of literacy practices in Childcare and issues arising from our study for learning and teaching in this and similar vocational areas.

The policy context

The macro-policy initiatives of England and Wales and of Scotland posi-tioned Childcare and Early Years Education courses as direct routes into the occupation and workplace. However, these courses were also meant to provide the potential for student progression into higher education. This was part of wider reforms in the labour market to provide career progres-sion for those who begin working with children in less qualified positions. College Childcare courses can therefore fulfil a dual role. However, while there are similarities between England, Wales and Scotland in overall policy, a major area of difference is in the meso-level between overall policy and classroom practice, in particular in relation to awarding bodies and curriculum development.

In Scotland, the Scottish Qualifications Authority (SQA) was the sole, non-departmental, body responsible for the development, accreditation, assessment and certification of qualifications pertaining to Childcare. The introduction of the Scottish Credit and Qualifications Framework (SCQF) led to the potential for clear progression for students to higher levels of study. All parties involved – employers, learners and college staff – could track (in principle) which level of qualification led to the next, how many credits each qualification had and how they related one to the other.

In England and Wales, there was a separation between awarding bodies and curriculum development. While the Qualifications and Curriculum Authority (QCA) provided quality assurance for courses that receive further education funding, there was a plethora of awarding bodies that designed, developed and verified qualifications. Consistency of levels was maintained across these qualifications through the regulatory criteria within the National Qualifications Framework (NQF), which was managed by QCA. The QCA regulated and developed the curriculum, assessments, examinations and qualifications. But qualifications were granted by the different awarding bodies. An awarding body had to gain recognised status from the QCA before it could propose qualifications for accreditation within the NQF.

In England and Wales, there were two main awarding bodies for Childcare: the Council for Awards in Children's Care and Education (CACHE) and Edexcel. CACHE was a niche awarding body, only delivering qualifications related to working with children. In contrast, Edexcel was the UK's largest awarding body. Unlike CACHE, Edexcel delivered a wide range of qualifications from the Standard Assessment Tests in schools (SATs) through to higher education qualifications. In terms of Childcare courses, one of the major differences between these was in the level of intervention and prescription by the awarding body. CACHE provided a very prescriptive and detailed approach with textbooks produced for each level of the course and organised according to the units that students study and assignment briefs written by the awarding body. Edexcel were less prescriptive in their approach: providing Business and Technology Education Council (BTEC) courses with specifications to which tutors were expected to write their own assignment briefs. There was no one textbook used on the BTEC courses.

CACHE courses also had an end-of-course three-hour exam, while BTEC required an integrated assignment written by the awarding body. The BTEC route at Level 3 was seen to be slightly more academic than the CACHE Diploma and required a higher GCSE points tariff. Joanne, the lecturer in Childcare profiled in Box 5.1, felt that the BTEC better prepared students for university because of the way the assignments needed to be written as the students needed to do more of their own research. CACHE courses were seen to be more practical and hands-on. Some confusion existed among employers in England who find that different qualifications seem to be operating at the same level but have different curricula and assessment criteria, and carry different credits. The complexity arising from the qualifications structure in England and Wales therefore differed from the more rationalised Scottish system.

The units, tutors and students

Childcare was studied in each of the five participating colleges. In each college, two Childcare units were researched, as far as possible, one at each of two levels: these are set out in Table 5.2. It was the intention of the LfLFE project that the units chosen for the research would cover different levels of study, different student populations and different learning settings. However, the practicalities of working in the dynamic naturalistic settings of colleges meant that the final selection became focused more on full-time units and full-time students than we would have liked. Only one of the units came from a part-time programme. Across the five colleges, we looked at six units within the higher HNC Level/Level 3 and four units at lower levels. Each unit consisted of approximately 40 hours of learning and teaching.

Each of the five college-based researchers in Childcare had previously worked in childcare settings as nursery nurses, nursery managers or primary school teachers. In both formal and informal discussions with them, this experience was one they valued when working with the students. They talked about the need to relate what they were doing in the classroom to the world of work. They felt that their experience helped them 'fill in the cracks' not covered by performance criteria for the units they taught. Rosheen in Anniesland College explained one example of such a crack in the unit 'Promoting Play'. The learning outcomes required the students to 'explain the benefits of play' and 'investigate the role of the adult in the promotion of play'. As part of the planning process for providing play scenarios in the childcare setting, she had developed exercises in which the students had to think about providing opportunities for children to explore and use new language appropriate to the setting; for example, 'caring/patient' in a hospital corner and 'selling/customer' in a shop corner. As a former primary school teacher, she recognised that it was not enough to supply the physical resources to establish such activities, but that the childcare practitioner had to provide the language resources too.

Within each unit in Scotland and England, we worked with four students to examine their literacy practices in and out of college. Apart from the three students who were on the Edexcel National Certification in Early Years (Level 3) programme in England, which was aimed at mature students, our student participants were learners aged 16 to 19 and on full-time courses. With one exception, the thirty-two students were female. Colley et al. (2003) found when studying colleges that Childcare continued to be a feminised vocational area and this was confirmed in the teaching of Childcare and Early Years education in all three countries (Scotland, England and Wales) in our research.

Table 5.2 The Childcare units in the research sample

Level	Name of programme	Name of unit	Country	College	CBR
HIGHER LEVEL					
SCQF 7 (Level 3)	HNC Childcare and Education	Curriculum Approaches	Scotland	Perth	Joyce Gaechter
SCQF 7 (Level 3)	HNC Childcare and Education	Assessment Approaches		Anniesland	Rosheen Young
Level 3 (SCQF 7)	CACHE Diploma in Childcare and Education (DCE)	Preparation for Employment	England	Lancaster and Morecambe	Christine Phillipson
Level 3 (SCQF 7)	Edexcel BTEC National Diploma in Early Years	Professional Practice		Preston	Joanne Knowles
Level 3 (SCQF 7)	Edexcel BTEC National Diploma in Early Years	Diet and Nutrition; Childcare Practice	Wales	Meirion-Dwyfor	Margaret Lewis
LOWER LEVEL					
SCQF 4 (Level 1)	NC Early Education and Childcare	The Pre-school Child, Food, Clothing and Play	Scotland	Perth	Joyce Gaechter
SCQF 4 (Level 1)	NC Early Education and Childcare	Care and Feeding of Babies		Anniesland	Rosheen Young
Level 2 (SCQF 5)	CACHE Certificate in Childcare and Education	Practical Work, Personal Development and Anti-discriminatory Practice	England	Lancaster and Morecambe	Christine Phillipson
Level 1 (SCQF 4)	Foundation Childcare Award (FCA)	Play and Practical Activities		Preston	Joanne Knowles

N.B. The other country equivalent is in brackets.

Literacy practices in learning Childcare

A range of artefacts and practices were used in the textual mediation of learning Childcare, with their use arising out of a complex interplay of factors. Tutors' choices of classroom material and assessments were influenced by:

- the unit descriptors from which they were working;
- other forms of guidance from awarding bodies;
- the culture of college departments;
- the tutors' professional training and expectations;
- the perceived demands of the workplace;
- the anticipated practices of higher education.

All of these were mediated through the judgement of the lecturer on the approach to be adopted in teaching specific topics in specific ways. Most relied on what we suggest are fairly traditional styles of pedagogic mediation, entailing continual use of a relatively limited range of types of reading and writing. In particular, Childcare was distinctive as not only were the students using texts to learn about their curriculum area, but also the teaching and learning of literacy was one of the topics of the curriculum.

Across all levels students were expected to engage with a wide range of literacy artefacts. They read overhead transparencies (OHTs), locally and nationally devised handouts, PowerPoint presentations, information sheets, worksheets, magazines, flipcharts, instruction leaflets, commercially produced advisory and information leaflets, internet sites, journals and books. As they progressed through the levels, the patterns of *participation* changed: students were increasingly expected to undertake these tasks independently and teachers were more likely to expect that the students could engage with practices around the texts unproblematically. In addition, the *modes and technologies*, and *genres, styles and designs* of texts students had to read changed as the levels increased. At the lower levels students could expect to read more publicly available, multi-modal texts such as leaflets and magazines and were less likely to be presented with official or extended texts such as policy documents. Pedagogic texts were more likely to be 'simplified' by reducing the content to a series of bullet points. This reduction posed challenges for students because the reading had been decontextualised to the extent that it became a list of information to be remembered rather than embedded within wider practices. This process of 'simplification' made it more difficult for students to relate the information to the practical context. In contrast, at the higher levels, students were more likely to be expected to read extended academic or official text with fewer images. Across all levels, reading was perceived to be less of a potential 'problem' for students than writing. As a result, few lecturers taught or discussed reading practices explicitly, especially at the higher levels.

The Childcare courses involved a lot of writing as well as reading. Students were involved in note taking from OHTs, PowerPoint presentations and videos; completing worksheets; drawing spider-grams; preparing presentations and wall displays; writing menus, lists and schedules; producing leaflets and posters; making notes when researching topics using internet or books; writing essays and reports; completing logbooks and designing game shows. As with reading, some of these written tasks embedded in practical activities were 'invisible' in the sense that tutors did not recognise the demands they were making in terms of reading and writing.

The variety and extent of literacy practices on Childcare courses was, for the most part, a surprise to the tutors, who tended to think only of 'writing essays' as 'literacy'. Expecting students to find 'essay writing' difficult, special classes were sometimes provided on this issue, usually at Induction, taught mainly by core/key skills teachers. The practice of teaching essay writing in discrete sessions as a set of generic skills which can be transferred later is part of an autonomous view of literacy as decontextualised skills that can be applied and transferred across learning sites.

In contrast, some tutors chose to work with the existing repertoires that students brought with them, and to use them as a context for developing a critical awareness of what is involved in writing. At Lancaster and Morecambe College, Christine encouraged students to bring aspects of their everyday lives into class. For example, she allowed them to play music of their own choice as they worked, and one of the presentations she asked them to do was on a subject of their choice which related to their outside interests. This proved to be a good starting point for students to consider the nature of their audience, and to decide on a clear and attractive way of presenting material.

Greater differences between levels than between countries

As suggested above, there was a marked difference between the levels of programmes in the range of literacy practices with which students were expected to engage. This was consistent across all colleges. At the lower levels the college-based researchers built the types of reading and writing which might be used in nurseries and pre-school centres into their courses. For example, students were asked to design posters and displays – often in themselves about words, letters and numbers – of the sort that might appear on the walls of a play area of a childcare centre. The college domain therefore anticipated the demands of the projected workplace.

Not only were there more practical activities at the lower levels (which might be expected), but perhaps more surprisingly there was also a greater variety of literacy demands. The tutors' reasons for adopting this variety were to engage the students in a positive way, to keep them interested in

Box 5.2   Producing a handbook for parents: a Childcare assessment task

An assessment task for an SCQF Level 5 group in Scotland was to produce a booklet for parents to help them understand their child's developmental stages between 0 and 5 years. The students had to develop a complex set of new literacy practices to deal with booklet production. The students could not draw on their own literacy experiences as no members of the group were parents or came from a background of media production. Their concerns centred around how to address this audience, how to get a professional finish so that the booklet looked neat, the layout they would have to adopt, and which images to use, if any, as well as how to organise the content. These were concerns about the production of the booklet, which in the end got in the way of them passing the assessment that required them to demonstrate their knowledge about developmental stages. In this particular case, all the students had to remediate their assessment because aspects of the performance criteria had not been fulfilled.

Both students and staff enjoyed the experience of producing the booklet because it was practical, they could work collaboratively, they could use pictures either drawn by themselves or taken from magazines, it was multimodal and multimedia, non-linear and generative. As a learning activity, it had many benefits. But in giving the students something different and potentially engaging to do, the teacher had added a new dimension to the task of demonstrating knowledge. This was thought to be unproblematic, as they had passed their basic skills assessments. This assumption that literacy is a unitary set of transferable skills ignores the complex range of activities that surround the production of any literacy artefact.

This may well have been a legitimate learning experience if the students would have to produce such a document when qualified or if subsequent assessments required similar literacy practices. However, their teacher said that they would be unlikely ever to have to do this in the workplace. The *actions and processes*, the *genre,* and the conventions of *style and design* were not related either to the course or future area of work. Writing a leaflet aimed at parents is a highly specialised literacy practice. There were too many *purposes* and too many *audiences* for this task to be successful as an assessment. While the lecturer's intention had been to make the assignment more *interesting*, it is not necessarily made more *relevant* by imposing a literacy demand which will be useful neither in the workplace, nor if the student progresses to higher level courses.

the subject and to help them to integrate learning, assessment and the world of childcare. In other words, the lower the level of unit, the more diverse the literacy demands made upon students, while the higher the unit level, the more narrowly focused the literacy demands. While variety was seen by the tutors as a motivating force for students, the complexities of developing such diverse literacy practices were not always addressed. In terms of their literacy careers, students were receiving inconsistent messages about what the appropriate forms of writing were, as exemplified in Box 5.2. Thus, while the mobility and multiplicity of literacy practices was apparent at lower levels, this increased the complexity the students encountered. Nevertheless, as in the examples from Catering and Hospitality in Chapter 4, when literacy practices had clear purpose, relevance and authenticity either for their future roles as childcare professionals or for learning, the students did not treat them as 'reading' or 'writing', but as part and parcel of what they were doing.

It would seem logical for students' literacy careers to increase in diversity and complexity as they progress educationally. Starting with the more practical work-placed activities, more academic literacies would be gradually introduced on top of the developing practical and occupational literacies. The research revealed much greater variety from a literacy perspective on lower level courses than on higher level courses. As a result, the lower level students' literacy careers may be diverse and possibly fragmented, whereas the higher level students are focused on developing a narrow range of reading and writing, usually associated with education rather than occupational progression. This does not mean that teachers should limit their curriculum, but that the relevance of literacy practices to students' futures, and the additional requirements they are placing on students need to be taken into account. The framework for analysing literacy practices introduced in Chapter 3 provides a useful tool for thinking about these issues.

Despite Childcare courses being designed to help students to encourage children to learn through play, these practical literacy practices disappeared from the programmes at the higher levels. As the students proceeded through the levels, the variety of texts that they had to read and write diminished. Students at the higher level expected to be reading and writing fewer texts and using visual as well as verbal modes of communication. They associated reading magazines and children's books, and designing posters and leaflets with the lower levels of courses and positioned them as 'childlike' or 'fun'.

At the higher levels students received a more consistent message about appropriate forms of reading and writing, which relate to progressing to higher education. There was thus greater consistency in the literacy careers they were being required to develop. This is not to say that students at the higher levels had fewer literacy challenges. They faced different demands with an increased textualisation of assessment based upon more extended academic reading and writing rather than work-related activities. The literacy demands of assessment were often additional to any literacy practices that students needed to develop within the workplace, as there was an anticipation of the demands to be faced by students in progressing educationally rather than entering the workplace.

These differences in literacy demands between lower and higher level courses were noticed in all four colleges in Scotland and England. (In Wales, only higher level courses were studied.) Although there were specific characteristics to each course, these were determined more by the specific content of the course and the tutors' individual dispositions than by the policy contexts within which they were operating.

The use of information and communication technologies

There was a limited use of information and communication technologies (ICT) in teaching Childcare across contexts. While at a national level in all three countries significant investment had been made into the ICT infrastructure of colleges, the students were provided with very few opportunities to use ICT in the Childcare courses we researched in Scotland and England. There were statements in policy documents across all five colleges about the value of increasing the use of ICT in the classroom. Departmental managers spoke about their commitment to these policies and teachers spoke often of their desire to change their teaching to incorporate ICT. However, when it came to actual classroom practice, we found very little evidence of the impact of this. In the classrooms which were primarily designated for Childcare provision, there were no dedicated personal computers for students' use. Indeed, in one college, PCs were brought into every classroom for an inspection visit but when the inspectors left, the computers were taken away. In this respect then, the learning environment was less rich than that experienced by many students in their everyday lives or in their prospective workplaces, especially when we take into account the huge growth of technological toys (Luckin *et al.* 2003).

Some Childcare lecturers did not have computers on their desks: if lecturing staff themselves do not engage with ICT with any regularity, they are not able to act as role models for its use. Additionally, the time pressures Childcare lecturers felt they were under meant that they were less likely to consider adopting innovative practices involving ICT. Some of them experienced a lack of technical support, and did not want to risk something going wrong and wasting class time. If they knew the equipment would be there on time, would work efficiently and be available consistently, they said they would use it more.

All five colleges had a Virtual Learning Environment (VLE), but where material had been provided for student use within Childcare, it was invariably presented exactly as it would be in a paper-based format, or as copies of OHTs available on a CD. Reflecting on the VLE, one of the lecturers felt that if a student missed a session on the course, the information was so complex that the student would still need the teacher's input rather than be able to catch up by remotely accessing the resources. Childcare tutors used ICT in the classroom when they could, such as video material and PowerPoint presentations. However, where PowerPoint presentations were observed, this practice seemed to be very similar to the use of OHTs: PowerPoint slides had linear bulleted text. This reflects a view of ICT as merely another means of communicating with students in the same way as through traditional technologies, rather than as a new resource with multimodal semiotic affordances and non-linear processing potential.

All colleges had one or more central resource centres where a large number of PCs were available for students' use. But many of the students in Childcare said they did not like to use the learning centres for a number of reasons:

- There were too many distractions.
- They had to book machines in advance.
- They had to remember to bring a disk or USB pen drive.
- They had to remember their password.
- They were only allowed to use the computers for specified purposes.

These constraints within the educational domain regulated their use of technology, which in other domains is characterised by its flexibility and capacity for multi-tasking, to the extent that these students preferred not to use the resource centres. In a focus group interview at the end of their programme, one of the students said she would prefer the computers to be in the classrooms:

> I think that would be actually really good because [the tutor] could say to me 'Right I want you to start this assessment today.' If we get it started then that means I can start typing it up right away and I don't have to go down to the [learning centre] – I've got my own computer sitting there right there in front of me and no matter where I sit there would be a computer where I could log on and do the work whereas now you've got to go all the way down to the [learning centre] and book it and say how long you want it for and if you don't get it done then you've got to go and say can I have it for another hour.

For such reasons, many students said that, when they had work that involved the use of PCs, they preferred to work at home if they had access to a computer there. When students did use the learning centres, it was for information gathering activities as an integral part of class time. Students would find the relevant sites and download lots of material to be read at home. This points to a tension between the spaces of educational practices and the spaces of learning practices: the way in which the official educational spaces were organised and regulated was not conducive to learning; the students reconfigure these arrangements and choose their own spaces in which to learn in ways that suit them.

At the higher levels, students used PCs when they had extended texts to produce such as essays or reports, but again this was more likely to be carried out at home. Most of the students talked about a requirement to present these assignments as word-processed text. However, very few of the Childcare students created the text using a PC. Rather they handwrote the text and used the PC to make it look neat and check spelling.

The data from the Childcare units clearly show that we are a long way from making the most of the pedagogical possibilities opened up by new information and communication technologies and that students can have more sophisticated multimodal and multimedia literacy practices in their everyday lives than they do in colleges. This finding was common across the different contexts of our research.

Literacy practices on Childcare placements

Childcare placements have particular literacy practices associated with them compared with other curriculum areas, as the job itself includes providing the children with opportunities for the emergence of literacy, as shown in Figure 5.1. In addition to bureaucratic uses of literacy similar to those in any work placement, such as keeping timesheets, updating records and communicating with colleagues, it is part of the job for Childcare workers to engage in reading and writing activities with young children, and to create a literacy-rich environment for them.

One important aspect of Childcare work placements was child observations. One English student disliked these more than any other aspect of the course, describing them as 'boring'. It became clear that what she found boring was not observing the child, but writing up the observation. She said: 'You have to do twenty and it takes ages to write them up.' This is a case of the literacy practice becoming a demand on top of the task itself.

Students of Childcare were also required to mediate between their work placements and their college-based courses through the maintenance of a logbook. While all the students appreciated and valued the actual placement experience, writing the logbook was seen as a chore by many of them, partly because it consisted of completing proformas. These logbooks differed in format across the qualification bodies but their function was essentially the same. Within the placement time, each student is expected to undertake a variety of tasks which cover the range of activities they would be expected to meet in a childcare setting. The logbooks are designed to provide opportunities for students to capture this experience:

Figure 5.1 Childcare placements: children's literacy development is part of the job

to record what has taken place and to reflect on their own development during placement. For many of the students, recording the activities presented few problems. However, the reflective element caused considerable challenges, as it consists in moving from a descriptive mode of writing to an analytical mode and is a particular genre of writing with which many students are unfamiliar. Thus, the *modes and technologies*, the *genre* and the associated conventions of *style and design* of the logbooks were not supportive of their *purpose*.

In Scotland the logbook consisted of fifty planned learning experiences (PLEs), twenty observations and ten reports. Some of the students talked about completing five or more proformas at one time. The physical space of the box in the proforma limited the amount of writing the students undertook, which is in tension with the purpose of writing reflectively, which entails more extended text based upon personal learning. These logbooks were designed to be read by the placement staff and/or the college tutor as *audiences* and then discussed with the student: a *participation* structure which might have made this a valuable literacy practice. However, all the project students reported that this discussion happened infrequently and, when it did, it covered a number of proformas at one time. One of the students commented that: 'I don't think she reads them really. She just signs them.' It therefore seemed to the students that these documents served no real *purpose*. Students often repeated similar phrases each week. One student wrote in over half of her PLEs 'I think my organisational skills could be improved'. She did not refer to her previous notes citing this as a problem, nor did she reflect on how this could be achieved.

The lecturers commented on the entries lacking a reflective quality, but the support that was offered to students was not having the desired effect. The lecturers thought that as long as the students had a good vocabulary and learnt to write extended text and to spell correctly, then they would be able to write reflectively. This skills-based approach to the teaching of writing was inadequate since it did not address key aspects which are entailed in the literacy practice of writing reflective documents such as *purpose, audience, processes, content*, and *flexibility and constraints*. In particular, both lecturers and students needed a more explicit under-standing of what is involved in adopting the *roles, identities and values* associated with being a reflective practitioner.

Bilingual literacy practices on Childcare courses

The textual mediation of learning on the two Early Years units at Coleg Meirion-Dwyfor was more complex because these units were part of a bilingual course. The students were reading, writing and talking about texts in Welsh and in English in class, in their assignments and in preparing for, carrying out and keeping a log of their work placements. Bilingual education has, for some years, been developed and consolidated in this FE college. In 2008, it was the leading institution in Wales with regard to provision for Welsh-medium and bilingual education in the FE sector. The language policy context for the research conducted in Wales is discussed in some detail in Chapter 7.

The thirteen young women enrolled in the Early Years course in the Welsh college when the research was carried out engaged in a similar range of literacy practices to the students in the Childcare courses in England and Scotland. The most striking difference was that these practices, and many of the texts they used and produced, were bilingual. Most of the time, the Early Years lecturer, Margaret Lewis, used teaching/learning materials that she had gathered or developed herself, because of the paucity of suitable bilingual or Welsh-medium materials for Early Years courses. One Welsh textbook was available but it was closely geared to the requirements of the CACHE courses. The students worked with bilingual texts and texts that had been originally produced monolingually, in English or in Welsh. The classroom conversations were usually bilingual, even when the texts they were engaging with were monolingual. This bilingual teaching/learning approach made it possible for all students with differing degrees of confidence in Welsh and in English to participate. It also made it possible to re-contextualise texts originally produced in English in this Welsh setting. See Box 5.3 for an example.

Box 5.3   Re-contextualising legislative texts in a bilingual Early Years course

In one class during the Childcare Practice Unit (*Ymarfer Gofal Plant*), Margaret Lewis was introducing UK-wide Health and Safety Legislation that had been published in English. She began by writing three English acronyms on the flip chart: HASAWA (The Health and Safety at Work Act), COSHH (Control of Substances Hazardous to Health) and RIDDOR (Reporting of Injuries, Diseases and Dangerous Occurrences Regulation). She then explained the term HASAWA using a bilingual OHT (with Welsh in one column and English in the other). She switched fluently between languages as she spoke. After this, the students were asked to work in groups and to come up with a list of four things which employers in Early Years settings were required to do to comply with HASAWA. Each group then had to select a scribe to prepare their list. One group discussed the task in English and the other three groups worked in Welsh. The plenary discussion based on the tasks was bilingual.

Margaret Lewis then returned to the flip chart and explained COSHH in the same way, using a bilingual OHT. Students were then asked to give examples of hazardous substances that might be encountered in Early Years settings. A handout in English was then passed round. This detailed the COSHH regulations. The content of the handout was discussed in Welsh. Margaret Lewis then turned to the flip chart for a third time and explained the RIDDOR regulations. This led to a bilingual discussion of the literacy practices in Early Years settings for recording accidents; for example, writing, in Welsh or English, in an accident report book or on report forms. Finally, a written task relating to the legislation was passed around. This had been photocopied from an English textbook, so the written task was completed in English. The students were given about 25 minutes to do the task. During this time, Margaret Lewis moved around the class and discussed the task with individual students, in Welsh and in English. Once the students had completed the task, it was discussed in Welsh.

Most of the students did their work placements in bilingual settings, such as local playgroups, nursery schools (*Ysgolion Meithrin*) or primary schools. Before embarking on these placements, they had to complete the standard CBR (Criminal Record Bureau) form. They had to choose to complete an English or a Welsh form and about half the group selected the Welsh form. In the bilingual school settings, they were required to produce bilingual wall displays and to prepare bilingual or Welsh-medium learning materials. Preparing both the displays and the illustrated learning materials involved decisions about multimodal and bilingual design; in other words, decisions about how to align words in Welsh and in English, along with images, within the overall text. In this bilingual course, the guiding principle was that all materials produced for the children that they were working with should be bilingual or Welsh-medium, in keeping with the language policy of Gwynedd Local Education Authority.

Since their lecturer was bilingual, the students could opt to do their assignments in either Welsh or English. The question of language choice for assignments was raised early on with prospective students, when they were interviewed and then offered a place on the Early Years course. The language choice options open to them at the college were clarified at this point. Once they had embarked on the course, most of the students in the cohort that participated in the BiLfLFE project employed the same language for all their assignments. Most chose Welsh, but those who had had less experience in using Welsh at secondary school chose to write in English. However, all students were encouraged to use Welsh for their placement portfolios, especially when they were reporting and reflecting on the Welsh or bilingual materials that they had produced for the workplace.

Childcare education as textually mediated hybrid space

In comparing literacies for learning on Childcare units in five colleges in three countries, there would appear to be more similarities than differences in the literacy practices in Wales, Scotland and England. Indeed, the differences may be as significant within countries as between them, in particular in England where different awarding bodies, CACHE and Edexcel, provide different curriculum contexts within which to operate or in Wales, where some Childcare courses are delivered bilingually, in Welsh and in English, and some only in English. As shown in this chapter, there were significant differences between lower and higher level units; other differences appeared to be as much to do with the pedagogic stance of the tutor as any other factor (see Miller and Satchwell 2006).

In our study of Childcare courses, we noted a significant tension between educational imperatives and occupational imperatives in terms of literacy practices, types of texts and types of engagement with texts required by students, especially as they progress to higher levels. This raises the most fundamental of questions: if Childcare is to enable students to progress in both directions, then the curriculum expectations and pedagogic practices of courses will need to address the issues around what is valued as literacy, and what resources are necessary for preparing students for participation in an increasingly multimodal and multimediated the world. The research has shown first that, at present, literacy tends to be too narrowly defined, with the literacy practices of practical activities and the workplace going largely unrecognised. Second, it has shown that the uses of ICT in many Childcare classrooms are not keeping pace with the rate of change and increase in usage and diversity of ICT in the students' lives outside college. Our research shows that students and tutors respond well to suggestions for more detailed attention to the different aspects of literacy practices to be incorporated into the enactment of the curriculum, in order to make more explicit the connections to the students' intended occupation and to their academic development.

At the broader conceptual level, this study points to the centrality of semiotic practices to students' learning careers, and suggests that greater pedagogical consideration of their literacy careers could enhance learning, not only in Childcare courses, but also for all students. The literacy practices of their imagined futures need to be scaffolded and modelled. Literacies for learning are fostered not simply by focusing on the development of individual skills, but by increasing the meaningfulness of tasks to students, taking into account that many students are still exploring what they might do as well as seeking preparation and qualifications in a certain subject area.

In Part III we show how the lecturers involved in this research took account of these issues in their own practice.

Part III

What are the implications?

Chapter 6

Making a difference

The conception, implementation
and analysis of changes in practice

Research actions for understanding that we have explored in previous chapters provide the basis for research actions for change. There is a degree to which this process is sequential, that is, a change in practice follows on from a research-informed understanding of existing practice. However, it is not always as straightforward as this, because the boundary between the different actions is not a firm one. Some of the lecturers in the project began to make changes in practice while still engaged in actions for understanding. Emerging understanding of literacy practices influenced their own practices. Similarly, understanding continued to develop as the actions for change were undertaken. Such is the nature of undertaking research in naturalistic settings. Understanding through analysis of the data collected for the project has continued to develop beyond its funded lifespan.

Many lecturers began by identifying a perceived difficulty experienced by students in their class in relation to the reading and writing demands of the course. The focus of the project had enabled tutors to recognise literacy-related aspects of the requirements of the curriculum and to make adjustments accordingly. For example, as shown in Chapters 4 and 5, the literacy demands of writing assessments or providing evidence were surfaced, as were some of the often hidden literacies of the workplace, such as reading or writing plans, reports, checklists and specifications.

**Box 6.1   Ian Gibb: lecturer in Catering and Hospitality
and member of the research team**

Ian Gibb had spent twenty years lecturing in hospitality. After leaving school he studied catering at Perth College, he then studied part time whilst doing an apprenticeship. Ian started working with the Western Hotel group who gave him a scholarship to work and study in Dallas, Texas. Towards the end of his contract he decided to return to Perth and

---

continued

obtained a lectureship position at Perth College. He then progressed to doing a Masters of Arts in Catering and Hospitality at Dundee University part time whilst lecturing. Ian finished this in 2001.

Ian recalls when he left college after a year and started working with British Transport hotels, the head chef who met him on the first day said: 'You probably think you know a lot after being at college for a year but just forget about what you've learnt at college because now you have to learn how the real world works.' This made a big impact on Ian, who has since worked towards bringing college and industry closer together and working more in partnership. Ian's experience of the abrupt transition from college to workplace practices was the inspiration behind him developing the Gleneagles patisserie chef qualification in partnership with the Gleneagles Hotel (described later in this chapter). Now all the further and higher education courses in Catering and Hospitality have some element of partnership with industry. Ian thinks that the work placements and the links with industry that the college has developed help to make that transition from college to work a lot smoother for the students.

Ian's motivation for collaborating in the research was to find new ways of reaching out to students who have previously had difficult educational experiences. Ian was very aware of the gap between industry-type literacy practices and those of being a student and had been actively introducing more elements of the industry-type literacy practices. The research he did with the students has allowed him now to think more about how the curriculum literacies can connect with the literacy practices engaged in by students in their everyday activities. He has introduced different types of multimodal texts and also different types of activities that engage the students in a more creative process and allow them to design their own texts as a way of assimilating the knowledge and presenting work for assessment. (A change in practice designed and implemented by Ian Gibb is described at the end of this chapter, and a different one is featured on the project DVD, Pardoe and Ivanič 2007.)

As a response to the difficulties identified, lecturers drew on what the research team had uncovered about the literacy practices that students engaged in from other domains of their past, present and imagined future lives, as presented in the list at the end of Chapter 2. The lecturers were influenced by their understanding of students' everyday literacy practices and attempted to bring dimensions of these into the classroom for teaching the curriculum. Lecturers' approaches to students' everyday literacies were to some extent influenced by their own personal and political positioning – often still dominated by the prevailing deficit discourse of literacy as something that students are lacking. Some lecturers found it more difficult than others to see the value of students' everyday literacies for learning of the curriculum. The lecturers' professional standing in terms of college hierarchy, length of service, whether full or part time, and previous professional practice also impacted on their changes of practice in terms of how confident they felt to introduce a new approach and whether they involved other members of their teams in order to expand the approach across the curriculum. Nevertheless, the majority of lecturers did find ways of incorporating some dimensions of students' everyday literacies into the teaching and learning of the curriculum.

The changes of practice implemented by the college lecturers were intended to improve or enrich the 'learning outcomes' for the students involved. The narrow definition of learning outcomes as laid out in the unit descriptors was expanded on by the students and lecturers themselves. For example, the students thought that the literacy events they were engaged in should be fun, interesting, relevant to their aspirations and useful in terms of moving them on to where they wanted to be or what they wanted to achieve through studying their course. Lecturers often identified practices which would be important for the students' futures which were not covered by the unit descriptors. So, we were not just looking at achievement and retention figures but taking a broader approach to learning outcomes by asking the students and lecturers through focus groups and interviews what they thought of the changes of practice and in what ways they may have 'worked'.

This chapter focuses on a selection of changes in practice out of a total of approximately forty-six across the project. We will look at how the changes in practice implemented by the college lecturers who were involved in the research process were conceived, carried out and evaluated. We discuss the factors that influenced lecturers' choices and the different work these changes of practice were designed to do in terms of the requirements of particular courses of study. We also consider how the changes of practice align the literacy practices of learning particular subjects within college with those of the everyday. Four particular changes of practice are discussed in more detail to illustrate the different kinds of work they were able to do. We use the framework for analysing literacy practices which we introduced in Chapter 3 to discuss the features of each of these examples.

Categorising changes in practice

The changes in practice were designed by the lecturers and developed collaboratively with the university researchers. They were research-informed attempts to bring elements from the literacy practices of students' everyday lives into their learning in college. Sometimes the changes developed into other areas and sometimes they had unexpected results.

During our analysis of the changes in practice, three overlapping ways of categorising them emerged:

1   according to which aspects of college life they addressed;
2   according to the pedagogic intentions underlying the activity;
3   according to the bordering work that they did in attempting to relate everyday literacies to curriculum literacies.

The aspects of college life addressed by the changes in practice

We took the four categories for literacy practices in college life which we introduced in Chapter 4, and looked at how the tutors' changes in practice were distributed amongst them. For each of the aspects of college life identified, we give the number of changes in practice which were directed towards it. We then give brief descriptions of a representative sample of the changes in practice in this category implemented in Scotland and England in order to provide an overview of the extent and variety of this work.

Literacy practices involved in becoming and being a student – 0

No lecturer focused specifically on this category, but Perth College as a whole reduced the quantity of paperwork provided at induction in response to findings that students did not read them.

Literacy practices for learning content – 27

Most changes in practice were in this category. Examples included:

* adding to a glossary of scientific terms on the whiteboard throughout lessons in Forensic Science;
* conducting research in Childcare using catalogues of educational toys;
* using real published company accounts in Business Administration;
* bringing a selection of everyday texts into class in AS Level English Language and Literature;
* designing subject-based games to enhance understanding of course content in Level 1 Business Administration;
* using mind-mapping software to understand concepts in HNC Childcare;
* writing accounts of music business networking in Music Production;
* producing a reflective log including photos in Construction;
* producing a presentation based around what had been learnt on a course for adult literacy teachers;
* designing kitchen layout plans in order to engage with theory and regulations about food hygiene and their impact on the construction and design of food premises;

- teaching note-taking in A Level Human Biology;
- drawing and labelling diagrams using an interactive whiteboard on a Graphical Detailing course;
- handwriting letters in Childcare.

Literacy practices for assessment – 14

Changes in practice were categorised here if the tutors were deliberately addressing an assessment aspect of the course. Examples included:

- production of a CD-ROM in Multimedia;
- production of biographies in Music Production;
- giving choice of modes of assessment in Travel and Tourism;
- collaborative working on portfolios in Painting and Decorating;
- production of a restaurant journal to facilitate completion of new logbook in Catering and Hospitality;
- additional sessions for explaining assessment criteria to students in Science.

Literacy practices relating to the students' imagined future – 5

Some of these changes in practice also addressed other aspects of college life, such as learning content, or assessment. If the change in practice was related to making an activity more relevant to future work, it is included here. Examples were:

- the use of recipes from a real restaurant in the Hospitality kitchen;
- improving the layout of the workbook in Travel and Tourism to have more relevance to future work;
- using real published accounts to relate more realistically to the workplace in Business Administration;
- creating web-based musician's biographies in Music Production.

This categorisation provides a useful overview of all the changes in practice, and the aspects of college life which they addressed. The individual lecturers' preferences and priorities were important here. Lecturers' choice of change of practice was largely pragmatic and influenced by the demands of the curriculum they were teaching at that time. Most of the changes were related to literacies connected with learning the content of courses. Some of the changes in practice spanned two or even more aspects of college life. For example, the use of real published accounts in Business Administration, and the design of kitchen layouts in Food Hygiene Practices concerned both learning content and relevance to the students' imagined futures.

The pedagogic intentions underlying the changes in practice

We identified four pedagogic intentions underlying the new activities. Lecturers introduced changes in practice which attempted to:

a)   make reading and writing on courses more resonant with students' vernacular literacy practices, that is, more multimodal, multimedia, interactive, participatory and collaborative, non-linear (i.e. with varied reading paths), agentic (i.e. students having responsibility and control), purposeful to the student, have a clear audience, generative, self-determined in terms of activity, time and place, varied – not repetitive;

b)   make the students more aware of the reading and writing in their everyday lives which could act as resources for their learning;

c)   make the communicative aspects of learning more explicit and visible; and/or

d)   make the reading and writing on courses more relevant to learning.

Intention (a) was the response we anticipated, since the research had been set up in order to achieve such resonance. It is not surprising therefore that this principle did indeed underlie the majority of the changes in practice designed and implemented by the lecturers, as will be demonstrated in the examples later in the chapter. Many of the changes of practice drew on aspects of literacies from home and/or from the workplace. The lecturers responded enthusiastically and imaginatively to the insights they gained from the research described in Chapters 2 and 3, using the understandings they had gained about reading and writing in students' lives to fine-tune or reconceive the literacy practices on their courses. What was more surprising was that the lecturers did not stop at this, but took other, unexpected ideas for practical applications from their involvement in the Actions for Understanding phase of the research. Intentions (b), (c) and (d) sometimes accompanied intention (a), and sometimes operated independently.

Intention (b) was occasioned by the lecturers' sense that the research we had conducted into students' everyday literacy practices had been so significant for the students themselves, and that the research methods were in themselves a useful pedagogic resource. Becoming aware of the extent, diversity and complexity of the reading and writing they did in other domains of their lives had increased students' sense of their own worth and achievements – indeed, had challenged their view that they did not read and write anything, and given them confidence in their literacy, in the lay sense of the term. One lecturer instituted a questionnaire which students completed and discussed in their induction week, providing him with an understanding of the reading and writing they did in other domains of their lives which he could use as a basis for his pedagogy in the year ahead. Other lecturers took 'the clock activity' which we describe in the Appendix and incorporated this in their programmes of work at the beginning of the following year.

Intention (c) resulted from the lecturers' insights gained from the research described in Chapters 4 and 5 of this book. This had made visible the communicative, and particularly the literacy dimensions of their pedagogy, and had revealed the demands these were making on students. The lecturers thought that it would help students if they drew more attention to these literacy demands, and gave them explicit help with them. Examples of this were activities devised by Joanne Knowles to help Level 3 Childcare students grapple with more theoretical terminology, and the glossary of scientific terms which Sandra Mulligan built up on the whiteboard during Forensic Science classes. The focus on literacies had drawn attention to these new literacies and had surfaced the need for them to be addressed explicitly.

Intention (d) arose partly from the careful consideration of the purpose(s) of reading and writing on units, and how far they were actually contributing to learning. It arose partly also from the lecturers recognising differences between the reading and writing on their courses, and those of the futures for which the courses were supposed to be preparing students. These considerations often went hand-in-hand with intention (a), as achieving resonance with vernacular literacy practices often amounted to ensuring that reading and writing were purposeful, and were serving their intended purpose. The main aim of many of the changes of practice was to increase the students' sense that what they had to read or write was meaningful and worthwhile.

The bordering work of the changes in practice

The changes in practice which fulfilled pedagogic intention (a) above sought to draw aspects of literacy practices from other domains of students' lives into the educational domain. For example, conducting research in Childcare using catalogues of educational toys drew on the students' leisure-related practice of reading catalogues and magazines. By contrast, using real published accounts in Business Administration linked to the students' future in a real workplace. The ways in which changes in practice mobilised resources across these borders are represented in Figure 6.1.

Figure 6.1 represents the three different domains of students' lives at which we were looking and a selection of the lecturers' changes of practice to show the borders addressed by their changes – whether they were drawing on dimensions of students' home, college or work-related literacies for learning the curriculum. Those in the middle were changes of practice which mobilised both home and work literacy practices for pedagogic purposes. Those on the left drew on dimensions of home literacy practices and the ones on the right drew predominantly on work-based literacies. There were a few changes in practice which remained only in the college domain and were not bordering either home or work. These were focusing

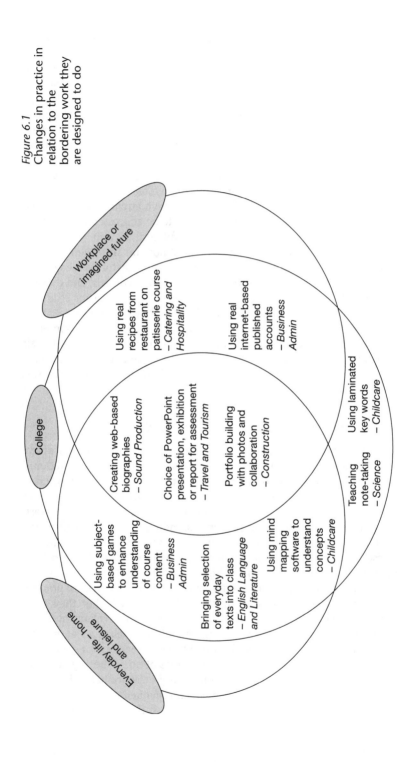

Figure 6.1
Changes in practice in relation to the bordering work they are designed to do

Workplace or imagined future

College

Everyday life – home and leisure

Using real recipes from restaurant on patisserie course
– *Catering and Hospitality*

Using real internet-based published accounts
– *Business Admin*

Creating web-based biographies
– *Sound Production*

Choice of PowerPoint presentation, exhibition or report for assessment
– *Travel and Tourism*

Portfolio building with photos and collaboration
– *Construction*

Using laminated key words
– *Childcare*

Teaching note-taking
– *Science*

Using subject-based games to enhance understanding of course content
– *Business Admin*

Bringing selection of everyday texts into class
– *English Language and Literature*

Using mind mapping software to understand concepts
– *Childcare*

on academic literacies because the tutors recognised that this was the aspect of the course that caused the students the most difficulties.

However, this way of categorising the changes in practice became problematic as the project progressed. We have already indicated that there was a greater porosity between the domains of college, work and home than we had initially conceived. As we looked more closely at the data, so our understanding of domains broadened, as we identified in Chapter 2, to embrace family, leisure, work, religion and community, as well as college. These domains are not firmly bounded. Similarly, as we started to identify the elements of a literacy practice outlined in Chapter 3, the specification of what was being mobilised from one domain to another became more nuanced. The sense of creating a connection between literacy practices through establishing a border began to fray, as we will examine in Chapter 8. Bordering literacy practices between domains began to feel conceptually and metaphorically inadequate to the data, as borders exclude as well as provide opportunities for crossing, and that which was being drawn into learning from the everyday seemed to be not so much a full-scale literacy practice as more fine-grained elements of a literacy practice. It was this insight which led us to develop the framework presented in Chapter 3.

Changes in practice

We will now look in more detail at examples of particular changes of practice, discussing them in terms of the categorisation systems introduced here, the students' preferences identified from their everyday literacy practices in Chapter 2, and the framework introduced in Chapter 3. It is important to note that the latter emerged after the changes in practice were put into effect, as we tried to make sense of data from the actions for understanding and from the effects of the changes themselves. In other words, the understandings which informed the changes in practice preceded the framework that arose from analysis of the project as a whole. It was only after the event that we were able to analyse the changes in this way. In future, the framework can be used alongside the preferences of students identified in Chapter 2 and the domains and purposes of literacy practices to conceive of more fine-grained changes in practice. Here, we pick out in italics aspects of literacy practices from Figure 3.1 and characteristics of students' preferred literacy practices from Box 3.1 the first time we mention them, for the purposes of cross-reference.

'Tourist Destinations' in an English Level 3 BTEC National Diploma in Travel and Tourism

This unit was described as 'dry', 'academic', 'boring' by tutors and students alike. David Jarratt, the lecturer responsible for teaching this unit in the first year of the research, commented:

I do think it's a bit of a dull unit though, if I'm honest, the fact that it is academic and it is quite thorough means that it's not going to be their favourite unit. For example at the same time they were doing a unit on repping, [where] there's a lot of standing up and taking them out on trips, doing welcome meetings which was obviously more fun and they prefer that.

The students also admitted they did not enjoy the written part of the course, 'like big assignments – they bore me a bit', and that they would prefer 'more active stuff'. They all said they would prefer to do PowerPoint presentations. One said: 'It would be easier because you don't have to go into details if you're doing PowerPoint.' They also thought 'you can talk a lot faster than what you can write'. Another student added that he would prefer doing 'visual presentations as well like pictures and writing on like a big piece of paper', in comparison with writing, even on a computer, which he described as 'Just black and white isn't it?' The students admitted that although they could see the relevance of the assignments, they did not always think about that when they received another one. One said: 'You just think about getting it done.'

When we first encountered the unit, the students were required to write a series of three reports, each about three contrasting tourist destinations. The two lecturers who taught the unit both thought that the repetition that was implied by the programme specifications, while having the advantage that students would become familiar with the genre required by the assignment, was unnecessary and put students off:

they start to lose interest because they don't see the relevance of . . . I mean they can probably see the relevance of doing like the first three destinations, provided that covers all the possible transport routes you could have. Then they would feel well why do another six on top of that?

However, the lecturer felt the external verifier would require this 'so you've got to do it – there's no flexibility on that'. Here perceived *constraints* weighed against *flexibility*. Although the *content* of the assignments was specified by the awarding body, it was possible for material to be presented in different ways. Students indicated they preferred *multimedia* and *active* work – characteristics of literacies in the other domains of their lives – and preferred talking to writing. Sarah Wilcock, the lecturer who taught the unit in the second year, wanted to give them *variety* and to make it *interesting*, but she acknowledged that for the students, 'interesting' on its own was not sufficient. The activity also had to have a clear *purpose* and *relevance* – again, characteristics of their preferred literacy practices in the rest of their lives. For students looking to a future in the tourism industry, Sarah thought that the production of exhibitions and talks using PowerPoint would be nearer to the types of literacy practice that would be required in a job.

After consideration of these factors, Sarah decided that, as a change in practice for this unit, she would give the students a choice of producing a PowerPoint, an exhibition, or a report. These activities would tap into the resources of students whose preferred everyday literacy practices tended to be *collaborative, multimodal, generative, non-linear, using multimedia* and *determined by their own choice*. In activities such as a presentation or an exhibition, there is a real *audience*, in addition to the assumed or imagined audience of the external verifier or the awarding body. The exhibition was open to other members of staff and their students at a specified time and date, which, although perceived as 'a bit embarrassing' by the tourism students, provided a focus and *purpose* for their work. Sitting or standing by their own exhibition also gave the students a real sense of *ownership* of their work and their attention to this audience was notable in the beautifully presented leaflets, posters and models.

For the presentation, it was evident that, although the students had said they preferred talking to writing and they did not like writing extended texts, they still produced slides with substantial amounts of text, and wrote scripts or copious notes for themselves. This indicates that students differentiate between writing an essay and producing a PowerPoint presentation, a distinction that has arisen in interviews with other students who see the latter as being not just 'doing a piece of writing', but engaging in 'a publishing exercise' or '*design work*'. When the writing is part and parcel of an activity with which they *identify* and which they *value*, the clarity of the *purpose* is heightened and the onerousness diminished. Students preferred producing a PowerPoint presentation to writing an essay, seeing it as 'more visual' and 'less boring'. It was a useful literacy practice which had purpose and value in the 'real world' of work, rather than an 'academic' literacy practice, serving no purpose other than to provide evidence of learning.

This change in practice was concerned both with learning content and with demonstrating knowledge and understanding for assessment purposes. It also related to students' imagined futures in the travel and tourism industry, unlike the previous types of assignment. It made the reading and writing more resonant both with students' everyday literacy practices and those of the world of work for which most of them were preparing (pedagogic intention a). It also made the reading and writing on the course more relevant to learning (pedagogic intention d), as the students could see not only that this literacy practice would be useful in the industry but also that they were learning a lot by engaging in it. It was bordering aspects of literacy practices from both home and work, harnessing them to enhance students' learning on the course. (For further discussion of this change in practice see Ivanič *et al.* 2007.)

'Language Production' in AS Level English Language and Literature

One of the colleges in our project was responsible for delivering academic courses at Level 2 and 3 to a number of Muslim schools. One of these was a girls' boarding school where the students were restricted in their activities and, during term time, did not have access to popular newspapers or magazines. The AQA AS Level in English Language and Literature contains a unit called 'Language Production' which requires students to write in a recognised *genre*, such as a women's magazine or a holiday brochure, using particular conventions of *style* for specific *audiences* and *purposes*. The students were perceived to be at a disadvantage in terms of the variety of different genres, styles and designs of literacy practices in which they regularly engaged by comparison to students who had unrestricted access to texts, computers, mobile phones, TV, adverts and so on. Their lecturer's interviews with them revealed that the students did not use mobile phones or watch TV at school, but they did have access to computers, phones, magazines and so on at home. In the previous year, although the girls did well in their results overall, they did not achieve well on this particular unit. Angela Brzeski, the lecturer responsible for this course, said:

> the students fell down heavily on this particular unit. Some students were getting a perfect score for poetry. One of these students got 90 out of 90 for the poetry, got an E for Language Production and the whole group either got an E or a U. Nobody got higher than an E, so that was quite staggering . . . The girls at the Muslim Girls School certainly did fare far worse on Unit 1 than the students at the main site – with the odd exception – but generally speaking the results were quite appalling.

The descriptor for this unit demonstrated that the examination board had recognised the need to draw upon the everyday, but in this particular case it had backfired to some extent, because it did not account for the fact that the school did not itself enable access to these resources for the students. At the main college site access to these texts could be taken for granted, although still these texts would not necessarily be brought into the classroom as teaching and learning texts. Because the girls lived in at the Muslim Girls School, their everyday texts were regulated by their teachers and supervisors: school life becomes part of their everyday lives. This example complicates any simple distinction between everyday and educational contexts.

As a response to this situation, the tutor brought in a folder of extracts from many different kinds of everyday text to give the girls an idea of the types of *genre* they needed to use in the exam. The exam also required students to name the publication that they would expect their 'article' to appear in. The examples provided gave students these names. They found the folder very useful, particularly as they were not expected to read it all in detail, but to get a flavour of the different *genres* of writing, their associated conventions of *style and design*, and the *modes and technologies* through which they were produced.

The *participation* in this change in practice involved a certain amount of *interaction and collaboration*, and physical *actions and processes*. When the magazines were brought in, the students went over to the box and got some out to look at, and the folder was handed round and discussed. These changes in practice were successful on different levels: for the students there was more enjoyment, collaboration, and increased engagement; the tutors found that students performed much better in the exam than the previous year; and the college could claim higher pass rates.

This change in practice was concerned with learning content and with preparation for one of the assessment requirements on the course. It was an unusual example of pedagogic intentions (a) and (b), as the students did not have immediate access to non-school domains of life, and therefore these had to be provided for them. It was bordering aspects of literacy practices from home, which was particularly crucial, since these were, in this case, being valued by the awarding body.

HNC Childcare unit 'Theoretical Approaches'

An HNC in Scotland is considered to be the same level as the first year of a degree, so students are expected to be doing more independent investigation and self-directed study. The introduction of the SCQF has made this more visible, while the SQA has been keen to make all HNCs of a consistent standard. The more streamlined approach they have introduced has meant that there are fewer assessments per unit and a graded unit which could be either an exam or a portfolio. Childcare had opted for a portfolio. There had been a drive to increase independent learning as a preparation for university and the Childcare sector wanted to develop a more 'professional' as opposed to practical approach in its HNC. In colleges, however, students often came from many different backgrounds and often had poor school experiences or may not have studied for a number of years.

Joyce Gaechter, the lecturer on an HNC Childcare course (SCQF Level 7) introduced a change of practice which involved using mind-mapping techniques. The important aspect of this was not the mind-map as such but rather the *process* that the students went through in order to produce the mind-maps. The introduction of mind-mapping came about in response to the emerging insights from the research that suggested that students enjoyed learning using *multimodal* texts which were often *non-linear* and *interactive*. For example, many students were adept at navigating and writing websites or using art software to design posters and logos in order to keep up with their hobbies, interests and work activities. These literacy practices used *modes and technologies* which involved manipulating colour, images and icons in creative *design work*, and had specific *purposes* which were *valued* by the students and often involved *relating to others*, particularly family, friends and their peers.

Joyce wanted to introduce a change of practice which would draw on dimensions of these home-related literacy practices, address the demands of the new HNC framework and also ultimately relate to workplace literacy practices. By drawing on aspects of literacy practices which were valued in other domains of the students' lives, the lecturer intended to help the students achieve their qualifications and enrich the learning process. In Joyce's experience, while students were adept at handling the literacies required by their practical work, many found academic literacy practices, such as report and essay writing, difficult. The HNC Childcare students often found the concepts involved in the units 'Language Development' and 'Theoretical Approaches' very difficult to understand and link to practice and other areas of study. Also, it was often a concern to lecturing staff that some students did not actually learn what was being taught in any meaningful way, but picked bits out to pass the assessments without making the connections in their own minds.

Mind-mapping techniques were introduced to help students make these connections as they allow connections to be illustrated through the use of colour and symbols. Use of the mind-mapping technique aimed to help students understand the wider picture and therefore be more effective learners. Initially the change in practice was to use a mind-mapping software package called *Mind Genius Education* with the class to allow the students to research, organise, illustrate and make up their own notes on early educationalists. It was hoped that this would help the students to plan and write essays and understand concepts better. Although Joyce, like the other Childcare lecturers described in Chapter 5, had not previously made a great deal of use of ICT in the classroom, she persevered with this because of the unique benefits it would offer students. The software allowed the students to take notes in an individual way using colour, lettering, pictures, diagrams, connections to websites, to connect up ideas and present them in a variety of ways. This allowed the students to *design* their own texts using different *styles, modes and technologies* in a *flexible* way rather than simply taking down notes or reading handouts. Drawing on various modes incorporated the processes of transformation, as they reorganised information onto their maps, and transduction, as they incorporated semiotically meaningful images, icons and colours into their maps. (See Kress 2003 for the distinction between 'transformation' and 'transduction'.)

Joyce described the *flexibility* of the approach:

> One mature student told me she thought this was a good idea but she would not be able to use it because at her school they were not allowed to use colours, diagrams, pictures and I had to tell her that I was giving her permission. We then had a discussion about a note taking system

she had developed for herself – which was a form of mind-mapping but in linear form – minus colour. I explained to her that there were different ways of mind-mapping and the software would allow her to do it in a non-linear way. One student was very excited about this technique as she had worked with mind-maps before and really enjoyed using them. The students worked very hard on these and I feel it was a very successful class that expanded their understanding greatly.

This *flexibility* meant that students could *design* the maps according to their *own preferences*. Some of the students preferred to design their maps by hand and explained that the *actions and processes* of drawing the maps helped them to remember the concepts in the map. Although the students enjoyed working *collaboratively* during the design process, they all produced an individual map of their own, which meant that they were able to take *ownership* of the text. All the students interviewed said that the group work involved in producing the maps was important, as they were able to exchange ideas and work things out collectively. Joyce described how she did this initially:

> Near the end of the class when one group of mature students were still particularly struggling with their mind-map – mainly because they wanted everything to fit into a neat box – I decided to split them up and send one each to another group and get the group to explain their mind-map to them. They found this useful and it was good for the other students to have to explain what they meant and their reasoning to someone else. The rest of the class then looked at other groups' mind-maps and were also given explanations, which often resulted in additions or changes to their own. This was a really good class. The students worked hard and were very motivated. I feel they deepened and clarified their understanding of 'language development' by constructing the mind-map but also by the amount of discussion that it generated. We also decided that this is a good technique to use when preparing for the closed book assessments they have this year – explain notes to someone else.

The students emphasised the *interaction and collaboration* in designing the maps as being very important to them: 'the talking about what to put in the mind-maps with each other really helped me understand the theoretical bits'.

As the students started working with mind-maps, it became evident that they were useful in a number of different ways in relation to studying their curriculum area. However, importantly they were also useful in the other domains of students' lives for work and leisure activities. Students began to use mind-maps at home to organise and plan domestic activities; they also used them in their work placements to scaffold activities with children. In other words, the folding of practices from one domain to another began to flow both ways. The students interviewed about this intervention reported successfully using mind-maps as intended for note taking and as an assessment tool, but also they were useful for understanding how they learnt. The group work that resulted from using mind-maps as classroom texts promoted informal peer learning, which again resonated with the way students participated in literacy practices outside the college domain.

The other lecturers teaching the programme were also involved in this change of practice and found ways of using mind-maps across the curriculum. Some of the students had already used mind-mapping techniques at school, while some of the older students were actively opposed to using colour and non-linear texts as this was not how they had been taught at school. However, after being involved in the collaborative process of producing maps, students found that they could adapt them to their own particular styles. Lecturers found that as a result of this change in practice, students engaged in a more analytical process in relation to the curriculum. (For further discussion of this change in practice see Miller and Gaechter 2006 and Pardoe and Ivanič 2007.)

This change in practice was concerned with learning content and with engaging with it in such a way that students could be more successful in the assignments they needed to complete for assessment purposes. It drew on the multimodal characteristics of literacy practices in other domains of students' lives for an educational purpose (pedagogic intention a), and introduced a new pedagogic literacy practice which was highly relevant to learning (pedagogic intention d). It was harnessing aspects of literacy practices from students' out-of-college lives to enhance their learning on the course.

Gleneagles Patisserie Chef Certificate

The last example is a change in practice which focused on workplace literacies. The Gleneagles Patisserie Chef Certificate is part of the professional chef award and is not strictly speaking a unit but rather an added value certificate assessed jointly between Gleneagles and the college. Ian Gibb, the lecturer for this award, started off this certificate as a way of bringing the college more in line with the catering and hospitality industry. As mentioned in his profile in Box 6.1, Ian had started his career in the industry and wanted to maintain close links to avoid the college courses being accused of being out of touch with real industry practices.

Ian invited the head pastry chef from Gleneagles Hotel to spend the day with the students producing pastries as they would be produced at Gleneagles in terms of quality and quantity. The head pastry chef brought in the recipes used at Gleneagles. The students had to work in groups to produce industrial quantity and quality of various different types of pastries. The recipes were simpler than the recipes they were used to receiving in that there was not so much information on what to do with the ingredients. In this way they were more authentic as a chef at Gleneagles would be expected to have the background knowledge required. This meant there was a fair amount of discussion between the groups working out who was going to do what and when.

The lecturer explains the change of practice:

> And the reason for that was to get industry involved, and for the industry to actually bring in the recipes for what the students were actually doing on that day. Students prepared . . . quantities that they would prepare in industry, like instead of four portions of scones – they would do forty . . . The students actually worked in . . . little sections like how they would do it in industry, in like, groups of three or four, and they actually had their instructions exactly what they had to do, scones, and cakes, all different sort of breads . . . or biscuits, so they worked in sections and they actually got time limits there to meet . . . And if they didn't meet the deadlines they would not get the grades. . .
>
> The students . . . referred back to [the recipes] to check quantities.

With this change in practice, the lecturer was focusing on the workplace side of literacy practices in that he was trying to make the training more realistic in order to prepare them for working in fully commercial kitchens. The recipes were authentic as were their surrounding practices, while the group work related closely to working practices in a fully commercial kitchen.

The reading was embedded in and to some extent incidental to the main *activity* of cooking the breads and pastries, rather than being the focus of attention. The reading *processes* themselves were thus authentic to the workplace setting. Both the larger activity within which the reading was embedded and the reading itself had a clear *purpose*, as the students were producing real food products, which would later be sold, and the reading was essential to this goal. The purpose could also be seen as a learning outcome, whereby the students gained experience and understanding of working with authentic recipes to produce industry-standard goods.

The *timing* element of the reading process was quite different from the reading of pedagogic texts, with moments of reading integrated into the food production. The interpretation of the texts involved *collaboration*, with groups of students pooling their knowledge in order to achieve their goals: this collaborative element resonates both with the students' everyday literacy practices and with the practices of the workplace. Through this change in practice, the lecturer had brought an element of the working practices from the Gleneagles Hotel to the college. Hence, although the *places and spaces* were actually the college kitchens and the more public spaces for the cake sale, elements of a real workplace were introduced into the college domain. In this way the lecturer crossed the boundaries of space and brought industry literacy practices closer to college and college literacy practices closer to those of the industry. The success of this change in practice indicates that the purpose was sufficiently *valued* and *identified with* by the students involved.

This change in practice was concerned with reading for the learning of new kitchen processes, and also with learning the reading practices of the students' imagined futures in the catering and hospitality industry. It made the reading more resonant both with literacy practices of the world of work for which most of them were preparing (pedagogic intention a). It made the literacy practices on the course more relevant to learning (pedagogic intention d), as the students could see that this literacy practice was authentic to the industry. This change in practice operated at the border between college and work. It was a case of a literacy practice being mobilised almost wholesale from work to college, the only difference being in the actual location in which it was being practised.

Conclusion

The majority of the changes in practice made use of an understanding of the characteristics of students' everyday literacy practices (as summarised in Box 3.1) in order to fine-tune literacies for learning. In particular, students responded well to activities in which the literacy practices were characterised by collaboration, choice and variety, creativity and the generation of meaning. When students could see the relevance of reading and writing on their courses, they valued these literacy practices and were more likely to take ownership of the artefacts and the learning which was generated. When students identified with the potential future inscribed in the literacy practice, they were more likely to engage effectively with it. In this way, bordering work between domains was attempted, some of which flowed in unexpected ways. While in some cases this led to better results in terms of students' achievement in assessments, interviews with staff and focus groups with students indicated wider learning outcomes were enhanced, in particular students' capacity for engagement and recall and their confidence in their literacy practices and careers.

We have given only four illustrative examples of changes in practice in detail here. These examples give a flavour of the variety of ways in which the understandings from the research reported in Chapters 2 to 5 can impact on practice. As the examples demonstrate, all changes in practice must be situated in time and place, according to the particular students involved, the subject, the course, the level, and the experience of the lecturer concerned. What may be an innovation for one lecturer will be established practice for another. Different lecturers will use an understanding of students' everyday literacy practices, and of the communicative aspects of learning, in different ways. To illustrate this, in the next chapter, we show how the research was recontextualised in a very different pedagogic context: three curriculum areas at Coleg Meirion Dwyfor in Dolgellau, the leading provider of bilingual and Welsh medium education at college level in Wales.

Chapter 7

Recontextualising the research

Bilingual literacies for learning in Wales

The focus of this chapter shifts to the project on 'Bilingual Literacies for Learning in Further Education' (BiLfLFE) (*Dwyieithrwydd, Llythrennedd a Dysgu mewn Addysg Bellach*), to the college in North Wales where this project was based – Coleg Meirion-Dwyfor – and to the lecturers and students in three curriculum areas: Agriculture, Early Years (Childcare) and Welsh (including Welsh as a first language and Welsh as a second language). The research design and research strategies for this bilingual project were broadly similar to those adopted for the larger project in England and Scotland. The only major difference was that the research was carried out bilingually. Thus, for example, two-thirds of the students (in our sample of forty-six) chose to be interviewed in Welsh.

There were clear similarities between the findings of this project and those of the project in England and Scotland. Take, for example, the students' accounts of their out-of-college literacies: the widespread use of mobile phones and MSN for the exchange of messages and for keeping in touch; the ease with which students navigated digital media and employed pictures and symbols as well as written language; the importance of literacy practices associated with learning to drive (access to and use of a car was especially valued in this rural context). However, there were also significant differences in this project's findings which need to be understood with reference to the particularities of the sociocultural, linguistic and historical context: to the ways in which the lives of the students and lecturers had been touched by the Welsh Language Movement, to the changes taking place in policy and provision for bilingual and Welsh-medium education and to the wider context of language legislation and political devolution in Wales. This chapter will foreground these distinctive findings, set them in context, and then show how we developed small-scale changes in bilingual teaching/learning practice, taking account of the findings.

The chapter is organised into five broad sections as follows: the first section provides a brief overview of the wider context and details the specific nature of the cultural, communicative and political changes taking place in contemporary Wales. This includes an account of the shifts, over time, in language education policy and moves that have been made towards the development of bilingual teaching/learning environments within the college sector. The second section sketches out the local setting, in North Wales, where the project was based: it introduces the college, the three curriculum areas which provided the main focus for our project, the three lecturers who were seconded to the project and the bilingual students with whom we worked.

The third and fourth sections detail some of the distinctive findings. Here we describe some of the ways in which students' everyday lives were mediated by bilingual texts and practices and some of the ways in which these texts and practices were embedded in this specific social and cultural context. The fifth section describes the small-scale actions for change in bilingual teaching/learning practice introduced through our project. These changes fell into two of the broad categories outlined in Chapter 6: (1) bilingual literacy practices for learning content; (2) bilingual literacy practices related to imagined futures.

The sociocultural and historical context

In order to contextualise the research we conducted in the BiLfLFE project, along with the findings from the project, we need to draw attention to two main processes of change that are at work in Wales and briefly trace their origins. The first is global in nature: it is the fundamental transformation of the communicative landscape. Wales is no different in this regard from the rest of the UK. This far-reaching process of change and its impact on literacy practices was described in detail in the opening pages of Chapter 1. With the advent of new technology, and with the globalised spread of new technoscapes (Appadurai 1990), we have seen the rapid diversification of artefacts and textual resources for communication within institutional and life world contexts and we have seen the opening up of new possibilities for literacy. Our concern with these changes in contemporary literacy practices and with the textually mediated nature of contemporary social life provided one of the main conceptual links for us with the LfLFE project. However, in our project, we also needed to take account of the additional level of complexity resulting from the fact that we were working in a bilingual context (in North Wales) where two languages are widely used in different domains of social life. Moreover, we needed to take account of variation in the use of Welsh, for the following reasons: the difference between standard written Welsh and vernacular forms of the language is considerably greater than it is for English; bilinguals in Wales use Welsh in reading and writing, with different degrees of confidence in different institutional and life world spaces, because they have had very different educational histories.

The second process of change is cultural and political in nature: this is the gradual shift in the status and value of Welsh that has been taking place since the mid-twentieth century and which has been accelerated by political devolution and by the establishment of the National Assembly for Wales (*Cynulliad Cenedlaethol Cymru*) in May 1999. In Wales, a linguistic market (Bourdieu 1977) has been created in which the Welsh language carries high value. Knowledge of spoken Welsh and considerable capability in the reading and writing of Welsh are real assets when applying for many public sector posts (e.g. in education) or for jobs in the Welsh media. There is also a burgeoning language industry, which encompasses a range of activities from translation and interpreting to the provision of bilingual websites for local businesses or research related to Welsh language planning. The status of the language is also underpinned by legislation, notably the Welsh Language Act of 1993, which stipulates that Welsh and English are to be treated on a basis of equality in public sector institutions in Wales (Jones and Martin-Jones 2004).

This significant shift in the status and value of Welsh has its origins in the Welsh language movement and, particularly, in the mobilisation of Welsh speakers around a campaign for the language, led by the Welsh Language Society (*Cymdeithas yr Iaith*) from the 1960s (Phillips 2000). Grassroots demands, in different domains of Welsh life, in education, in the media and in the legal system, led to significant policy shifts over the decades that followed. Echoing the terminology first introduced in Catalonia, this process has come to be known in Wales as 'normalisation', that is, the restoration of legitimacy to the language in public life. In education, parental demand was a significant factor in the establishment of bilingual and Welsh-medium nursery and primary provision. Local education authorities then played a significant role in the expansion of bilingual secondary education (Jones and Martin-Jones 2004). By 2007, 24 per cent of all secondary schools (fifty-four in all) were offering more than half of the subjects of the National Curriculum in Welsh (WAG 2007a, 2007b). Since devolution, there has also been a significant expansion in provision for Welsh as a second language. Since 1999, all students in schools in Wales have been required to study Welsh, as a first or second language, for eleven years (from age 5 to 16) (WAG 2007b).

However, at Further and Higher Education levels, provision for bilingual education has been much slower to develop and is still unevenly distributed across Wales. We focus here on the situation regarding bilingual provision at college level. In 2008, there were twenty-three colleges in Wales and two further education institutions (www.fforwm.ac.uk). Fourteen of these were listed as providing some bilingual or Welsh-medium courses, though the overall picture was variable. However, most of the bilingual and Welsh-medium provision was offered by six colleges: four in North Wales and two in West Wales (FEFCW 2000; Heath 2001). Coleg Meirion-Dwyfor, where the BiLfLFE project was based, was the leading provider of bilingual education in the sector.

There have been some attempts to co-ordinate the development of bilingual education at college level. For example, in the late 1990s, the

Allwedd Iaith project (literally, the Language Key project), based at Coleg Meirion-Dwyfor, facilitated collaboration between the six colleges mentioned above. The focus was on the production of new bilingual materials, the setting of standards in Welsh and the training of staff in bilingual approaches to teaching (Baker and Jones 2000; Williams 2000). In 2001, *Allwedd Iaith* was replaced by *Canolfan Sgiliaith* (the Language Skills Centre). Since 2001, *Sgiliaith* has continued to support professional development and the production of bilingual learning materials for the college sector. Its mission has been broader than that of *Allwedd Iaith* as it has also been expected to liaise with the school and HE sectors in seeking to widen participation in bilingual and Welsh-medium education post-16. *Sgiliaith* has also contributed to debates about future policy directions.

However, possibilities for co-operation across colleges providing bilingual education were curtailed with the reorganisation of the further education sector under the terms of the 1992 Act and with the incorporation of colleges in 1993. During the early 1990s, there was actually an overall decline in bilingual and Welsh-medium provision, although two colleges in North Wales, Coleg Meirion-Dwyfor and Coleg Menai, continued to expand their provision (Baker and Jones 2000). This local expansion was, in part, a response to the growing demand for bilingual and Welsh-medium vocational education, as the need for Welsh language and literacy abilities in different occupations and in different sectors of the economy increased, particularly in the service sector and in professional and technical occupations (Williams and Morris 2000).

Since political devolution, the national language policies of the Welsh Assembly Government have become the main drivers of change. Within its first few years, the Welsh Assembly Government moved towards a pro-active approach to language policy. In its first strategic plan, *BetterWales.com,* the government articulated a commitment to 'fostering Wales' unique and diverse identity and the benefits of bilingualism' (statement reported in WAG 2002: 4).

In 2002, a Welsh language policy statement, *Dyfodol Dwyieithog* (Bilingual Future) (WAG 2002), was published. This policy document sets out the Welsh Assembly Government's vision of a bilingual future for Wales:

> in a truly bilingual Wales both Welsh and English will flourish and will be treated as equal. A bilingual Wales means a country where people can choose to live their lives through the medium of either or both languages; a country where the presence of two national languages, and other diverse languages and cultures, is a source of pride and strength to us all.
>
> (ibid.)

This policy statement was followed by a National Action Plan (WAG 2003). This Action Plan, entitled *Iaith Pawb* (Everyone's Language) states:

'we are committed to facing up to the paucity of Welsh-medium provision in Higher Education and . . . in Further Education' (WAG 2003: 43).

This, then, was the sociocultural and historical context in which the BiLfLFE project was situated. The policy shifts that we have described here and the changes in the communicative landscape ushered in by the advent of new technology have intersected in significant ways. Thus, for example, new virtual worlds for the use of Welsh have been created and new possibilities have been opened up for using Welsh in both institutional and life world contexts. These intersections also give rise to a tension between globalising and localising trends (e.g., the tension related to the ubiquitous presence of English on the World Wide Web or the global dominance of software in English). By focusing in on local literacies, in Welsh and in English, in one college setting, we were able to capture some of the ways in which these global processes of change were shaping the day-to-day lives of the students and the lecturers at Coleg Meirion-Dwyfor, both in the college context and outside the college. In the next section, we take a closer look at the college and at the three curriculum areas that provided the main focus of our work.

The research context

Coleg Meirion-Dwyfor was first established in 1993. It is set in a rural context in North Wales. There are three campuses at Dolgellau, Pwllheli and Glynllifon (near Caernarfon), with a distance of about 65 km/40 miles between them. The main college site is at Dolgellau, in South Gwynedd. Each campus is located in a region of Wales where a substantial proportion of the local population is Welsh-speaking. The *Sgiliaith* unit, which played a key role in co-ordinating and promoting bilingual education across the college sector in Wales, is based on its Pwllheli campus. The language policy of the college, like that of other colleges in Wales, was formulated under the terms of the Welsh Language Act of 1993. It is overseen internally by the bilingual co-ordinator for the college and the senior management team and externally by the nationally constituted Welsh Language Board. The college has a distinctly Welsh ethos and has an explicit policy on the equal use of Welsh and English in written communication internal to the college (e.g., email correspondence, memos, forms and noticeboards) as well as in all external communication (e.g., brochures, websites). The college also has its own, in-house, translation unit.

The three curriculum areas

The three curriculum areas, the courses and the units selected as the focus of our project, the college-based researchers and the awarding bodies are all shown in Table 7.1.

Table 7.1 College-based researchers, curriculum areas, main units and levels
in the Welsh research

College-based Researcher/ campus	Curriculum area	Course/unit	Level/ awarding body
Margaret Lewis (Dolgellau)	Early Years/ *Blynyddoedd Cynnar*	Early Years – Childcare Practice/ *Ymarfer Gofal Plant*	BTEC ND Level 3
		Early Years – Diet and Nutrition/*Diet a Maeth*	BTEC ND Level 3
Anwen Williams (Glynllifon)	Agriculture/ *Amaethyddiaeth*	Specialised project/ *Prosiect Arbenigol*	BTEC ND Level 3
		Agricultural Business/ *Busnes Amaethyddiaeth*	City & Guilds NCA Level 2
Beryl Davies (Dolgellau)	Welsh/*Cymraeg*	Welsh/*Cymraeg* Poetry/*Barddoniaeth*	WJEC AS Level
		Welsh as a second language – Film and Oracy/*Ffilm a Llafaredd*	WJEC AS Level

These three curriculum areas were linked, in two broad ways, to the
wider processes of cultural and political change described in the section
above. First, in creating these bilingual learning environments, the lecturers
were part of the college's response to the wider policy shift, under the
Welsh Assembly Government, towards extending bilingual education
provision in the college sector in Wales. Second, each curriculum area was
connected in particular ways to the grassroots campaign for the normalisation of the Welsh language in public life. The Early Years course
attracted a significant number of students who wanted to work in Welsh-
medium or bilingual settings. Agriculture and other land-based industries
are the traditional sources of employment for those who have been brought
up in the rural areas of Wales. After leaving college, many of the young
people attracted to bilingual courses, in this area of the curriculum, seek
jobs in environments where Welsh is likely to be the main working
language. The teaching of *Cymraeg* (Welsh) as an academic subject, at
advanced level, to those for whom Welsh is a first language, is the main
stepping stone to HE Level study of the language, giving access to highly
valued linguistic knowledge and highly standardised forms of Welsh. The

students enrolled in the Welsh as a second language course, during the period when we were carrying out the research in the college, had different aspirations, some academic and some vocational: some had chosen Welsh as one of several AS Level subjects, as part of their preparation for HE Level study. Others had enrolled in this academic course alongside vocational courses which would lead to public sector employment in Wales (e.g., in the tourism and leisure industries).

The students

There were forty-six students in our sample. They were all in the 16 to 19 age range and were all bilingual in Welsh and English, though they had diverse language and literacy histories. Some had learned Welsh as a first language at home and others had learned it as a second language at school. Some had been born in Wales and others had moved to Wales with their parents during a particular point in their schooling. Some were from households where everyone spoke Welsh. Others were from households where only one person (either an adult or a sibling) spoke Welsh and yet others were from households where no one, apart from them, spoke Welsh.

The students had different educational histories and thus had different levels of confidence in using Welsh across the curriculum. Most students had grown up in Wales and had had access to Welsh-medium or bilingual education in both primary and secondary school, though the schools had varied in the degree to which a Welsh ethos had been embedded. Some had had a bilingual primary school experience but had received their secondary education through the medium of English while studying Welsh as a subject. A range of attitudes towards Welsh was expressed by the students in the sample. Their attitudes and values depended on their school experience, their family backgrounds, their peer group networks and their aspirations for the future.

A further dimension of diversity in our sample – and one often commented on informally by their lecturers – related to the particular region of North Wales where they lived. Some of the students studying *Cymraeg* (Welsh as a first language) and Early Years came from Dolgellau or the surrounding rural areas. Others travelled in to college from towns such as Bala (a market town and tourist destination) and Blaenau Ffestiniog (an industrial town in the slate mining area). Both towns are known in Wales as having high proportions of Welsh speakers. Most of the students studying Welsh as a second language came from the anglicised seaside towns on the north-west coast of Wales. The students enrolled in Agriculture courses came from farms and small holdings across North Wales, from Môn (Anglesey) to Aberdyfi in South Gwynedd. The distances were too great for them to travel in to college every weekday so the Agriculture courses were partly residential, with accommodation being provided for students from Monday to Friday.

As well as regional differences in patterns of enrolment to the bilingual courses in these three curriculum areas, there were also gendered patterns. Thus, all those who were taking the Early Years course (thirteen in all) were young women, echoing the finding of Colley *et al.* (2003) regarding the feminisation of this area of the vocational curriculum. Young women also predominated in the Welsh as a first language unit whilst there was more of a gender balance in the Welsh as a second language cohort. In contrast, all the students in the Level 3 Agriculture unit (Specialised Project) were young men (eight in all) and so were all but two of the students in the Level 2 Agricultural Business unit (seven in all). Patterns of work in this rural context are still quite gendered: daughters tend to seek work outside the farm whilst sons are typically encouraged to work on the family farm, especially if there is scope for diversification and for expansion of economic activity on the land (see Martin-Jones *et al.* 2009 for more details).

In the next two sections, we highlight findings that distinguished this bilingual context from Scotland and England bringing out the main comparisons and contrasts with the ideas and findings presented in Chapters 2, 3, 4 and 5. We begin with the bilingual literacy practices associated with different aspects of life at college. We then focus on bilingual literacies in the students' lives outside college.

Bilingual literacies at college

When students first enter Coleg Meirion-Dwyfor, they enter a communicative space that is mediated by texts in two languages. Many of these texts are in Welsh, some are bilingual texts with different kinds of bilingual design, and some are solely in English. We describe here some of the ways in which these texts mediated college-wide and classroom-based activities, drawing upon the four uses of reading and writing across different phases of college life identified in Chapter 4. In our account, we take up this four-way distinction, primarily with a view to capturing the distinctive communicative landscape of bilingual colleges such as Coleg Meirion-Dwyfor. Our account is based on observations and interviews carried out between 2005 and 2007.

Bilingual literacies in becoming and being a student

Before applying to Coleg Meirion-Dwyfor, prospective students visited the college's bilingual website or they read the Welsh or the English version of the college brochure. They then filled in a bilingual application form. On arriving at the college to register, they were guided by bilingual signs to different parts of the college. The printed and handwritten notices on the noticeboards in different areas were also in Welsh and in English. When new arrivals and the returning students signed up for their chosen courses, they were asked to complete forms in their preferred language. The bilingual design of the forms enabled them to make this choice: some forms had Welsh on one side and English on the other; others had both languages, side by side, in each of the sections that needed to be completed. At this point in their college life, students also received a stack of bilingual printed texts about college facilities, college policies, timetables and details of their courses. In addition, they could request a bilingual application pack for the means-tested Educational Maintenance Allowance (*Lwfans Cynhaliaeth Addysg*), which could be filled in at home and, where appropriate, with the assistance of a parent or guardian. At different points in the academic year at college, students could also retrieve further college information online, using screen-based literacies and making digital language choices.

Bilingual literacies for learning content

The day-to-day routines of reading and writing associated with the learning of content, across the curriculum, were quite similar to those described in detail in Chapter 4, but they were accomplished in two languages. These bilingual literacy practices included: reading handouts, booklets, overhead projector transparencies and textbooks; doing in-class and out-of-class writing tasks (individually or as group work); making notes in Welsh or English from lecturer presentations or from books; interpreting and producing diagrams and doing research on the internet.

There was some variation across curriculum areas, in terms of the amount and type of reading and writing in Welsh and in English. The students in the Early Years units were required to produce the widest range of texts, in different genres, including reports, essays, wall displays, booklets for parents and learning materials for use in nursery school placements. Moreover, the production of these texts sometimes involved considerable multimodality and complex alignment of verbal and visual resources as well as decisions about the bilingual design of the texts.

The availability of published materials in Welsh varied across curriculum areas. They were particularly scarce in the vocational areas. This meant that the lecturers needed to rely on teaching/learning material published in English and either translate it themselves or mediate such texts bilingually in the classroom context. For example, in vocational courses, reference was made to UK-wide legislation related to health and safety or to measures for protection of the environment. Texts related to such legislation were invariably in English though they were discussed in Welsh, or bilingually, in the classroom context. Similarly, some visual resources such as DVDs were only available in English. For example, in one Agriculture class we observed, the lecturer showed a DVD on the disposal of toxic substances which had been made by the Environmental Agency. The film was in English but the classroom activities based on the film were mostly in Welsh: following the showing of the film, the whole class discussed key points with the lecturer and then individual students drew a map of a farm that they were familiar with, identifying areas where sources of toxic substances or potentially toxic substances were to be found.

One major constraint for the development of bilingual courses at college level in Wales lay in the fact that, when our project was being conducted, course specifications were mostly produced in English by awarding bodies such as Edexcel, which are based in England. The one awarding body that offered qualification specifications in Welsh (the WJEC) had only a narrow range of vocational qualifications. In some colleges where Welsh-medium and bilingual vocational courses were offered, the lecturers translated the course specification themselves. In other colleges, such as Coleg Meirion-Dwyfor, assistance was sometimes provided by the Translation Unit. Some awarding bodies do now provide translations, but there is a time lag between the publication of the English specifications and the Welsh translations. This makes course planning quite difficult for the bilingual lecturers.

Bilingual literacies for assessment

A good deal of assessment, in Welsh or English, was focused on traditional academic genres such as formal written assignments, complete with references, bibliography and appendices. In the higher level vocational courses, students were also expected to conduct and write up research on a particular topic, often using the internet and relevant search engines. For example, in the Level 3 Specialised Project unit in Agriculture, students had to create an action plan, then carry out a practice-oriented project, such as building a feeding trough for livestock or selecting animal breeds for a particular environment or market. They then had to write a final report, with appropriate referencing, and evaluate the work they had undertaken.

Students could choose to be assessed in Welsh or English. In principle, they could write different assignments in different languages, although, in practice, they continued to use the same language. As long as the lecturers are bilingual, this flexibility of language choice for the student does not pose a problem for internal assessment or for internal verification, However, we noted that external verification did sometimes present a challenge: awarding bodies occasionally had difficulty recruiting specialist verifiers with the appropriate language abilities.

Bilingual literacies for imagined futures

The two vocational courses offered at Coleg Meirion-Dwyfor included work placements in bilingual or Welsh-medium settings. The Early Years course included a number of different placements in bilingual schools and other Early Years settings. The students took on a range of literacies as part of these placements, preparing learning materials and games for children and preparing signs and wall displays for the bilingual print environment of classrooms.

The Agriculture students enrolled in the Level 3 BTEC course did work placements on farms, between Year 1 and Year 2. The placements were often arranged, in partnership with parents, through local community contacts. In this way, students could be placed on farms with people who knew them. As part of their work, they engaged in or assisted with a range of literacy practices in Welsh or English associated with farming. These are 'hidden literacies' since farming is seen as a primarily practical activity. The paperwork varied in nature, depending on the type of farm, but usually involved record-keeping activities such as documenting vaccines administered to livestock or filling in animal movement forms on going to auction. It could also involve use of high-technology farming equipment such as computer-assisted milking on large dairy farms.

As shown in Chapter 4, students engaged in the reading and writing in their work placements with relatively little difficulty or comment and saw it as 'getting the work done'. However, they found the preparation of evidence related to work placements much more challenging, that is, when these work-related literacies were re-presented in more conventional academic form, as 'portfolios' or 'logbooks' for assessment. For all students, monolingual or bilingual, this was a specialised genre, one only encountered in educational settings. For bilingual students, where Welsh was still being extended into new institutional contexts and used in new genres, portfolio production presented an additional challenge.

Bilingual literacies outside college

As was the case for the Scottish and English students, we found that the students engaged in a much wider range of literacy practices outside college than they did in college. Their literacy practices also had characteristics similar to those identified at the end of Chapter 2. In this section, we will focus on findings in Wales that differed from those in Scotland and England as a result of the bilingual repertoires of the students and the sociocultural context in Wales.

Domains of literacy and language choices

The domains of literacy mentioned by bilingual students varied considerably in the possibilities they afforded for reading and writing in Welsh. The domains can be placed on a continuum from those which offered most possibilities for reading and/or writing in Welsh to those which offered the fewest. Figure 7.1 shows this broad continuum.

For the majority of students, who came from Welsh-speaking homes, home and family offered most opportunities for using Welsh. For those who came from English-speaking homes (about a quarter of those in our

Home/family → Community/peer group → Religion → Leisure/media → Work

Figure 7.1 Domains of literacy: a continuum of possibilities for the use of Welsh

sample), it was not their home or family but the local community and their peer-group that offered most opportunities for using Welsh. Their networks were often quite far flung because of the distances they travelled to college and so literacy helped to maintain these ties.

Only a couple of students mentioned religion as a domain. Rowena mentioned affiliation to a local chapel, where all the religious texts were in Welsh. She was often asked to do the reading from the Bible in Welsh during the chapel service, including one occasion when the service was on BBC *Radio Cymru.* Sometimes she was also asked to sing. Danielle said that she and her family attended a local church that was part of a UK-wide religious denomination. She played bass guitar with her worship group. They exchanged lists of hymns by email before the morning and evening services. She also contributed to the running of the Sunday school activities. This included reading stories with a moral content in English to 3 to 8-year-olds or doing activities such as writing 'agony aunt letters with pretend problems' with the 9 to 11-year-olds. The children swapped the letters and tried to write answers to them. For both Rowena and Danielle, the domain of religion was an extension of the domain of community and peer group and their religious observance involved engaging with texts in either Welsh or English.

Most of the young bilinguals were involved in reading during their leisure activities, moving between text and screen and reading magazines, newspapers, Ceefax and Sky, the internet, Facebook and Ebay. So, in this domain, their options for the use of Welsh were more limited. There were exceptions to this. For example, most of the young people had access to the Welsh television channel (*Sianel Pedwar Cymru* – S4C) and sometimes used Welsh teletext or watched films in Welsh with English sub-titles. A couple of students mentioned reading *Golwg,* a weekly news magazine published in Welsh. Surprisingly little mention was made of computer games, though ample use was made of the internet, almost always in English.

Work was the domain where there were fewest opportunities to use Welsh. Most of the students had part-time jobs. Some worked for companies with a national reach, such as supermarkets, DIY or sports stores, launderettes or hotel and restaurant chains. All the reading and writing they did in these workplaces were in English. A few worked for local businesses or had jobs in the public or voluntary sector where bilingual services were provided. These reported reading and writing in both English and Welsh at work.

One group of students did make frequent mention of workplace literacy in Welsh: these were the students studying Agriculture at Glynllifon –

fifteen students in all. All these students had part-time jobs. Some worked, on weekends and during the vacations, in neighbouring farms. Others were running small businesses on the family farm to bring in additional income. They either did this single-handedly or with another family member.

Bilingual uses of reading and writing

Cross-cutting all these domains were different uses of reading and writing, in Welsh and in English. The bilingual students' uses of literacy were broadly similar to those of the Scottish and English students, the main difference being that the Welsh students' uses of literacy were bound up with language choices. The choice of language added an extra element of meaning to each reading and writing activity. We will briefly illustrate this below.

Communication

Mobile phones figured prominently in the lives of the Welsh students. They kept in touch with each other and organised their social lives using the phones. They chose different languages in their SMS messages to different friends and family members. All were proficient in the conventions for abbreviating English and found these quick and easy to use. However, the conventions for abbreviating Welsh were still quite variable and there were fewer available, so texting in Welsh took more time. Nevertheless, some students preferred to send messages in Welsh. As Rowena put it: 'Because I think in Welsh, I text in Welsh.' The students also chose greetings cards and made birthday posters according to their own language preferences and those of their addressees. Haf told us that she sent Christmas cards to everyone in her village, choosing the language she thought was appropriate for each individual.

For the Agriculture students, the choice of language for communication at work also carried considerable significance. For those running small businesses on a part-time basis, the choice of language was determined by the type of customer they were aiming for. For example, Bryn came from a large sheep and cattle farm in Ynys Môn (Anglesey). He ran a specialised business venture with his mother. They had established a small pedigree sheep flock and used artificial insemination methods to develop the flock. Their customers included local Welsh farmers and others, from much further afield, who were interested in their particular pedigree breed. They travelled to agricultural shows in the summer with a view to selling rams and sheep from the flock. Some of these shows were in Wales and others were in England and Scotland. Communication with customers was in both Welsh and English, depending on their language background. Bryn created a website for this business in his second year in college. The website was designed bilingually.

In contrast, Ceunant was brought up on a large hill farm in south Gwynedd. While the main farm business revolved around sheep and cattle, his parents had also established a campsite on the farm. When he was home from college, Ceunant was involved in assisting his parents with the running of the campsite business, dealing with word-processed correspondence and email, mostly in English. As part of a project for college, he designed a website for this small business and chose to construct it entirely in English. Most of the campers were English-speaking hill-walkers or tourists.

Organising life

The students gave us several examples of ways in which literacy in Welsh and in English was used to organise their lives on a day-to-day basis. Individual family members left hand-written messages and lists for each other in either Welsh or English or in both languages. A couple of students mentioned that they planned their lives using a diary or a wall calendar printed in Welsh. They said they usually wrote in Welsh but sometimes in English, depending on the event. Among those who had opened bank accounts, there were a couple who said that they had requested a bilingual chequebook from the bank. They all made digital language choices, between Welsh and English, when withdrawing funds from their accounts at the ATM machines of their local banks.

Documenting life

As in the LfLFE project, the Welsh students had their particular passions and documented these aspects of their lives using photographs and/or text. They did this in either Welsh or English.

One particular theme that recurred in interviews with the Welsh students was that of documenting work-related activities. As we have already noted above, all the Agriculture students were employed, in some way, in land-based work alongside their studies. Those who were involved in running small businesses on the family farm had to keep records of their business transactions and, where livestock were involved, had to maintain animal husbandry logs. They did this documentation in both English and Welsh.

Several of these students were also involved in assisting family members with general farm paperwork (*gwaith papur*). For example, Dave helped his father with correspondence relating to their small-holding. His father drafted letters in Welsh or in English and then Dave helped with the word processing. Another aspect of the farm paperwork was linked to the increasing regulation of agriculture across the European Union (EU). This has transformed the working lives of farmers. The literacy burden of documentation is heavy, particularly on farmers rearing livestock. It includes documentation such as registering animal births; ensuring that individual animals have ear tags (or 'animal passports'); filling in animal movement forms and keeping track of medicines or vaccines administered. Whilst previous studies of working farms (e.g., Ashton 1994; Jones 2000) have drawn attention to the primary role of women in farm households in dealing with this paperwork, the interviews in this research revealed that young people were also involved, particularly as the record-keeping was becoming more digitised. Young people were contributing their expertise with computing and their facility with digital literacies to the task of keeping the farm documentation up to date. This collaboration sometimes extended across generations, with one adult in the household taking the main responsibility for leading on the paperwork. (For further details, see Martin-Jones *et al.* 2009.)

Finding things out and taking part

Continuing with our focus on the Agriculture students, we also found that they made regular use of the internet in their part-time work lives outside college. The advent of these new technologies has transformed the working practices and routines of farm households. Thus, for example, those farmers who have access to the internet can now obtain information about new agri-environmental schemes or they can apply for grants or loans for small infra-structure developments. When we first met him, Dave and his father were making plans to convert a garage on their smallholding into a farm shop. Dave was searching the web for information about grants or loans to fund this conversion.

Literacy was also drawn upon in leisure-time activities, in finding out about events. Steven played football for his local seaside town team and his training sessions and match fixtures were all arranged, in English, by text message. He was also an avid reader of football magazines in English, such as *FourFourTwo*. In addition, he said he was a Liverpool fan and visited the website of this Premier League club 'quite a lot . . . to see if players are injured or if they find a new player'. Luke was a qualified ski instructor. He was also registered as a racer. He arranged his participation in English via the relevant UK websites. He also had to fill out race entry forms which were sent by post. In addition, he kept a logbook with details of his races, his fitness and his coach's comments. Meredydd was active in the Young Farmers' Association in South Gwynedd. He helped to put up posters and send out leaflets in Welsh about events such as local barn dances or the Young Farmers' *eisteddfod* (cultural festival) and regularly used text messages in Welsh to arrange meetings with other members.

Learning and sense-making

The bilingual students used literacy in both Welsh and English to expand their knowledge or find out how things worked. For example, Cadwaladr ran a small business from the family farm, on a part-time basis. This work was mainly done in the summer months since it was a grass-cutting business. He had started the business while he was still at school. Cadwaladr drew on a number of literacies in running this small business; for example, when he acquired new equipment, he had to turn from time to time to the instruction manuals in English to check on the workings of particular parts. Figure 7.2 shows him consulting a manual related to a particular piece of grass-cutting equipment that he used in his work and Figure 7.3 shows him sitting at his computer, preparing the invoices for his customers.

Reading and writing for pleasure

Few of the Welsh students mentioned reading and writing fiction or non-fiction in either Welsh or English as a leisure activity, though those who were studying Welsh mentioned reading Welsh fiction at home in preparation for college classes. Most of the reading reported by the students involved newspapers or magazines. Most of the time, they read in English for recreational purposes. *The Daily Post,* the main regional newspaper for

Figure 7.2
Cadwaladr consulting instruction manual for lawn-mowing equipment

Figure 7.3 Cadwaladr preparing invoices for his customers

North Wales, was mentioned frequently. One student also said she read the *Cambrian News,* a bilingual newspaper published weekly and distributed in West Wales. Another referred to *Golwg,* the weekly current affairs magazine in Welsh. Others mentioned their local newsletter or *papur bro* (literally 'regional paper'). These newsletters are produced, in Welsh, by local community groups. There was also a gendered pattern of reading across our sample, with the young men studying Agriculture mentioning that they read *Farmers' Weekly* and with the young women in the Early Years and Welsh courses reporting that they read magazines such as *Hello, More, Sugar, Elle* and *Marie-Claire.*

   In this section, we have focused just on those aspects of the domains and uses of literacy that were distinctive in this Welsh context, as the LfLFE project design and its analytic lenses were re-contextualised. Working in this way, at the interface of research on bilingualism and literacy, we have gleaned the insights which are summarised in Box 7.1.

**Box 7.1   Characteristics of the Welsh students'
everyday literacy practices**

* The students engaged in a much wider range of reading and writing in Welsh and in English outside college than they did in college.

---

continued

- They employed different literacy technologies, often combining different modes of communication, both verbal and visual.
- The characteristics of their literacy practices were similar to those described in Chapter 2, that is, their practices were purposeful, oriented to a clear audience, generative (involving meaning-making and getting things done), shared and interactive, in tune with the students' identities and values, specific to times and places, multi-modal (combining verbal and visual signs), non-linear (with varied pathways), multimedia (combining paper and electronic media), agentic (with students having control), varied and not repetitive, and learned through participation.
- Opportunities for reading and writing in Welsh were more constrained in some domains than in others, particularly in the worlds of work and the media; in other words, students' language choices were bound up with contemporary conditions for Welsh language and literacy use in public spaces in Wales.
- The students' uses of literacy in Welsh, in their local life worlds, were linked to their sense of identity, to their language values and to their participation in peer group networks and communities of practice where Welsh is spoken.
- Their uses of Welsh in these life world contexts were also shaped by their own language capabilities and preferences.

Making a difference: changes in practice

The changes in bilingual practice introduced by the three lecturers at Coleg Meirion-Dwyfor related to two broad aspects of college life: bilingual literacy practices for learning content and bilingual literacy practices related to imagined futures. Seven changes were introduced altogether, and most of these related to bilingual literacy for learning content. There were innovations in each of the three curriculum areas which are summarised in Tables 7.2 and 7.3. The right-hand columns of the tables show the aims of the changes in practice.

The bordering work of the changes in practice in the bilingual context

As with the changes introduced in the four colleges involved in the LfLFE project, the changes in bilingual practices made linkages across different domains of the students' lives. This is represented diagrammatically in Figure 7.4.

Table 7.2 Changes in literacy practice related to learning content

Course and unit	Level	Innovation in practice	Specific aims
Welsh as a second language – Film & Oracy/ *Ffilm a Llafaredd*	AS Level	Students developed a bilingual website for future students related to Hedd Wyn – Welsh poet and pacifist. This project involved viewing a film about the life of the poet, gathering materials (e.g., visiting HW's home) and doing library research as well as designing a bilingual website (Figure 7.5 shows the home page).	To involve students in the development of a new, web-based learning resource. To enable them to produce and use texts in different media in Welsh.
Cymraeg (Welsh) – Language in Use/ *Defnydd Iaith*	AS Level	Students carried out a small-scale project on the everyday literacy practices of bilingual members of their own households, including different domains of literacy: home, community and work. They chose between two different approaches: using a questionnaire or a literacy diary.	To build on and extend their awareness of the everyday uses of literacy in Welsh and in English. To make links between the curriculum content and the wider context for reading and writing in Welsh.
Cymraeg (Welsh) – Twentieth-Century Poetry/ *Barddoniaeth yr Ugeinfed Ganrif*	AS Level	The Welsh poet Gwyn Thomas was invited to the class to meet the students. The dialogue revolved around questions that they had prepared after reading his work.	To give the students the opportunity to ask their own questions about the poems they were reading, face to face, instead of providing answers to written questions designed just to assess their knowledge.

Table 7.2 Continued

Course and unit	Level	Innovation in practice	Specific aims
		The whole encounter was audio-recorded and transcribed as a learning resource for future students.	To involve students in the development of a new learning resource.
BTEC ND Early Years – Diet and Nutrition/ *Diet a Maeth*	Level 3	Working with a local health visitor, students prepared a bilingual wall display for a local doctor's surgery on the topic: *The nutritional needs of young children during the weaning process.*	To build on the students' existing capabilities in combining text with images. To provide experience of communicating with a different kind of audience.
BTEC ND Early Years – Communication and Interpersonal Skills in Early Years Work/ *Cyfathrebu a Sgiliau Rhyng-bersonol ar Gyfer Gweithio yn y Blynyddoedd Cynnar*	Level 3	Students investigated the literacy practices involved in bilingual home–school communication in the work placement schools. They jointly produced a questionnaire (ten questions) for an interview with the head of the school. They then wrote up their findings individually and compared notes in class.	To build on and extend their awareness of different forms of bilingual written communication in Early Years school contexts. To enable them to use their own bilingual literacy abilities to find out more about the context in which they were working.

Table 7.3 Changes in literacy practice related to imagined futures

Course and unit	Level	Innovation in practice	Specific aims
BTEC ND Agriculture – Work experience/ *Profiad Gwaith*	Level 3	Students developed a PowerPoint presentation based on their workplace experience on two farms over the summer and took turns at presenting in class. They included maps, photographs and text in their presentations, using relevant software.	To make more visible in class their bilingual workplace experience and associated literacies.
			To provide opportunities to talk in Welsh about texts and images in a formal setting.
			To connect with the students' future aspirations with regard to employment in Wales.
BTEC ND Agriculture – Specialised Project/*Prosiect Arbenigol*	Level 3	Each student constructed a bilingual website for a small agricultural business (in some cases, their own business).	To make links between the learning content and the students' out-of-college experience of work in small agricultural businesses.
			To build on the students' interests and expertise in computer-assisted literacy.
			To connect with the students' future aspirations with regard to employment in Wales.

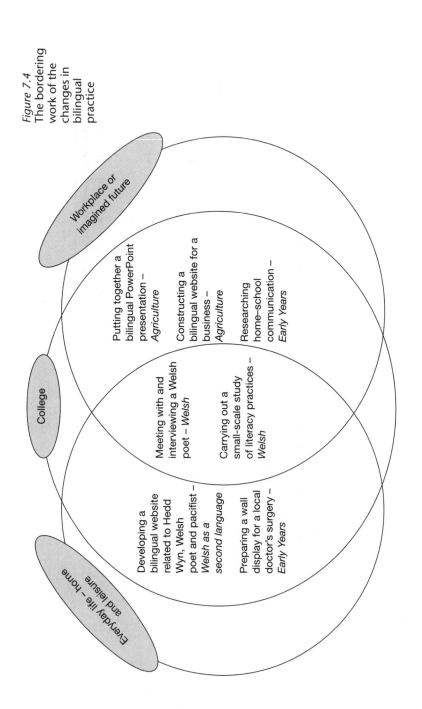

Figure 7.4
The bordering work of changes in bilingual practice

Workplace or imagined future

College

Everyday life – home and leisure

Putting together a bilingual PowerPoint presentation – *Agriculture*

Constructing a bilingual website for a business – *Agriculture*

Researching home-school communication – *Early Years*

Meeting with and interviewing a Welsh poet – *Welsh*

Carrying out a small-scale study of literacy practices – *Welsh*

Developing a bilingual website related to Hedd Wyn, Welsh poet and pacifist – *Welsh as a second language*

Preparing a wall display for a local doctor's surgery – *Early Years*

Pedagogic intentions underlying the changes in practice in the bilingual context

The right-hand column of Tables 7.2 and 7.3 sets out the aims we formulated at the time when each of the innovations in bilingual practice was undertaken. These original statements relate to the different pedagogic intentions outlined in Chapter 6. Here, we take three of these intentions in turn and draw out the similarities.

First, all of the projects were designed to make reading and writing in college more resonant with the students' everyday experiences with bilingual literacy outside college, that is, to take account of the specific characteristics of the students' everyday practices, as summarised in Box 7.1. Second, several of the innovations had the explicit aim of extending students' awareness of the uses of literacy in Welsh and in English and of the textually mediated nature of contemporary social life; for example, the small-scale projects carried out by the students studying *Cymraeg* (Welsh) and by the Early Years students in the unit on Communication and Personal Skills Early Years Work. Third, several of the innovations were adopted with a view to making the college-based production of bilingual texts by students more relevant to their vocational learning and to their preparation for working futures in settings where Welsh literacy was likely to be a valuable resource. These included the following innovations: the preparation of a wall display for a doctor's surgery by the Early Years students, the PowerPoint presentation by Agriculture students based on their summer work experience on two farms and the design of bilingual websites for small agricultural businesses by the same students.

In all of the changes in practice, the lecturers were guiding the students towards reading, writing and text production in Welsh in new ways. They were also extending their capacities in designing bilingual communication in print (such as the wall display) or on screen (such as the websites and PowerPoint slides).

An analysis of one change in practice: designing a bilingual website

The creation of a bilingual website by the students in the Welsh as a second language unit on Film and Oracy represented a considerable departure from previous learning and teaching practice. Nearly all the work that students had done prior to this had been of a more traditional academic nature, involving genres such as essays or individual oral presentations. The lecturer had, however, built in activities to the unit such as the viewing of a full-length feature film, in Welsh with English sub-titles, about the life of Hedd Wyn, the Welsh poet and pacifist, who was forced to join the British army and was killed in combat during World War I. Prior to working on the website, the students had been to visit his home – *Yr Ysgwrn* – in the village of Trawsfynydd. They had also been to a local heritage centre and viewed a statue of the poet. In addition, they had had the opportunity to go to see a theatrical production, in Welsh, based on his life. So, when the idea of developing a bilingual website was first mooted, it was agreed that it should include pages on the students' reactions to these visits.

The *process* of producing a website brought about significant changes in the bilingual literacy practices that the students normally engaged in when learning about the life of Hedd Wyn. Most obviously, they were drawing on a new *mode* of communication (screen literacy), a new literacy *technology* and a *genre* which was quite different from those that had previously been expected of them on the course. One student, who had greater facility with and experience of digital literacies, led the work of the group. We now analyse some of the other changes in the students' reading and writing practices with reference to the aspects of a literacy practice presented in Chapter 3. The *purpose* of the activity was to create a long-lasting learning resource for future cohorts of students. This would be made available to future students, through the Learning Resources Centre, on both the Dolgellau and the Pwllheli campuses. There were two *audiences*: the lecturer and other students learning Welsh as a second language at Advanced Level. This activity thus involved more than just displaying knowledge to the lecturer for assessment purposes. Moreover, the website incorporated sections on their own reactions to the visit to Hedd Wyn's home and to the play about his life. These sections allowed them space to express their own *values*.

The students assumed the *role* of bilingual web designers. Unlike previous activities where they mostly responded to questions or to set tasks, here they had considerable scope and *flexibility* to design the website in ways that they considered appropriate. Moreover, since the website was bilingual, they could choose to draft the textual elements in their strongest *language* and then count on other students, or the lecturer, to assist with the translation of these elements. The students decided on the conventions they would adopt for the *style* and the actual bilingual *design* of the website. They also made their own decisions about how to represent the *content* they were focusing on. As shown below, the students chose to place a photograph of Hedd Wyn in the centre of the home page for the website. This photograph was surrounded by a wreath decorated with red poppies. This imagery anticipates the story of Hedd Wyn's early death, and deals with key *issues* which concern his life and work. In linking visual images to words, they were able to draw on characteristics of their everyday literacy practices, including their experience with *multimodal, non-linear and multimedia* communication. In setting up language choices for visitors to the site, they used colour contrast, with red for Welsh and green for English. And, to add extra meaning to the title (the actual name of the poet), they adopted a particular font which evokes the handwriting style of old Celtic texts.

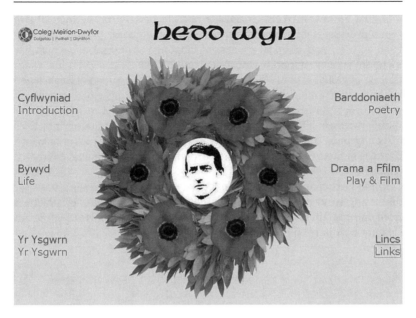

Figure 7.5 Home page of a bilingual website created by students studying Welsh as a second language

Each student in the group *participated* in the development of the website and contributed in different ways. Rather than directing the activity, the lecturer acted as a consultant and helped to provide occasional resources (e.g., a photograph of the poet's grave in Flanders taken during a visit that she had made). The *actions and processes* involved were complex and challenging. The students drew together material from different sources and engaged in *design work* to decide how they would present it bilingually and multimodally.

Conclusion

In this chapter, we have focused on the distinctive findings from the BiLfLFE project in Wales. Building on the tradition of ethnographic research into local literacies that has been developed within literacy studies, we have documented in detail the ways in which literacies in Welsh and in English mediated the lives of the young people in our sample, at college and out of college. However, we have also emphasised the need to understand the particularities of bilingual literacy practices with reference to the wider sociocultural and historical context. The domains of literacy, the students' language choices, the values associated with Welsh and the challenges that both students and lecturers faced in extending the use of Welsh into new written genres and learning activities at college – all these dimensions of bilingual literacy in Welsh social life need to be seen in the light of two broad processes of change taking place in contemporary Wales: first, the local cultural and political process of language revitalisation, which has increasing policy support in a post-devolution Wales; and second, the wider process of globalisation, which has contributed to the spread of English and to the reinforcement of its dominant status within the global communicative order. As researchers and practitioners, we need to keep sight of these processes, in describing and analysing the bilingual literacy practices of young people such as those in Wales and in exploring ways in which changes in literacy practices can be introduced in their bilingual courses at college.

In the next chapter we focus on a single curriculum area, as a basis for discussing ways of conceptualising the mobilisation of literacy practices from one domain to another: a theoretical construct which we identified in Chapter 6 as in need of refinement.

Chapter 8

Conceptualising the interface between everyday and curriculum literacy practices

In Chapters 2 and 3 the focus was on the richness, abundance and diversity of students' communicative practices in their everyday lives. In Chapters 4 and 5 we showed how learning, teaching and assessment are textually mediated. We have indicated that literacy practices are assembled from a set of what we have termed 'aspects' of a literacy practice. In Chapter 6 we showed how lecturers took account of these insights and made connections between these literacy practices to make changes in their teaching to enhance students' opportunities for learning. In Chapter 7 we showed how the research was recontextualised into a very different context – that of bilingual college provision in Wales. Here in this chapter, using one extended case study, we consider different metaphorical resources for conceptualising the connections between the everyday and curriculum literacy practices which lie at the heart of the research.

It is common to assume a one-to-one relationship between the world and how we describe it. 'Describe what you see' and 'tell it how it is' are common enough phrases that reflect such an understanding. It has a certain common-sensical ring to it. However, a language of description always has certain conceptual assumptions built in it. Our descriptions of the world are always mediated by language, as becomes very clear when we try to learn languages other than those into which we were born. One of the roles for research is to question those assumptions and find or develop conceptual framings that attempt to adequately describe and, in the process, make better sense of the data. The focus of this chapter is an exploration of some of the possible languages of description for the ways in which literacies from other domains in students' lives can become resources for learning in college settings. Indeed, it is virtually impossible to write about this topic without recourse to metaphor. In choosing the phrase 'become resources for', we have tried to choose a relatively literal way of explaining that to which we are referring. But even here, the term 'resources' in its literal sense refers to physical, material resources, and its use to refer to social phenomena such as literacy practices remains metaphorical, albeit a well established and heavily used metaphorical usage in educational discourses. In other words, often what we take to be literal descriptions are more often than not metaphorical (Edwards *et al.* 2004).

In this chapter we explore the conceptual framings offered by two metaphors that we have used to help us understand the relationship between everyday and curriculum literacy practices: 'border'/'bordering', and 'resonance'. Each of these opens up possibilities and has limitations. We have also used other metaphors in the course of our explorations that we do not explore here: metaphors of 'mobilising' and 'harnessing', among others, could also have been explored in more detail (for discussion of the 'mobilising' metaphor, see Fowler and Edwards 2005). However, we have focused on those we have found most productive in helping us describe our data. We first present a short case study of one of the units in the curriculum area of Music studied in the research, focusing on the interface between everyday literacy practices and the literacy practices in the curriculum. Ronnie Goodman (see Box 8.1) was the lecturer at Perth College who worked with us researching this area. We then discuss this case in terms of each of these metaphorical framings, focusing on the affordances and constraints offered by each.

Box 8.1   Ronnie Goodman: lecturer in Music and member of the research team

Ronnie Goodman has extensive experience in the music industry as a musician and as a composer. In Perth College, part of the University of Highlands and Islands, he lectures in Music and the Creative Industries, teaching a variety of subjects.

Ronnie is careful to recognise how the students link their hobbies, passions and interests with the gaining of qualifications in the subject area and the gaining of work in their industry. His pedagogical approach sometimes reflects this blurring of boundaries and the sociocultural context of the work. For example, there are performance opportunities for students' own bands during the year in the college. Ronnie is also the founding member of a community performance group, Rhythm Wave, a percussion band made up of Music students and graduates from Perth College. They bring their distinctive Latin sounds to public events and concerts including Glastonbury Festival.

In 2008, Ronnie took six months' research leave from his college to work on a Masters on ethnomusicology – a study of the social aspects of music playing, listening and making in Brazil where he has long-standing relations with some musicians. His involvement in this research had in some ways spurred him on to do this work and helped him understand the rigour and care needed around data collection, analysis and fieldwork.

Case study

This SCQF Level 7 unit, 'Working in the Creative Industries', was a requirement for three Higher National Diploma courses in Scotland: HNC Music, HNC Music Business, and HNC Sound Production. On this unit, according to the Higher National Unit Specification from the Scottish Qualifications Authority, the 'students [were] expected to learn effective knowledge required to explore employment opportunities'. The outcomes required were that students should:

- investigate skills required to develop a career in the creative industries;
- demonstrate a broad knowledge of commercial, legal, and financial issues;
- outline and develop a strategic plan for personal career development.

At Perth College, two main types of student were taking the unit: sound engineers (a small minority) and Music students who were performers, usually with membership of at least one band. Most of the students were between 17 and early twenties, and male. About 100–110 students took the unit overall. The classes took place in a theatre-style setting with sound and lighting facilities more akin to a stage environment. While classes were assembling, the lecturer would play some selections of music from his laptop through the sound equipment and discuss them informally.

In Boxes 8.2–8.4, we present three extended vignettes from our data related to this course: in 8.2 a portrait of the literacy practices of Laura, a student taking the unit; in 8.3 an overview of the first, less successful attempt made by the lecturer to draw on the students' everyday literacy practices within the curriculum; and in Box 8.4, the second, more successful change in practice drawing on the students' everyday literacy practices. Where relevant, we discuss the literacy practices in the examples using the concepts from the framework introduced in Chapter 3.

Box 8.2   Laura, a Higher National Music student: literacy practices in different domains of life

Laura claimed that music was 'the love of her life'. She was a member of several bands some of which were related to her participation in the course. A key text for Laura was her 'song book'. This was a focus for her own creative writing and a centrepiece for her literacy (placed in the centre of the map) – 'I love writing lyrics and stuff it's my way of, [I] suppose, of getting my emotions out'. She saw the activity of writing and 'doodling' as being related to her college course and her future career in the music industry: she eventually wanted to be a singer/songwriter. The literacy practices of writing songs and lyrics sometimes started with a

---

continued

melody or some lyrics. She often put these down in the notebook and this could happen almost any time of the day, such as when she was doing the ironing. She drew pictures in it too. Once there were some lyrics in place, she would get the guitar out and try to work out some chords for these pieces. The lyrics are the important part of the product for her but these records in her notebook were reminders of the melodies that she created for them. She did not write the full score (inclusive of rhythms and stave notation) for these songs, but was prepared to consider the usefulness of being able to do this.

Laura downloaded music from her CDs and catalogued them on her computer according to genre or type. She searched for and found music categorised under various terms, some of which were her own rather than the generic terms found in music stores, such as soul, classical and so on. She also pulled lyrics for songs she liked from the web and then read the lyrics and sang along to them.

Regarding technologies for literacy, Laura noted that the computer was a central player in her literacy but she tended to think of it as something she resisted by handwriting and working in her song scrapbook using non-digital technologies. She preferred book reading to internet sources and looked at websites only a couple of times a week when in college, as she had no internet connection at home. However, she said she would miss internet access if for some reason she did not have it.

Laura texted people a lot and her phone was 'always on'. She used a lot of short cuts when constructing texts. Texts tended to be about arrangements to meet folk. She thought that if the college started sending texts to students they would get read and would not be experienced by users as an intrusion. She felt it would get read 'straight away' and be replied to as appropriate. This new use might be as simple as letting people know if a lecture was cancelled. When she was abroad for six months, the internet provided her with a very important 'lifeline'. She felt emails were for family and friends at a distance and took the place of letter writing as a practice. Texts were 'for friends' she met everyday and they did not usually discuss college work. 'Live online chat' via MSN was not something she did much of (perhaps because of not having access to internet at home).

Laura loved reading books. She read books every night as a way of relaxing. She read books that were related to the music industry in some way. She not only read musicians' biographies, but also fictional novels that often related to music in terms of the plot or characters' interests in music. Some of these books were suggested to her by her parents, while others were sourced through reading about them in magazines. Book reading was an important literacy practice for her because:

I'm learning and I enjoy learning, even when it's fiction or non-fiction. . . . I like reading books like the Marley book [*No Woman, No Cry*] because it's showing how people got into the music business but also I've got another book, well it's called popular music it's a fiction but I haven't actually read it yet, just started reading it but it's about the person's love for music or something.

There was an overlap between reading for leisure and for college work as they were helping her with learning on the same topic. The differences appeared to be in how systematic and managed the reading and learning were. Also, books she read for leisure were usually purchased, while reading for the coursework was borrowed from the library. Recommended books seemed 'hard' and she had not read many of them, or, if she started, she did not get through them. Like many students in other subject areas, she thought reading fiction could be a useful starting point for innovative forms of coursework.

Her note taking on what lecturers said was a practice that is distinctive as it entailed writing usually full sentences and not some sort of individualised shorthand. Unlike handouts that told her what she was 'supposed to know', the note-taking practice was about the creation of personal meaning rather than an exact record of what the lecturer said. In other words she wrote in full sentences but not verbatim from the lecturer.

Interviewer: . . . do the notes feel different to, let's say if the lecturer gave you a transcript of what they said or gave you handouts, are they different?

Laura: Emm yeah, because when I'm writing it I know exactly what I mean by it.

Laura's notes were carefully filed in plastic sleeves and then placed into bigger folders. They were the sources of longer pieces of writing that emerged in her essay writing which she did on a computer. She felt that if students could see the relevance of what the essay does in terms of helping them go somewhere with the subject area that it would be less onerous and something they would want to do. Here we noticed how for her the literacy practices around essay writing for formal coursework were experienced as less purposeful than the book reading or the lyric writing.

Box 8.3   Change in practice 1: writing about personal experience of networking in the music industry

Part of the specification for the unit stated that students should 'produce an assessment and evaluation of their personal skills in preparing for employment'. The lecturer felt the need to meet this requirement while also making the topic relevant to his students. The purpose of the change of practice became therefore to get students writing about their own situated understandings of how networking had *already worked* for them in their everyday lives. In other words, it was hoped that the *content* of the writing would be relevant to their everyday lives and that the literacy would therefore be more engaging for them. In terms of *participation*, the lecturer encouraged a degree of collaborative authorship – a feature he knew was a preferred aspect of the literacy experience for many students.

> There's not a theory of networking that I can implant into the students' subconscious that they can in an empirical way swallow and then disgorge it later [as if] there is a [theory] of networking. . . . [I want] to draw out of them . . . it's a bit like a well. To bring out the literacy practice in that way . . . And then to try to draw out some kind of understanding of experience, projection or trajectory into the world that they wish to enter. So to draw from all the cues, the cultural cues if you want, the contexts that they have. [I want] to try and encourage that.
>
> (Tutor)

Students worked in groups, sharing stories and kept a written record of their ideas. Some of the strategies they wrote about included using contacts among their family and friends, attending gigs, word-of-mouth contacts, texting, going to the pub, taking on part-time work and so on. Students seemed to enjoy and value this time. The group work itself seemed to be a form of networking.

The tutor 'recycled' these stories by annotating the networking stories and passing these shortened and summarised versions back to the students. Thereafter, to meet the requirements of the assessment, they were asked to use these notes as a starting point for constructing a more reflective 500-word piece of writing which would evidence their knowledge about different aspects of networking.

There were a number of positive reactions to this task. Some noted the effects as personal:

> [Networking] made me realise that performing was what I wanted to do.
>
> (Student A)

Another student reflected:

> These experiences have made me really think to myself that whatever you want out of life you have to go after it with everything you have. I will never give up within this industry. I know the passion and excitement I feel within its environment.
>
> (Student B)

Most of the sound engineers felt that the task was more appropriate for the Music students, although one sound engineer who also played in a band noted that the classes were interesting because 'it fits in with my hobbies an' my pastimes an' that'. This flagged up how taking the cultural situation of students into account was critical but not easy to achieve for all. The *content* of reading and writing tasks may relate to the lives of some students but not to the lives of others.

Further, the *purpose, audience, genre* and conventions of *style and design* were problematic for some students:

> It was kinda the subject because we were writin' about our personal experience so there weren't really many rules about how you would put it.
>
> (Student C)

Others were thrown by the fact that the topic was personal and therefore easy to write about; as a result, some felt that it was not challenging enough. A male Music student said:

> It was so easy. It was just in my head. I didn't know why I had to write 500 words on it. Seemed a bit pointless.
>
> (Student D)

In feedback sessions, the students said they wanted to do something useful and relevant to their everyday lives as emergent musicians. In devising a change of practice that connected with everyday literacy practices, there was still some way to go:

Student M: If I'm goin' to get a gig in Glasgow . . . writing 500 words on it is going to do nothing. Showing a promoter a website I built is.

Interviewer: That connects to your world?

Student M: That's definitely relevant.

Box 8.4   Change in practice 2: writing bios rather than CVs

The second change of practice built on the first as the lecturer and researcher achieved a greater degree of awareness of what was critical in this context. The lecturer was faced with a unit assessment that specified that a curriculum vitae was a required submission. Bearing in mind what we had learnt from the first change in practice about paying careful attention to *genres, audience* and *roles and identities,* it seemed more appropriate to ask the students to produce web-friendly personal biographies (often part of a 'press pack') as these held greater currency among both the students and the target audience of promoters and potential music listeners. Students, particularly the Music students, reacted favourably to this idea. This would be worthwhile 'work' not unconnected to their 'band' lives, as they could see that they needed to network themselves into the music business by having a vibrant web-presence. They were also attracted by the practical focus. Examples of web-based biographies were discussed and key features identified. While the text was to be submitted for assessment, they were also able to 'go live' with their biographies (or 'bios' as they are called in the trade) online alongside sound files of their music, photographs and so on. The students generally took to the task:

> Last week I was asked to join a . . . band which was exciting and did a gig with them the same week. I am very keen to try new styles of music but my favourites include Jazz, Blues, and Classical but I am open to play different genres. When I join a band I am very enthusiastic and committed to myself and my band members.
>
> (Bio extract 1, male Music student)

> Music is what I am and what I want to do forever. I am a [name of instrument] player who has played for nearly nine years. During that period of time I have learned a lot by tutors, teachers, and other musicians. I have played in many bands such as [name] band, [name] band, [name] and [name]. I enjoyed these experiences very much, I love meeting other musicians and learning new things. I currently play in the [name] band, [name] Orchestra, and my new band called [name].
>
> (Bio extract 2, female Music student)

The reactions were generally positive:

> It's good because . . . we had examples of what we would . . . write if we were wanting to send away a press pack to like a promoter or

like a record company . . . it was good like how we got showed . . . how to like write a proper structure. And I think it did help me.

(Student M)

The sense of a different audience was palpable in how they discussed the bios afterwards:

If you are writing something to hand in to be graded you know, you don't stick in a lot of humour in it because normally the person who's reviewing it isn't wanting to be entertained by it.

(Student N, focus group)

It was completely different . . . at least I know how to go about kind of writing a press pack and bio stuff. There's other essays I mean, [you] write them and forget about them.

(Student P, focus group)

In all three vignettes, everyday literacy practices are serving as resources for learning. Laura is herself making connections between the reading and writing on her course and in other domains of her life. In 'Changes in practice 1 and 2', the lecturer is trying out ways of making these connections for the benefit of all students. In the rest of the chapter, we discuss the affordances and constraints of using different metaphors and framings to conceptualise these connections.

Affordances of the 'border/bordering' metaphor

As outlined in Chapter 2, we conceived our task initially to uncover the creativity in people's everyday semiotic practices, to identify border literacy practices and to support the border crossing of literacy practices from the everyday to the formal. We conceived of a sort of borderland, or third space, in which some literacy practices from students' lives outside college might serve as border literacies, which could act as resources to enhance learning. We envisaged that we would identify practices in students' everyday lives which potentially occupy this borderland, and/or might cross the border into college life in order to serve curriculum purposes. However, over time, we came to see certain limits to the concepts of border literacy practices and border crossing.

As data accumulated in the early phases of the project, we did not find any evidence of discrete literacy practices sitting clearly in-between the domains of college and the everyday, nor any regularly occurring, obvious mechanisms whereby literacy practices migrated between these domains. In effect, the idea that we had started with, that there were numerous and easily identifiable border literacy practices, was not refined enough as a description of what was going on. However, there was definite evidence that some sorts of *bordering* processes were in play and that there was every likelihood that lecturers could make better links across students' home, work, leisure and college domains. For example, it was clear that Laura was making her own links between her everyday literacy practices and the requirements of the course.

In the data collection phase with students, one method we used was the 'Icon Mapping Exercise' (for details about this data collection method, see Appendix; Mannion and Ivanič 2007; Mannion and Miller forthcoming). The rationale here was to explore students' own understandings of whether and how literacy practices were linked across domains and what this had to do with identification processes. The method was devised so that it allowed students to explore through the lens of literacy how these domains could be related to one another. First, a range of icons were presented to students, representing the sorts of artefacts (*modes and technologies)* that they seemed to regularly use, reflecting the abundant semiotic landscape of their lives. The icons could be interpreted differently by each of them to signify, or function as a label for, the sorts of literacy practices and events they had now become aware of because of participation in the project.

Working with these small laminated symbols, students were invited to design a map of reading and writing across the domains of home, college and work using a Venn diagram (see Figure A.1 in the Appendix). This map then allowed them to reflect on when and how reading and writing in various times and places were connected. The method also took cognisance of the idea that students work in a multimodal manner and can be viewed as 'designers' (Kress 2001) of the maps they produced. Individually, they were invited to pick a range of icons (maximum of ten) that reminded them of the sorts of reading and writing that were important to them and in which they engaged in their daily lives.

In order to generate salient data, the interviewers then asked students for comments on the sorts of reading and writing that:

• they would miss if they could not do them any more;
• were meaningful to them in some way;
• had led them to learn things that were important to them.

Students were invited to place the icons on the Venn diagram according to where they took place and/or for whom or for what context they had most relevance. The use of three overlapping circles meant that icons could be placed in any of the possible overlaps between any of the circles allowing for cross-domain relevance. This acted as a way of identifying practices that could border between two domains. The researchers then explored this

Home: texting, playing and reading music, playing CDs.	*Home/college overlap:* using computer, reading books.	*College:* taking notes (and writing assessments).	*Home/college/ work overlap:* writing lyrics.

Figure 8.1 Overlaps in Laura's literacy practices

map in more detail, probing for ideas about the relevance of certain literacy practices.

Laura talked about literacy practices that revealed a high degree of personal ownership and commitment. She indicated that she had in different ways 'made her own' even the literacy practices that directly related to college coursework. But, more importantly, the literacy practices she deemed important seemed intimately connected to *both* who she said she was – a band member and a Music student – and what she wanted to become – a songwriter/musician. Current context and imagined futures were both important to what she practised and what she valued.

Not all students were like this and we did encounter many students who had much less obvious connectivity between literacy practices across domains. For Laura, there were a number of literacy practices that appeared to relate to her more personal world, the course-related literacy practices (the college domain) and the literacy practices she imagined may become useful in the music industry (the work domain) – see Figure 8.1. Being a Music student, a band member and a musician/lyricist were important identifications associated with different and diverse literacy practices that she valued. We suggest it was these connected identifications that seemed to allow her literacy practices to be seen as relevant to more than one context thereby providing the possibilities for bordering across domains.

Lyric writing and reading biographies about famous musicians in particular served *purposes* which produced a borderland between being a student, being a band member and being an emergent professional musician. Understanding the practice contexts of the music industry, learning how to write songs and develop creative abilities, and 'passing the course' all interrelated for Laura. Here we are not seeing a simple transfer of literacy as a skill from one context to another, nor had we discovered practices we could viably call border literacies in the sense we had originally envisaged, as discussed in Chapter 1. Laura's vernacular practices were not imported wholesale into the context of course, since the context changed the practice. Rather, everyday literacies seemed to feed into the formal coursework in a subtle manner: in-college and out-of-college identifications and their related literacies *bordered* on one another, similar in their configurations of some aspects of literacy, but different in respect of others. So while Laura's literacy practices were not 'border literacy practices' per se, Laura was engaged in what we began to see as *bordering work*: mobilising aspects of literacy practices across the borders between domains.

In designing and implementing the changes in practice (Boxes 8.3 and 8.4), we recognised that we should stop looking for whole literacy practices which occupy the borderland between home and college. A socially situated view of literacy implies that a practice is shaped by its context and therefore that it cannot be the same in two different contexts. Instead we needed to first focus on the more fine-grained aspects of literacy practices, as discussed in Chapter 3; and second, pay attention rather to the work entailed in bordering – rendering aspects of the literacy practices in students' everyday lives more available as resources for learning. Thus, the new task of writing about personal experience of networking in the music industry was not a border literacy practice, but it was aiming to 'close the gap' between college work and everyday literacy practices by setting a *topic* to which students could relate, and offering a collaborative *participation* structure which we knew students preferred to writing in isolation. We saw the lecturer working to fine-tune aspects of the pedagogic task to border off students' everyday literacy practices.

Similarly, the new task of writing bios was not exactly the same as writing bios in the home or work domain, since it was done in a pedagogic context and would be assessed as coursework. However, it shared certain characteristics with students' home practices, in particular clarity of *purpose* and *audience*, and relevance of *genre*. It seemed useful to talk of lecturers' changes in practices as bordering work, and the idea that pedagogic practices might connect to aspects of everyday literacy practices by bordering off them in one or more respects was productive.

Thus, the concept of 'border literacies' ultimately became untenable, since it entailed talking about 'whole' literacy practices as if they could operate in more than one social context. We also realised that the border metaphor was inscribed in the method we had used to collect the data. There is a certain flatness, a static two-dimensionality about the Venn-diagram representations and mapped spaces which follow from talk of 'borders' and 'border-crossings'. In other words, the assumptions from Euclidian geometry that go into making Venn diagrams precisely produce borders. In laying out three overlapping contexts, we had assumed a border space, but as we moved to bordering as a practice rather than identifying border literacy practices as entities, we saw that the relationship between domains and practices was more complex and messy: they co-emerge.

The metaphors 'bordering', 'bordering work' and 'bordering off' were an advance on the concept of border, and provided us with an initial way of understanding and describing the relationship between college and everyday literacy practices. However, further questions were raised. How exactly do practices border off one another, along what dimensions and under what circumstances? To explore this we looked for alternative conceptual framings as a means of increasing our understanding and providing a more adequate language of description. One came from the very curriculum area which is the focus of our case study in this chapter: Music. This is the metaphor of resonance.

Affordances of the conceptual metaphor of resonance

As a term, *resonance* appears to offer much potential for exploring the links between the embodied experience of events (such as a musical sound or, a practice such as literacy), identification and learning. After reading a newspaper or magazine, you may have commented that some feature of the article 'struck a chord' with you: it could have been that it created an emotional response or perhaps enthused you to rekindle an old passion. This common-sense notion of 'striking a chord' and the theory of resonance in music can help extend our understanding of how the forms of reading and writing we do with students might be more attuned to the many contexts in which students lead their lives: home, leisure, work, as well as college.

In music, resonance is used to talk about two related phenomena: *consonance* and *dissonance*. Two musical notes are said to be dissonant when they sound harsh together and seem to require resolution. These are sometimes described as being unstable sounds. Consonance is used to describe when two sounds have wavelengths that coincide. Thus resonance embraces both coincidence and harshness, allowing us to explore the complex struggles within literacy practices and also their cultural situatedness, given that resonance takes different forms in different musical traditions, and even within musical traditions.

In literacy, we suggest the experience of reading and writing in one context is resonant (consonant and dissonant to varying degrees) with another depending on the configuration of micro-practices which are assembled as a literacy practice. When one sounds a note on an instrument, the fundamental or basic sound is always accompanied by higher frequency tones called overtones or harmonics. We suggest there is a parallel here with literacy and offer the view that the aspects of a literacy practice work in a similar way. We suggest the *harmonics of literacy* lie in how certain aspects are experienced and practised.

It also appears that people's cultural experience of music will condition what they find unpleasant and acceptable degrees of dissonance. In the West, for example, ears are being progressively culturally conditioned to accept new musical conventions and styles with associated degrees of dissonance often designed to elicit different emotional responses. Similarly, with literacy, what we deem acceptable, pleasant or comfortable, is affected by our previous experiences of reading and writing. In music some degree of dissonance will always be present. The resonant character of an individual note or chord (two or more notes played together) depends on the degree of both consonant and dissonant overtones that are inherent in them. In fact, without resonance, musical instruments simply would not have the rich timbre, colour, projection and tuning and the sound would be dull to the ear. It appears that all music, even music that we hear as harmonious, incorporates some degree of dissonance. As with music, in literacy, we can expect that there will be resonances that are made up of dissonances and consonances. Indeed, some degree of dissonance may even be essential for learning. (For further discussion of this metaphor, see Mannion 2006; Goodman *et al.* 2007.)

We illustrate this by comparing the two changes in practice in Boxes 8.3 and 8.4. We show how the initial change in practice was problematic because it was not sufficiently resonant with the kinds of communication found in some students' everyday lives. We then go on to show how the subsequent change in pedagogical approach was more effective because it made space for literacies that were resonant with elements in everyday life in relation to some critical aspects of our framework.

The lecturer's first change in practice was an attempt to increase the resonance of a reading and writing task with students' lives and identifications. He did so first by choosing *content* which was consonant with their interests and associated literacy practices, and second by organising the activity as group work, which is consonant with their preferred *collaborative participation* structures. However, too much was dissonant for many students. First, students had been asked to write without any *genre* being specified. Second, the 500 words produced by students had no clear or authentic *audience* other than themselves as students or the lecturers as assessors. The lecturer recognised that while the *content* seemed to be relevant and close to the students' experience, the lack of a clear *purpose*, lack of a clear *audience*, ambiguity of *roles and identities,* and uncertainty about the *genre* and conventions of *style and design* were also playing key roles. Not only were these factors contrary to the characteristics of the students' preferred literacy practices (as set out in Box 3.1), but neither did they find them relevant or conducive to learning. As a result, there was insufficient resonance and the activity had a mixed reception. The research team concluded that in order to achieve resonance, critical aspects of a pedagogic literacy practice need to be the same as or similar to literacies which students are familiar with and value.

By contrast, the second change in practice – the writing of bios – did achieve resonance for the majority of students. We concluded that the bios were more successful not only because the *content* was interesting and relevant to the students, but also because the *purpose* for writing was clear, and the *genre* and conventions of *style and design* for these texts were an authentic and accessible way of communicating to a real and important *audience* for these emerging musicians. Students also appreciated the *flexibility* the lecturer offered regarding *modes and technologies* for the production of their texts: they had the freedom to submit digitally and to create multimodal texts with sound files attached. Thus, there was a high degree of consonance with literacy practices in their lives outside college. In this case, however, there was also dissonance regarding *purpose* and *audience*: the students knew that these bios would also be used for assessment by an external verifier – something unique to the college context. In addition, this was a learning activity as well as an assessment task: the students were explicitly taught about the *genre* they would employ – a genre which would be of use in their lives outside college, not just a pedagogic genre. Overall, there was a judicious mix of consonance and dissonance to achieve the resonance which, we suggest, characterises a good learning activity.

Students did not all take to the changes in pedagogy equally. The engineers did not find the opportunity for engagement in 'bio' writing as resonant, perhaps because the genre lends itself more to the construction of a web-presence for musicians. This suggests that writing depends on a strong link with identification processes. Through writing (and reading one another's self-stories of networking and their 'bios'), students were using literacy to incrementally re-invent themselves through aligning themselves with new aspects of the *roles and identities* that were important to them. Taking the cultural situation of students into account was critical but not easy to achieve for all. The changes in practice allowed us to explore in a situated way, how we might *tune in* to different dimensions to enhance their resonant effects. As with resonance in music, there were degrees of consonance and dissonance within these effects.

As with many powerful metaphors, we found that not only had wave theorists, therapists, psychologists and others already used the notion of resonance in other contexts, but also communication theorists and cognitive psychologists. The concept of resonance is pervasive and generative of productive understandings. However, there were aspects of the interaction between literacy practices in different domains which were not sufficiently captured by this metaphor.

Beyond 'borders': future directions in conceptualising the interface between everyday and curriculum literacies

While the notion of resonance added to our understanding and provided a useful language of description for our data, it did not provide us with ways of conceptualising the actual relationships between practices in different domains of people's lives. In addition, achieving resonance between one practice and another through fine-tuning aspects of literacy practices, while intuitively attractive, does not bring out the power relations whereby certain literacy practices are privileged and perpetuated, and others are proscribed. To provide a more robust conceptualisation of the relationship between literacies in college and literacies in other domains of students' lives, issues of power need to be taken into account.

A possible direction is to consider the contribution that could be made by Actor-Network Theory (ANT). ANT has become increasingly influential in the social sciences since the 1980s (Star 1989; Latour 1986, 1987, 1993, 1999; Law 1994). In education, the use of ANT has been more recent (Nespor 1994, 2003; Edwards 2002, 2003; Fox 2000; Hamilton 2001; Clarke 2002). Its assumptions and language are unfamiliar, but ANT is part of the shift from individualised, psychological approaches to the understanding of learning to more social and cultural interpretations. It conceptualises social life as a 'messy' configuration of networks in which action is influenced by a constantly shifting set of factors, animate and inanimate. It pays particular attention to the workings of power and the effects of dominant values and beliefs in the 'translation' of practices from one context to another, and the 'stabilisation' of some and not others.

Literacy and learning can be seen as distributed through the range of networks within which a person is interconnected. These networks 'expand, contract and shift configuration over time, and even the most stable and predictable of them are constantly being reappropriated and redefined by the nature of the flows that animate them' (Nespor 1994: 12). Literacies and the power exercised in and around them therefore can be seen as actor-networks, ordered in time and space. This approach then, rather than assuming a movement of literacy from one context to another, examines the work that goes into *stabilising* certain situations as contexts through precisely the attempted exclusion of multiplicity. Here, despite the multiplicity of literacy practices which we have identified outside educational domains, only certain forms are stabilised in establishing an educational and educated context. Colleges are complex and contested organisational forms, within which there may be many tensions between the different pedagogical practices at play.

ANT is helpful here for it recognises the messiness of the world and that no context can be pure. To understand people acting in different contexts, it employs the metaphor of *translation*. Translation 'creates mixtures between entirely new types of beings, hybrids of nature and culture' (Latour 1993: 10). In terms of our case study, Laura was herself undertaking acts of translation, whereby she, in interaction with the technologies available to her and technologies of her choice, negotiated between the network of the Music course she was taking and the networks of her daily practices. Her writing of lyrics and her reading of fiction and non-fiction were networked across her home life and her college life: literacy practices which existed in both actor-networks, although subtly shifting in terms of the technologies and practices involved. Laura, then, was active in other networks as well as the course, and there was a constant translation and stabilisation of literacy practices between these networks, linking them and shifting their configurations over time. The two changes in practice, described in Boxes 8.3 and 8.4, are examples of how one lecturer successively challenged the processes operating in college. In the 'writing about networks' task, he intervened in the normalised *topics* and *participation* structures for written tasks. However, the *genre* of the written product itself was defined by the norms of the educational domain. In the 'writing bios' task he went a step further, challenging this normative regime. By introducing the writing of bios, a genre from the music industry, instead of CVs, a genre recognised in the educational domain, he engaged in a process of translating across networks, changing the connections in the pedagogic practice in an attempt to stabilise bios as a legitimate and legitimised educational practice. Here pedagogy is not just about content or process, but about networking various factors to enable learning.

While the term 'bordering' moved us forward in understanding what was occurring in our data, it still entailed an assumption of enabling literacy practices to move across different situations. Resonance pointed to the relatedness of aspects of practices, rather than whole practices. ANT could, we suggest, give us a view not only of the way in which literacy practices are mobilised and translated from one domain to another, but also of the stablisations and power at play in the practices of pedagogy. We do not see the processes we have been investigating as simple border-crossings or resonances, but as complex reorientations which are likely to entail effort, awareness-raising, creativity and identity work on the part of all concerned.

There are no simple answers, nor one completely satisfactory language of description for framing our data. Each metaphorical framing opens up pedagogical possibilities through describing the mobilisation of everyday literacies in the curriculum in particular ways. All have constraints, as well as affordances. In describing pedagogical landscapes there are different perspectives promoted by different forms of description. Our findings then are not tied to one language of description but to many, which will themselves be dependent on context, purpose and disposition. In each there are possibilities and constraints raised by being strangers in a strange land, which is at the heart of all educational endeavours.

.plications for learning
.n college and beyond

Large-scale research projects across many sites and subject areas generate
a large amount of data. This project has collected data through interviews
and other interactions with students and staff in colleges, through staff
participation in the project, and through observation. We have also
collected a large number of documents to do with the teaching and assessment in the various curriculum areas. While the focus of our study has been
on literacy practices, this data has provided us with many insights into
curriculum issues more generally within colleges. Many of the implications
go beyond the specific focus of the projects, as literacies for learning are a
part of any learning experience – in schools, universities, workplaces
and so on. Projects of this sort also raise issues and questions for further
research. What we focus on in this chapter are not only the specific
outcomes of the project in relation to literacies for learning in colleges but
also some of the broader inferences that can be drawn from them.

The relationship between people's everyday practices and the formal
curriculum has been explored in a range of ways over the years. The
distance between what goes on in educational institutions in terms of the
formal, codified, abstracted curriculum and the day-to-day learning in which
we all engage has been the basis of much debate about what is distinctive
about learning through education and its relevance to people's wider lives.
We see it in the discussion of formal and informal learning, dominant and
vernacular literacy, everyday and scientific knowledge, to name a few. Each
is identifying a gap between what goes on in educational institutions and
what goes on elsewhere in life. The gap is framed in understandings drawn
from different disciplines, including psychology, linguistics and education.

Not everyone would find that gap problematic. Insofar as education has
a unique role to play, then we would expect differences between what
people do in the institutional spaces of education and what they do elsewhere. Learning may take place in a workplace, but the organisation does
not have learning as its primary purpose. Similarly, the home, the community centre, the funfair may be sites of learning. However, learning does
take place in these other spaces, and people's practices and accomplish-
ments outside educational institutions are potentially rich resources for

learning. The recognition of these factors has raised issues about this gap and the ways in which education excludes by failing to draw upon the achievements people have developed in their everyday lives.

It is important to identify two types of finding from this project. First there are those findings that have emerged from an explicit focus on people's everyday literacy practices and those of the college curriculum. These are both descriptive and explanatory. These findings tell you the sorts of reading and writing people do in their everyday lives and attempt to develop pedagogic strategies through which to fold these literacy practices into the curriculum and college life. The second type of finding is that reached by using the study of literacy practices as a lens through which to re-read learning. These findings point to wider issues that need further exploration; for instance, the issue of academic drift in the vocational curriculum (Edwards and Miller 2008), and they open up different horizons through which such issues can be explored.

In what follows we provide a summary and overview of the insights and understandings reached by the research in the form of a set of sixteen findings listed in Boxes 9.1, 9.2 and 9.3. Alongside this we explore the potential implications of these findings for five areas of practice: resources students bring with them; curriculum; assessment; purposes and progression; and fine-tuning literacies for learning. This more discursive, open-ended discussion provides a way of opening up literacies for learning for fuller and further exploration. We then make suggestions about the application of the research to other sectors of education. We end by outlining possible future directions for research on literacies for learning.

What we present here are contextualised understandings, reached by our particular research activities in our particular contexts, and we suggest that these findings need to be 'recontextualised' in the particular contexts in which you work. In other words, rather than *generalise* from our research to all contexts, it is possible to *infer* how our findings might apply to other contexts. In order to establish the extent to which the inference is correct, it would be necessary to explore the issues within the specificities of those different contexts, just as the Bilingual Literacies for Learning in Further Education project recontextualised the research in Coleg Meirion-Dwyfor in Wales, as described in Chapter 7.

The resources students bring with them to learning

Box 9.1   Summary of findings about literacy practices in students' everyday lives

1   The literacy practices which students used in their everyday lives tended to have the following characteristics:

---

continued

- purposeful to the student;
- oriented to a clear audience;
- shared, that is, interactive, participatory and collaborative;
- learned through participation;
- in tune with students' values and identities;
- agentic, that is, with the students having control;
- non-linear, that is, with varied reading paths;
- specific to times and places;
- multimodal, that is, combining symbols, pictures, colour, music;
- multimedia, that is, combining paper and electronic media;
- varied, not repetitive;
- generative, that is, involving meaning-making, creativity and getting things done;
- self-determined in terms of activity, time and place.

2 Staff and students tended not to perceive the literacy practices associated with everyday lives as having value.

3 Students engaged not only in vernacular literacy practices – that is, those which arise from their own interests and concerns – but also in a wide range of bureaucratic, more formal literacy practices which are demanded by the practicalities of their lives.

4 A literacy practice has several 'aspects' or 'dimensions', as represented in the framework presented in Chapter 3. Each of these can be configured in many ways, and change in any one of them changes the nature of the practice.

In the course of the research, we discovered that the students we engaged with had certain preferences in their literacy practices, as listed at (1) in Box 9.1. We are wary of making too much of this in case it is over-generalised to students across time and context. The research indeed showed the importance of context to understanding literacy practices. We would not therefore expect to find a universal set of preferences. Designing teaching and learning around literacy practices that draw upon such preferences would not necessarily result in enhanced learning. However, the preferences we identified do point to the creative and social ways in which literacy practices emerge in student lives and, with that, certain possibilities for pedagogy. Above all, these findings indicate the value of lecturers' finding out about their *own* students' practices and preferences, so that these provide the resources for their own pedagogy.

A key finding from the research challenges some of the fundamental assumptions that inform the discourses and practices of literacy and learning in colleges. While there is a generalised view that students in colleges are *deficient* in terms of literacy, when one explores with them their everyday literacy practices, there is not a lack, but an *abundance* and *diversity*. Indeed, with the pluralisation of communication possibilities developing through the use of the screen as well as the page and the icon as well as the word, it is diversification and multiplication of literacy practices which is the issue and not the lack of them. If one seeks to impose a standardised view of literacy, then diversity and multiplicity will inevitably be problematic, but they could be a source of strength.

Yet it is precisely such deficit views that tend to inform much policy and practice in relation to literacy in education and it is this which has become a significant underpinning for what we might term the 'literacy industry' – those who are funded to 'put right' the deficits. Embedded in standards are hierarchies of value as to what constitutes literacy and what constitute valued literacy practices. Different interests are at play in establishing specific types of literacy practices as *universal* – to be valued irrespective of context. This results in the privileging of only certain literacy practices. The research challenges such privileging and indicates that a far wider range of practices should be recognised and rewarded by the education system. The research reported in this book suggests that there are grounds for further discussion of the assumptions upon which current approaches to literacy education are based. The research opens up to question the meaningfulness of the literacy practices which are treated as universal across contexts and are embedded in so-called 'standards'. This is not an argument that all literacy practices are equal but that practices have to be evaluated in relation to their relevance to the purposes to be achieved.

The projects established that neither staff nor students in colleges recognise a wide range of literacy practices as reading and writing. Anything other than the reading of books and handouts, and the writing of extended text was often dismissed as 'not reading or writing'. Students do not on the whole identify the reading and writing in their everyday lives as literacy, nor as practices they might draw upon in their college lives. What was overwhelmingly apparent in these projects was the surprise to both staff and students involved when we started to explore with them the literacy dimensions of their lives and of their teaching.

Insofar as they do identify these diverse practices as literacy and these are positioned as capabilities for learning, then it does become possible to make use pedagogically of the everyday for students to achieve their curriculum goals. Identifying the different aspects of literacy as presented in Chapter 3 of the book, and considering the ways in which the characteristics of students' everyday literacy practices can be drawn upon in their pedagogy is neither simple nor straightforward, not least because of the pre-existing dispositions and cultures of teaching and learning in colleges and in education more generally. Educators tend not to consider explicitly the communicative aspects of their teaching and often feel constrained by curriculum and assessment regimes.

These issues require explicit discussion and exploration among staff teams planning their teaching and their curriculum development. College staff need to recognise, value and harness what students *can* do with reading and writing. This may involve recontextualising the research in their own contexts, and then using the 'aspects of a literacy practice' as a way of 'calibrating' the reading and writing on courses so that they are more resonant with students' everyday literacy practices.

Box 9.2   Summary of findings about literacies for learning in college

5   While the general discourses of policy and practice focused on students' deficits in literacy, exploration of students' everyday literacy practices indicates it is the multiplicity and abundance of these which is an issue, when compared with the very specific sets of practices that are valued within the context of college.

6   There are four categories of literacies for learning:

- literacies for being a student – for example, registration, use of learning resource area;
- literacies for course-related learning – for example, content-focused learning;
- literacies for assessment;
- literacies related to an imagined future – for example, placements, work simulations.

The relative weight of these varies, but overall literacies for assessment dominate the learning careers of students.

7   Learning has three interconnected dimensions: theoretical, practical, communicative. While staff and students talked of theory and practice, the communicative aspect of learning, including literacy practices, tended to be left implicit. Students tended to be expected to understand the differences among genres of writing – for example, reflection or analysis – rather than these being made explicit.

8   Students received mixed messages about the genres and tasks which were expected of them. For instance, the notions of 'an essay' or 'a report' were used in a wide variety of ways, as are tasks such as 'to discuss', 'to research', 'to analyse'.

9   There was a view that the literacy requirements of more vocational courses were of a lower and less complex order. Our research suggests that this is misguided. While students on more academic routes are encultured into a specific set of literacy practices associated with developing extended reading and writing of academic texts,

those on vocational courses are often expected to engage in more diverse literacy practices, involving a wider range of genres, and requiring an understanding of the social context in which the texts they are reading and writing are situated; for example, producing pamphlets for parents on a Childcare course.

10 A focus on literacy practices revealed an ambiguity in curriculum purpose. More vocational courses often aimed for both employment relevance *and* academic progression. However, these two goals made different requirements in terms of literacy practices; for example, simulations of work tasks or essays.

Curriculum

The projects found that lower and intermediate level units tend to use a wider range of texts and require more diverse practices of reading and writing than the higher level courses. Much of the reading and writing on lower level courses is more vocationally relevant, and more resonant with students' everyday literacies. However, some of the diversity is introduced spuriously in order to make units more 'interesting' and 'stimulating' for students, as in the example in Box 5.2 in Chapter 5. Overall students on lower level courses often receive confusing messages about what literacy practices are necessary for them to succeed with their learning, as they are asked to engage with and produce a far greater range of artefacts and use a more diverse range of genres. As students progress to higher level courses, the literacy practices become more academic, and there is a more consistent message about the required forms of reading and writing: their literacy careers have a narrower, but clearer trajectory. If this difference in emphasis between the levels is not made explicit and worked with, the shift may impact upon progression.

College staff need to become aware of the literacies which mediate learning. The reading and writing on all courses at all levels needs to be scrutinised to ensure practices and tasks are relevant and meaningful for learning, and for the futures for which the students are preparing. The reading and writing needed for the course need to be recognised, and often explicitly taught. Fine-tuning the ways in which reading and writing are used on courses can help students to mobilise ways of reading and writing from their everyday lives as resources for their college learning. Small changes in one or more of the 'aspects of literacy' can make a big difference.

Assessment

One of the key findings of the research is that the majority of literacy practices and, in particular, of writing practices are associated with assessment. Given that colleges have been identified as sites in which there is not simply assessment *of* learning or assessment *for* learning, but also assessment *as* learning (Torrance *et al.* 2005), this is of particular significance. Building up knowledge, understanding and capacity beyond that required by assessment is often seen as necessary by lecturers, but the time constraints of the organisation of the curriculum and pressure to ensure student achievement do not always seem to make that possible.

We found a great deal of diversity and some confusion around the genres of writing required of students for assessment purposes. Tasks were set as writing 'essays' or 'reports', but the expectations of what was to be submitted could be very diverse from lecturer to lecturer in the same subject as well as from subject to subject. 'Learning logs' of various sorts have also become popular under the auspices of student-centred learning, but the genre of reflective writing for this purpose is not taught, and indeed seems to be thought of as a 'natural' form of self-expression. This was something the students struggled with and we would suggest that any task set by lecturers should first be undertaken by them to establish its viability and validity.

It also emerged that the reading and writing that the students do as part of the learning within the classroom is often very different from that which they have to do in the assessments. Some tutors seem to believe that if we give students the right information in an effective and interesting way, then they will be able to do anything with it and re-present it in the required ways. Yet transfer is not straightforward and talk around texts is crucial for this to occur. The use of texts is therefore as important as the complexity of their content. This calls for explicit strategies; for example, making links between the curriculum and the task in order that their meaning, relevance and significance is clear, and relating back to practice to give purpose and encourage ownership.

The insights from the research suggest that assessments for qualifications in vocational and subject areas should allow students to demonstrate and provide evidence of knowledge, understanding and capability in ways which do not require them to learn special 'assessment literacies'. Assessment for such qualifications should be reshaped in such a way that the students are assessed more by their capacity to engage in the actual literacy practices of the futures for which the courses are preparing them – both futures in employment and progression within the educational system.

The research also has implications for assessments for qualifications in key/core/functional skills of communication. It shows that the contexts provided by courses afford plenty of opportunities for students to develop and demonstrate communicative capabilities, and there need not be any communication assessment tasks apart from these. Assessment for such qualifications should be reshaped so that they accredit the literacies which are part and parcel of the courses themselves, particularly vocational literacies.

Purpose and progression

On many courses students engage in literacy practices associated with the prospective point of progression, that is, the workplace or further study. In relation to the former, either through work placements or simulations, students are introduced to the literacy practices they will face in their prospective occupation. These practices often have the real-life characteristics of the reading and writing involved in occupational tasks, but sometimes, in particular in simulated environments, they can involve hybrid literacy practices associated with college as well as the prospective workplace; for example, the writing of logbooks. If the course is intended for progression within the education system, including progression to university, then it may attempt to simulate the prospective literacy practices of the destination course. A difficulty arises when the progression is potentially towards both of these options, as the literacy practices of the prospective workplace and academic progression do not always sit easily alongside each other.

Educators need to recognise these tensions between educational (academic) imperatives and occupational (vocational) imperatives in terms of literacy practices, types of texts and types of engagement with texts required by students, especially as they progress in terms of level. Thus the same unit can be taught differently and therefore entail a different curriculum according to whether it is primarily perceived to be for preparing students for the workplace or for academic progression. This raises the most fundamental of curriculum questions: is the purpose of the programme to extend education or to fit occupational context? Each has implications for the literacy practices in which people participate, both students and tutors. If it is to do both, then the issues of what is valued as literacy and the resources necessary for the multimodality of the world will need seriously to be addressed in the curriculum expectations and pedagogic practices of courses.

So there are many dimensions to literacy practices in being a college student. When we factor in the different aspects of a literacy practice that we have identified, then there is a wealth and diversity of ways of fine-tuning pedagogic literacy practices in which lecturers and students might engage to the benefit of all.

Fine-tuning literacies for learning

Box 9.3   Summary of findings about fine-tuning literacies for learning

11 Lecturers made four types of change in practice in relation to literacies for learning:

- making the reading and writing on courses more resonant with students' vernacular literacy practices;
- making the students more aware of the reading and writing in their everyday lives which could act as resources for their learning;
- making the communicative aspects of learning more explicit and visible;
- making the reading and writing on courses more relevant to learning, and/or to the futures for which the students were preparing.

12 Lecturers were able to fine-tune the reading and writing on their courses in relation to one or more of the dimensions shown in Figure 3.1 in Chapter 3, so that they would resonate more with the literacy practices in students' everyday lives, and thus help students learn and demonstrate their learning, rather than acting as barriers to success.

13 Not all students wished to draw upon their everyday practices. Older students tended to view the use of pictures/icons/symbols other than writing text as 'childlike'. This was also the case for students on more advanced courses.

14 Tutors often felt themselves constrained to use existing assessments, which seemed to limit the possibilities for such changes. Often the most beneficial change would have been – 'change the assessment requirement'. Many college staff at various levels were hesitant to do this because of the exigencies of moderation, and/or because they felt that it was not within their power.

15 Changes in practice which engaged with students' everyday literacy practices tended to increase their capacity for engagement and recall, and their confidence.

16 The changes in practice depended on the tutors' own professional expertise and preferences: what amounted to a change in practice for one tutor might be an established practice for another. Changes in practice were not necessarily innovative, but could be new to the particular staff and students involved; for example, the use of mind maps.

The research found that 'whole' literacy practices in everyday life, as diverse as applying for child benefit or reading horoscopes, cannot be moved wholesale into educational settings, because the context changes the practice. Nor, at the other extreme, is the current notion of 'transferable skills' satisfactory, since reading and writing are shaped by the contexts of which they are part. Nor is it simply a question of bringing apparently 'authentic' texts from other domains into educational settings, because they are no longer 'authentic' to their new context (see also Breen 1985 for this argument). In order to pursue our original intention of identifying ways in which students' everyday practices might be harnessed for their learning on college courses, we needed a way of theorising literacy practices which allowed us to talk about their fine detail. We therefore focused on the aspects of a literacy practice as presented and discussed in Chapter 3 of the book. Each of these aspects can be configured in many ways, and change in any one of them changes the nature of the practice.

To frame our understanding of the relationship between the literacy practices of the everyday and those of college life we have used the metaphors of bordering, resonance and translating. In relation to resonance what we are asking is: if literacy practices are like music, how would we engender harmony between the practices of the everyday and those of college? What we like about this metaphor is that it is more subtle than some that are more generally used, such as learning as acquisition and learning as participation. Both of these latter suggest the idea, whether justifiably or not, that learning is a unitary process – one either acquires knowledge and understanding or not; one either learns through increased participation or one does not learn. By contrast the metaphor of resonance is more subtle. For a musical note to resonate, it will have aspects of consonance and dissonance within it, that is, things that relate to each other and things that do not. In other words, there is no one-to-one relationship, but a play of similarities and differences which produce an overall resonant effect. There are harmonious and discordant parts to the overall resonance that work in concert to support learning. Similarly, the metaphor of translation implicitly holds within it the possibility for being lost in translation.

The research has also pinpointed the centrality of identification in affecting engagement in literacy practices (see especially Ivanič 2006; Satchwell and Ivanič forthcoming). When students see the relationship of literacy practices to their sense of who they are or who they want to become, they participate in them wholeheartedly. By contrast, if students associate reading and writing practices with identities which they resist or are indifferent towards, they are unlikely to engage in them. Providing students with opportunities to identify with the 'selves' held out by reading and writing activities emerged as a key to harnessing the potential of literacies to enhance learning.

In a number of the changes the lecturers made in the literacy practices on their courses, they attempted to incorporate at least some of the students' preferences discussed in Chapters 2 and 3, and summarised in item 1 in Box 9.1. These changes did not work for all the students, nor did they always do the intended work, but in moving away from some of the established patterns of teaching, they were attempts to engage literacies to mediate learning in a far more explicit way. In some curriculum areas and situations there may be more possibilities than others, but we suggest that there is a great deal of scope for attempting one or more of the types of change in practice suggested in item 11 in Box 9.3.

Implications of the research for other educational sectors

The research was conducted in colleges of Further Education in the UK. These are very rich sites for educational research for several reasons. They are post-compulsory educational institutions, where students are, for the most part, studying by choice rather than compulsion. The majority of the full-time students are young people with an active engagement in the fast-changing landscape of modern life, with more autonomy and more freedom than children, yet giving insight into the developing interests of the younger generation. Because of the diverse backgrounds and possible futures of the students, the curriculum in colleges is extremely varied. Specifically, they are the main sites for vocational education, yet they also provide second-chance opportunities for the study of traditional school subjects, and of alternative subjects which are not always offered at schools. While our research is centrally relevant to educational provision in such colleges in the UK and elsewhere, we suggest that it has implications for other educational sectors and inferences can be made about how our findings can be recontextualised in very different contexts.

In schools in the UK, particularly for students aged 14 to 19, there is an increasing interest in the provision of vocational education, and a new policy move to teach 'functional skills' to all students. The research reported in Chapters 2 and 3 has shown how students aged 16 and above use reading and writing in their everyday lives, and discussions with secondary school teachers have suggested that research would reveal a similar richness in the literacy lives of their students, including those who are not succeeding in school subjects. Further, it is apparent that the insights about the textual mediation of learning in Chapters 4 and 5 have direct parallels in schools. A preliminary exploration has indicated that most secondary classrooms are what might be called textually saturated: children are reading and writing a wide range of multimodal texts as part and parcel of the activities devised by teachers.

A particular example is the reading and writing in the learning and teaching of Textiles – a subject which might at first glance appear to be 'practical' and therefore not dependent on 'literacy'. The teacher uses the actual texts of the fashion industry, both online and in the form of magazines, patterns and instruction booklets. In addition she provides a wide range of pedagogic texts – adapted for a younger age group, but similar in purpose to those we encountered in the colleges. The students need to write both as part of the planning of their practical work and in the production of their portfolio of work for assessment. In discussing the interaction between the children's everyday literacy practices and the reading and writing on the Textiles course, the teacher saw exactly the same sorts of connections as we discussed in Chapters 6 to 8. It was apparent that greater awareness of learners' reading and writing outside school, and of the textual mediation of learning in the classroom could lead to beneficial fine-tuning of the literacy practices for learning not only in Textiles, but in all subjects across the curriculum. This has implications not only for enhancing children's success in their chosen vocational and academic subjects, but also for the recognition of 'functional skills' which already exist within the broader curriculum.

Higher education differs from school and college education as students are expected to be far more independent in their study practices, and the dependence on textual mediation of learning is taken for granted. Yet it is increasingly apparent that students would benefit from greater explicitness about the nature of academic literacy practices, and the values which underpin them. Students in higher education have a lot in common with those in colleges – most of them are the same age, and participate in the same cultures and practices. In our view, educators in higher education would find it useful to pay attention to the literacy practices students bring with them from their everyday lives and from their previous educational experience, just as they did in our research. It is almost certainly an uphill task to consider fine-tuning the literacy practices which mediate learning in higher education, since they are so entrenched in the system. However, imaginative educators are beginning to pay explicit attention to the nature of the reading required on their courses, to recognise writing as a tool for learning as well as for demonstrating learning, and to envisage alternatives to traditional assessment tasks. We believe that the insights from our research could provide the basis for scrutinising the literacy practices of learning and teaching in higher education, unpicking the assumptions which underpin them, and experimenting with reconfigurations which allow for more resonance with ways of knowing and learning in students' everyday lives.

Conclusion

The particular focus of this research has been literacies for learning, investigating the social uses of reading and writing rather than literacy as an autonomous skill. In doing so, the research works within the grain of what is a wider critique of formal educational provision: that it is abstracted from contexts of use, out of touch, decontextualised, inauthentic, not relevant and so on. Over the years many such critiques have been offered of the curriculum in general. Indeed, one of the rationales for the development of a competence- or outcomes-based approach to the curriculum was that it would make it more relevant to the end contexts of use; for example, the workplace. The fact that employers, students and others still point to the gaps between learning a subject and working suggests there is more to it than simply a focus on performance in the curriculum. The research has foregrounded the importance of paying attention to the contexts and purposes for reading and writing. It has shown how the literacy-related aspects of social practices interface with and co-emerge with other aspects of context. The ongoing contextualisation of literacies in pedagogic contexts can be subtly reshaped to make them more powerful as resources for learning. This can be achieved by calibrating the elements in the framework we have developed.

We cannot separate what is to be learnt from the forms of interaction and communication through which the curriculum is enacted. These are the semiotic practices of which literacy is an essential dimension. What has become clear in our projects is that communication, which encompasses literacy practices, is an important part of the hidden curriculum in colleges. Yet all too often the communicative aspects of learning remain unacknowledged, literacies are treated as 'belonging' in college or out of college, and students' everyday literacy practices remain untapped as resources for learning. As long as these tendencies continue, literacy in colleges and in other educational institutions will remain a constant 'problem'. Indeed, this perceived 'problem' will probably increase given the multiplications of semiotic practices that are taking place. Without continual questioning and fine-tuning of the literacy practices which mediate learning, educational institutions could start to become museums rather than laboratories for life.

Researching literacies for learning

Research aims (LfLFE project)

1 To identify those 'border literacies' that enable people to negotiate successfully between informal vernacular literacies and formal literacies within the Further Education context, that positively affect learning outcomes, and that can serve as generic resources for learning through the life course.

2 To develop, implement and evaluate programmes based on these findings, aimed at mobilising students' use of their vernacular literacy capabilities and 'border' practices as means for learning in FE and other contexts.

3 To uncover what may be common within the FE experience of a range of learners across different areas of the curriculum in different FE sites in both England and Scotland, whilst also accounting for diversity of experiences.

4 To inform future practice and policy in the design of learning opportunities that will enable smoother articulation between informal vernacular literacy practices, formal institutional literacy practices and emergent demands upon literate persons in the wider society.

5 To engage FE practitioners directly in a research partnership to investigate (a) the literacy capabilities and practices of their learners; (b) the literacy demands of their curriculum subjects; and (c) the development of appropriate 'two-way' intervention strategies taking account of (a) and (b), and thus enable and directly support evidence-based practice within the FE context and to evaluate this process especially in terms of its sustainability.

Research design (LfLFE and BiLfLFE projects)

The research design for both projects was in three phases, as shown in Table A.1.

Phase One was an induction period in which we took a broad-brush approach to mapping the literacy practices required by students across the

Table A.1 The phases of the research

Phase	Focus	LfLFE timing	BiLfLFE timing
Phase One	Induction	Jan–July 2004	May–Sept 2005
Phase Two	*Actions for understanding*: Literacy Practices: • in students' everyday lives • in curriculum areas and focal units	Aug 2004–June 2005	Oct 2005–June 2006
Phase Three	*Actions for change*: Changes in Pedagogic Practice	July 2005–June 2006	July 2006–June 2007

colleges, particularly in those aspects of college life which are not about learning a subject such as registration and induction. During this phase we recruited college lecturers to act as college-based researchers for the project. This involved extensive collaboration with the host colleges, selecting curriculum areas and individuals to be involved in the research to fulfil college aims and interests as well as those of the research projects. Phase Two was an academic year in which the lecturers involved, supported by the university-based research staff, engaged in 'actions for understanding': research activities aimed at making visible the reading and writing which students do in their everyday lives, and making visible the communicative dimensions of their learning on the chosen units. Phase Three was an academic year in which the same lecturers (as far as possible) engaged in 'actions for change': designing, implementing and evaluating small changes in practice on the same units of study (as far as possible). These changes were designed to take account of and build upon the insights and inferences reached during Phase 2.

Partnership research

The research in Phases Two and Three of the projects was undertaken as a partnership between university-based researchers and college lecturers who were employed as researchers, whom we refer to as college-based researchers. Our aim was for the research process to be a valuable experience for the students and lecturers involved, most of whom had never undertaken any research before. To this end we followed the practitioner research model developed within Exploratory Practice (EP) (Allwright

2001). This approach to research critiques both 'reflective practice' and 'action research', proposing instead an integrated model in which research processes aimed at understanding provide the basis on which any changes in pedagogy are designed and implemented. We adopted the EP distinction between 'Actions for Understanding' and 'Actions for Change'. We devoted Phase Two to 'Actions for Understanding': research processes in which the college lecturers worked in partnership with university-based researchers to examine in depth the literacy practices of the students on their courses across the domains of college, work and home. In Phase Three the college lecturers engaged in 'Actions for Change', developing and evaluating changes in practice based upon the initial data collection and analysis, to try to establish whether there are ways of folding learners' everyday literacy practices into activities on their courses to support learning, retention and achievement. These research processes are the focus of the project DVD (Pardoe and Ivanič 2007).

Research methodology

The methodology informing this project was broadly ethnographic, hermeneutic and reflexive. It was ethnographic in that we sought to describe in as much detail as possible through fieldwork the literacy practices required by the study of particular subjects in becoming a college student and those that learners manifest in the diverse domains of their lives. We attempted to understand the culture and rituals of college, and the artefacts and totems through which literacy is folded into practices. Here we were contributing to a number of projects exploring the impact of policy on college practice (Coffield *et al.* 2005) and the culture of college teaching and learning (James and Biesta 2007). We were trying to obtain thick description from the inside rather than merely act as observers from the outside. A range of data collection methods were designed which could be used by the lecturers themselves to increase their 'noticing' of the characteristics of their own practices (Mason 2002). This resulted in a mixed-method approach to data collection in Phase Two, as described in detail in Boxes A.1 and A.2.

Box A.1   Methods used for researching the curriculum areas and focal units

The main aim here was to understand the existing and potential role of literacy in the learning of each of the selected units. In order to do this we needed to understand the syllabus and assessment requirements of the unit and the literacy demands which the lecturers were currently making. The following data were collected about each of the focal units:

continued

- an interview by another member of the research team with the lecturer of the unit about its aims, content, his/her plans for teaching it, and any existing mapping between the subject area and key/core skills;
- a comprehensive collection of texts associated with the unit – a copy, or other record, of texts which students encounter and produce in the course of taking the unit;
- a detailed study of three of these texts by the unit lecturer in terms of their nature and purposes, and the ways in which they are used;
- students' answers to the same questions on one of these three texts;
- reflective fieldnotes written every week by the lecturer about the literacy practices associated with the teaching and learning of the unit;
- a visit by a different lecturer to make comparisons and contrasts across curriculum areas regarding the relationship between literacy and learning;
- students' perceptions of what is involved in learning this subject and in achieving the qualification;
- data on enrolment, initial assessment, attendance, retention, achievement and any other indication of outcomes from learning such as satisfaction and progression for all students, to act as baseline data against which to compare data from the Changes in Pedagogic Practice Phase of the research (Phase Three).

Box A.2 Methods used for researching the students' literacy practices in different areas of their everyday lives

The main aim here was to find out whether students were engaging in literacy practices in aspects of their lives outside their study of the focal unit and, if so, what they read and wrote, when, where, how and in relation to which aspects of their lives. In order to do this each lecturer selected four students from each of their two focal units (eight students in total) to research. In practice, they often researched more students than this. Some of the following data was collected for each student:

- a pen-portrait, detailing who the student was, and why he/she had been chosen to participate in the project;
- one or two clock faces to elicit representations of what they did in the course of a day or part of a day, with detailed notes to say where,

and what reading and writing were involved, and further notes indicating how other days were different from this (see Figure 2.1; for more information on this method, see Satchwell 2006);

- a record of the reading and writing involved in a week of their life, collected through photographs on a disposable camera and a collection of (some of) the texts involved;
- an icon-mapping activity where students organised icons representing different kinds of reading and writing into different areas of their lives (see Figure A.1; for more information on this method, see Mannion and Miller 2005; Mannion and Ivanič 2007).
- an interview based around previous activities and artefacts. We used an interview scaffold to guide our questioning in these interviews.

Students found it extremely interesting and valuable to be involved in the research, and responded positively to the interest the researchers were taking in their lives.

Figure A.1 The icon-mapping activity

Through working with observations, clock faces, photo elicitation and icon mapping, focus groups and individual interviews, rich and varied data were collected about literacy practices. Individual and focus group interviews and observations were conducted, artefacts collected and changes in practice undertaken and evaluated in order to understand the role of literacy practices in learning different curriculum areas.

The research was hermeneutic in recognising the recursive role of interpretation in the understanding of practices, that is, the ways in which understanding is generated through the interrelationships between persons and artefacts and how these understandings help to shape future practices. We were therefore looking to *understand* as well as to *describe* literacy practices. Analysis in research entails a sense-making process. We do not claim the outcomes of our analysis as findings in any final sense. We have presented here what we prefer to call 'warrantable understandings': the sense we have made to date of the data as supportable by the evidence we have and the methodology of the project. The analysis is illuminative and capable of inference rather than quantifiable and capable of generalisation. The participation of the college lecturers and students in the research process and the confirmations of interpretations they have given have been part of the ways in which we have sought to warrant or confirm the interpretations we provide in this book.

Our approach to the research was reflexive as it entailed surfacing our own assumptions and rationales. A large distributed research project in naturalistic environments is not the same as conducting an experiment in a laboratory, nor would we expect it to be. However, it is the latter which often codes readers' understanding of research. It is important that this research is not read in this way. Similarly, the analysis we offer should not be read as exhaustive nor definitive. The understandings reached through the interpretive process are often coded as 'findings' and with qualitative data the notion of saturation is used to suggest that as much as is possible has been extracted from the data collected. Our view is somewhat different. While being rigorous, we do not believe data can be either saturated or exhausted. Data are always open to reinterpretation in the light of changing circumstances and different conceptual perspectives. Any finding also involves a covering up, since, in bringing to the fore key themes, others are placed to one side. Once again, this is for practical reasons but also, reflexively, we argue that this is inherent in sense-making processes. We follow Stronach and MacLure (1997) in recognising that every opening relies upon a closing and vice versa. In opening up our understandings, thereby producing a particular map of a landscape, we are closing other roads that we might have travelled. We would claim the recognition of this to be a methodological strength of this project. Our own sense-making of the project has changed over time and the understanding we offer in this book is that which we have arrived at for now. (See Mannion and Ivanič 2007 and Ivanič and Satchwell 2007 for further discussion of these methodological issues and consequent methods of data collection and analysis.)

Bibliography

Allwright, R. (2001) 'Three major processes of teacher development and the appropriate design criteria for developing and using them', in B. Johnston and S. Irujo (eds) *Research and Practice in Language Teacher Education: Voices from the Field*, Minneapolis, MN: CARLA Working Paper 19. Also (dated 1999) at www.ling.lancs.ac.uk/groups/crile/epcentre/readings/ep_reading_contents.htm.

Appadurai, A. (1990) 'Disjuncture and difference in the global cultural economy', in M. Featherstone (ed.) *Global Culture: Nationalism, Globalisation and Modernity*, London: Sage.

Ashton, S. (1994) 'The farmer needs a wife: farm women in Wales', in J. Aaron, T. Rees, S. Betts and M. Vincentelli (eds) *Our Sisters' Land*, Cardiff: University of Wales Press.

Baker, C. and Jones, M.P. (2000) 'Welsh language education: a strategy for language revitalization', in C. Williams (ed.) *Language Revitalization: Policy and Planning in Wales*, Cardiff: University of Wales Press.

Barton, D. (2000) 'Researching literacy practices: learning from activities with teachers and students', in D. Barton, M. Hamilton and R. Ivanič (eds) *Situated Literacies: Reading and Writing in Context*, London: Routledge.

Barton, D. (2001) 'Directions for literacy research: analysing language and social practices in a textually-mediated world', *Language and Education*, 15 (2): 92–104.

Barton, D. (2007) *Literacy: an Introduction to the Ecology of Written Language*, 2nd edn, Oxford: Blackwell.

Barton, D. and Hamilton, M. (1998) *Local Literacies: Reading and Writing in one Community*, London: Routledge.

Barton, D. and Hamilton, M. (2005) 'Literacy, Reification and the Dynamics of Social Interaction', in D. Barton and K. Tusting (eds) *Beyond Communities of Practice*, Cambridge: Cambridge University Press.

Barton, D., Hamilton, M. and Ivanič, R. (eds) (2000) *Situated Literacies: Reading and Writing in Context*, London: Routledge.

Baynham, M. (1995) *Literacy Practices: Investigating Literacy in Social Contexts*, London: Longman.

Beavis, C. (2002) 'Reading, writing and role-playing computer games', in I. Snyder (ed.) *Silicon Literacies: Communication, Innovation and Education in the Electronic Age*, London: Routledge.

Bloomer, M. (1997) *Curriculum Making in Post 16 Education*, London: Routledge.

Bourdieu, P. (1977) 'L'économie des échanges linguistiques', *Langue Française*, 34: 17–34.

Breen, M.P. (1985) 'Authenticity in the language classroom', *Applied Linguistics*, 6 (1): 60–70.

Britton, J. (1970) *Language and Learning: the Importance of Speech in Children's Development*, Harmondsworth: Penguin.

Burbules, N.C. (2002) 'The web as a rhetorical place', in Snyder, I. (ed.) *Silicon Literacies: Communication, Innovation and Education in the Electronic Age*, London: Routledge.

Chaiklin, S. and Lave, J. (eds) (1996) *Understanding Practice: Perspectives on Activity and Context*, Cambridge: Cambridge University Press.

Clark, R. and Ivanič, R. (1997) *The Politics of Writing*, London: Routledge.

Clarke, J. (2002) 'A new kind of symmetry: actor–network theories and the new literacy studies', *Studies in the Education of Adults*, 34 (2): 107–22.

Coffield, F., Steer, R., Hodgson, A., Spours, K., Edward, S. and Finlay, I. (2005) 'A new learning and skills landscape? The central role of the Learning and Skills Council', *Journal of Education Policy*, 20 (5): 631–56.

Colley, H., Hodkinson, P. and Malcolm, J. (2003) *Informality and Formality in Learning*, London: LSDA.

Cope, B. and Kalantzis, M. (2000) *Multiliteracies: Literacy Learning and the Design of Social Futures*, London: Routledge.

Edwards, R. (2002) 'Mobilizing lifelong learning: governmentality and educational practices', *Journal of Education Policy*, 17 (3): 353–65.

Edwards, R. (2003) 'Ordering subjects: actor-networks and intellectual technologies in lifelong learning', *Studies in the Education of Adults*, 35 (1): 54–67.

Edwards, R. (2007) 'It ain't (simply) what you know, it's the way you communicate it: curriculum knowledge and communication', in *What's Missing from C__riculum? Influencing Design and Delivery*, Stirling: SFEU.

Edwards, R. and Fowler, Z. (2007) 'Unsettling boundaries in making a space for research', *British Educational Research Journal*, 33 (1): 107–23.

Edwards, R. and Miller, K. (2008) 'Academic drift in vocational qualifications? Explorations through the lens of literacy', *Journal of Vocational Education and Training*, 60 (2): 123–31.

Edwards, R. and Smith, J. (2005) 'Swamping and spoonfeeding: literacies for learning in Further Education', *Journal of Vocational Education and Training*, 57 (1): 47–60.

Edwards, R., Biesta, G. and Thorpe, M. (eds) (2009) *Rethinking Contexts for Learning and Teaching: Communities, Activities and Networks*, London: Routledge.

Edwards, R., Nicoll, K., Solomon, N. and Usher, R. (2004) *Rhetoric in Educational Discourse*, London: Routledge.

Fawns, M. and Ivanič, R. (2001) 'Form-filling as a social practice: taking power into our own hands', in L.Tett, M. Hamilton and J. Crowther (eds) *Powerful Literacies*, Leicester: NIACE Publications.

Fforwm (2008) www.fforwm.ac.uk (accessed June 2008).

Fowler, Z. (2008) 'Negotiating the textuality of Further Education: Issues of agency and participation', *Oxford Review of Education,* 34 (4): 425–41.

Fowler, Z. and Edwards, R. (2005) 'Mobility and situatedness in literacy practices: the case of further education', paper presented at the British Educational Research Association Annual Conference, University of Glamorgan, September 2005. Available at Education-line: www.leeds.ac.uk/educol/documents/143407.doc (accessed February 2007).

Fowler, Z., Hodgson, A. and Spours, K. (2002) *Strategies for Balancing Learning and Earning: Student, Teacher and Employer Perspectives in the Context of Curriculum 2000,* London: University of London Institute of Education.

Fox, S. (2000) 'Communities of practice, Foucault and actor-network theory', *Journal of Management Studies,* 37 (6): 853–67.

Further Education Funding Council for Wales (FEFCW) (2000) *A Study of Welsh-Medium Provision in the FE Sector in Wales: Final Report.* Cardiff: FEFCW.

Gee, J.P. (1992) *The Social Mind: Language, Ideology, and Social Practice,* New York: Bergin and Garvey.

Gee, J.P. (2000) 'The New Literacy Studies: from "socially situated" to the work of the social', in D. Barton, M. Hamilton and R. Ivanič (eds) *Situated Literacies: Reading and Writing in Context,* London: Routledge.

Gee, J.P. (2003) *What Video Games Have to Teach Us About Learning and Literacy,* New York: Palgrave/Macmillan.

Gonzalez, N., Moll, L. and Amanti, C. (eds) (2004) *Funds of Knowledge: Theorizing Practices in Households and Classrooms,* Mahwah, NJ: Lawrence Erlbaum Associates Inc.

Goodman, R., Mannion, G. and Brzeski, A. (2007) 'Reading, writing and resonance: an experiential workshop for practitioners', *Research and Practice in Adult Literacy Journal,* 61 (Special issue for RAPAL Conference 2006): 10–14.

Green, J. and Bloome, D. (1997) 'Ethnography and ethnographers of and in education: A situated perspective', in J. Flood, S. Heath and D. Lapp (eds) *A Handbook of Research on Teaching Literacy through the Communicative and Visual Arts,* New York: Simon and Schuster Macmillan.

Greenfield, P.M. and Subrahmanyam, K. (2003) 'Online discourse in a teen chatroom: new codes and new modes of coherence in a visual medium', *Journal of Applied Developmental Psychology,* 24 (6): 713–38.

Hamilton, M. (2000) 'Expanding the New Literacy Studies: using photographs to explore literacy as a social practice', in D. Barton, M. Hamilton and R. Ivanič (eds) *Situated Literacies: Reading and Writing in Context,* London: Routledge.

Hamilton, M. (2001) 'Privileged literacies: policy, institutional process and the life of the IALS', *Language and Education,* 15 (2): 178–96.

Heath, R. (2001) 'Language, culture and markets in Further Education', unpublished Ph.D. dissertation, Cardiff University.

Heath, S.B. (1983) *Ways with Words: Language, Life and Work in Communities and Classrooms,* Cambridge: Cambridge University Press.

Hull, G. and Schultz, K. (eds) (2002) *School's Out: Bridging Out-of-School Literacies with Classroom Practice,* New York: Teachers College Press.

Hymes, D. (1962) 'The ethnography of communication', in T. Gladwin and

W. Sturtevant (eds) *Anthropology and Human Behavior*, Washington, DC: Anthropological Society of Washington.

Ivanič, R. (1998) *Writing and Identity: the Discoursal Construction of Identity in Academic Writing*, Amsterdam: John Benjamins.

Ivanič, R. (2004) 'Discourses of writing and learning to write', *Language and Education*, 18 (3): 220–45.

Ivanič, R. (2006) 'Language, learning and identification', in R. Kiely, P. Rea-Dickens, H. Woodfield and G. Clibbon (eds) *Language, Culture and Identity in Applied Linguistics*, London: Equinox.

Ivanič, R. (forthcoming) 'Bringing literacy studies into research on learning across the curriculum', in M. Baynham and M. Prinsloo (eds) *The Future of Literacy Studies*, London: Routledge.

Ivanič, R. and Satchwell, C. (2007) 'Boundary crossings: networking and transforming literacies in research processes and college courses', Special Issue of *The Journal of Applied Linguistics* on *New Directions in Academic Literacies Research*.

Ivanič, R., Edwards, R., Satchwell, C. and Smith, J. (2007) 'Possibilities for pedagogy in Further Education: harnessing the abundance of literacy', *British Educational Research Journal*, 33 (5): 703–21.

James, D. and Biesta, G. (2007) *Improving Learning Cultures in Further Education*, London: Routledge.

Jones, D.V. and Martin-Jones, M. (2004) 'Bilingual education and language revitalisation in Wales: past achievements and current issues', in J. Tollefson and A. Tsui (eds) *Medium of Instruction Policies*, Mahwah, NJ: Lawrence Erlbaum.

Jones, K. (2000) 'Becoming just another alphanumeric code: farmers' encounters with the literacy and discourse practices of agricultural bureaucracy at the livestock auction', in D. Barton, M. Hamilton and R. Ivanič (eds) *Situated Literacies: Reading and Writing in Context*, London: Routledge.

Keddie, N. (ed.) (1970) *Tinker, Tailor. . .: The Myth of Cultural Deprivation*, Harmondsworth: Penguin.

Kress, G. (2001) '"You've just got to learn how to see": curriculum subjects, young people and schooled engagement with the world', *Linguistics and Education*, 11 (4): 401–15.

Kress, G. (2003) *Literacy in the New Media Age*, London: Routledge.

Latour, B. (1986) 'The powers of association', in J. Law (ed.) *Power, Action and Belief: a New Sociology of Knowledge*, London: Routledge and Kegan Paul.

Latour, B. (1987*) Science in Action*, Cambridge, MA: Harvard University Press.

Latour, B. (1993) *We Have Never Been Modern*, London: Harvester Wheatsheaf.

Latour, B. (1999) *Pandora's Hope*, Cambridge, MA: Harvard University Press.

Lave, J. and Wenger, E. (1991) *Situated Learning*, Cambridge: Cambridge University Press.

Law, J. (1994) *Organising Modernity*, Oxford: Basil Blackwell.

Lea, M.R. and Nicoll, K. (eds) (2002) *Distributed Learning: Social and Cultural Approaches to Practice*, London: RoutledgeFalmer.

Lee, A. (1996) *Gender, Literacy, Curriculum: Rewriting School Geography*, London: Taylor & Francis.

Lemke, J. (1998) 'Multimedia literacy demands of the scientific curriculum', *Linguistics and Education,* 10 (3): 247–71.

Lillis, T. (2001) *Student Writing: Access, Regulation and Desire,* London: Routledge.

Low, B.E. (2005) '"Sayin' it a different way": adolescent literacies through the lens of cultural studies', in Street, B. (ed.) *Literacies Across Educational Contexts: Mediating Learning and Teaching,* Philadelphia: Caslon.

Luckin, R, Connolly, D., Plowman, L. and Airey, S. (2003) 'Children's interactions with interactive toy technology', *Journal of Computer Assisted Learning,* 19: 165–76.

Mahiri, J. (ed.) (2004) *What Kids Don't Learn in School: Literacy in the Lives of Urban Youth,* New York: Peter Lang.

Mannion, G. (2006) 'Viewpoint: "Striking a Chord"', *Broadcast,* 71: 40–1.

Mannion, G. and Miller, K. (forthcoming) 'Literacies for Learning in Further Education: promoting inclusive learning across boundaries through students' literacy practices', *Pedagogy, Culture and Society.*

Mannion, G. and Ivanič, R., (2007) 'Mapping literacy practices: theory, methodology, methods', *International Journal of Qualitative Studies in Education,* 20 (1): 15–30.

Martin-Jones, M., Hughes, B. and Williams, A. (2009) 'Bilingual literacy in and for working lives on the land: case studies of young Welsh speakers in North Wales', contribution to a thematic issue of the *International Journal of the Sociology of Language* on 'Welsh in Wales and its diaspora: social and subjective issues', (edited by N. Coupland and M. Aldridge): 39–62.

Mason, J. (2002) *Researching Your Own Practice: the Discipline of Noticing,* London: RoutledgeFalmer.

Miller, K. and Gaechter, J. (2006): 'Thinking about learning the curriculum in different ways', *Broadcast,* 72: 20–1.

Miller, K. and Satchwell, C. (2006) 'The effect of beliefs about literacy on teacher and student expectations: a Further Education perspective', *Journal of Vocational Education and Training,* 58 (2): 135–50.

Miller, K., Smith, J., Carmichael, J. and Edwards R. (2007) 'Researching literacy for learning in the vocational curriculum', in M. Osborne, M. Houston and N. Toman (eds) *The Pedagogy of Lifelong Learning: Understanding Effective Teaching and Learning in Diverse Contexts,* London: Routledge.

Nespor, J. (1994) *Knowledge in Motion,* London: Falmer.

Nespor, J. (2003) 'Undergraduate curricula as networks and trajectories', in R. Edwards and R. Usher (eds) *Space, Curriculum and Learning,* Greenwich: IAP.

New London Group, The (1996) 'A pedagogy of multiliteracies: designing social futures', *Harvard Educational Review,* 66 (1): 60–92.

Pahl, K. and Rowsell, J. (2005) *Literacy and Education: the New Literacy Studies in the Classroom,* London: Paul Chapman.

Pardoe, S. and Ivanič, R. (2007) *Literacies for Learning in Further Education: Making Reading and Writing Practices Across the Curriculum More Useful for Learning,* DVD and accompanying booklet, Lancaster: PublicSpace Ltd and Lancaster University.

Phillips, D. (2000) 'The history of the Welsh Language Society 1962–1988', in

G. Jenkins and M. Williams (eds) *Let's Do Our Best For The Ancient Tongue: the Welsh Language in the Twentieth Century,* Cardiff: University of Wales Press.

QCA (2004). Key Skills Standards and Guidance: Communication Level 3 www.qca. org.uk/libraryAssets/media/6341_com_level3.pdf.

Russell, D. (1991) *Writing in the Academic Disciplines: a Curricular History,* Carbondale, IL: Southern Illinois University Press.

Russell, D. (2009) 'Texts in context: theorizing learning by looking at genre and activity', in R. Edwards, G. Biesta and M. Thorpe (eds) *Rethinking Contexts for Learning and Teaching: Communities, Activities and Networks,* London: Routledge.

Satchwell, C. (2006) 'Literacy around the clock: an examination of the clock activity', in J. Caldwell, P. Cleary, B. Crossan, R. Edwards, J. Gallacher, P. Gray, K. MacFarlane, K. McGavock, T. Mayes, D. Miller, M. Osborne, R. Remedios, J. Smith and N. Toman (eds) *What a Difference a Pedagogy Makes: Researching Lifelong Learning and Teaching. Proceedings of 3rd International CRLL Conference* (2005), Glasgow: Centre for Research in Lifelong Learning.

Satchwell, C. and Ivanič, R. (2007) 'The textuality of learning contexts in UK colleges', *Pedagogy, Culture and Society,* 15 (3 Special Issue on *Contexts, Networks and Communities*): 303–16.

Satchwell, C. and Ivanič, R. (2009) 'The textual mediation of learning in Further Education', in R. Edwards, G. Biesta and M. Thorpe (eds) *Rethinking Contexts for Learning and Teaching: Communities, Activities and Networks,* London: Routledge.

Satchwell, C. and Ivanič, R. (forthcoming) 'Reading and writing the self as a college student: fluidity and ambivalence across contexts', in K. Ecclestone, G. Biesta and M. Hughes (eds) *Lost in Transition? Change and Becoming Through the Lifecourse,* London: Routledge.

Smith, D. (1990) *Texts, Facts, and Femininity: Exploring the Relations of Ruling,* New York: Routledge.

Smith, J. (2004) 'Furthering literacies: a study of literacy practices in Further Education', unpublished MSc. dissertation, University of Stirling.

Smith, J. (2005a) 'Further education and the literacy debate – a Scottish perspective', *Scottish Educational Review,* 37 (2): 153–62.

Smith, J. (2005b) 'Mobilising everyday literacy practices within the Curricula', *Journal of Vocational Education and Training,* 57 (3): 319–34.

Smith, J. (2006) 'Students' everyday literacy passions (practices) and those required for study within the FE curriculum', in J. Caldwell, P. Cleary, B. Crossan, R. Edwards, J. Gallacher, P. Gray, K. MacFarlane, K. McGavock, T. Mayes, D. Miller, M. Osborne, R. Remedios, J. Smith and N. Toman (eds) *What a Difference a Pedagogy Makes: Researching Lifelong Learning and Teaching. Proceedings of 3rd International CRLL Conference* (2005), Glasgow: Centre for Research in Lifelong Learning.

Smith, J. and Edwards, R. (2004) 'Telling tales of literacy', in *SCUTREA Proceedings. Whose Story now? (RE)generating Research in Adult Learning and Teaching,* University of Exeter. Available at *Education-line*: www.leeds.ac.uk/educol/documents/00003606.doc (accessed February 2007).

Star, S.L. (1989) 'The structure of ill-structured solutions: boundary objects and heterogeneous distributed problem solving', in L. Gasser and M. Huhns (eds) *Distributed Artificial Intelligence,* vol. I, London: Pitman.

Street, B. and Lefstein, A. (2007) *Literacy: an Advanced Resource Book for Students*, London: Routledge.

Stronach, I. and MacLure, M. (1997) *Educational Research Undone: the Postmodern Embrace*, Buckingham: Open University Press.

Torrance, H., Colley, H., Ecclestone, K., Garratt, D., James, D., Jarvis, J. and Piper, H. (2005) *The Impact of Different Modes of Assessment on Achievement and Progress in the Learning and Skills Sector*, London: LSDA.

Tuomi-Gröhn, T. and Engeström, Y. (eds) (2003) *Between Work and School: New Perspectives on Transfer and Boundary-Crossing*, Amsterdam: Pergamon.

van Leeuwen, T. (1993) 'Genre and field in Critical Discourse Analysis: a synopsis', *Discourse and Society*, 4 (2): 193–223.

van Leeuwen, T. (1995) 'Representing social action', *Discourse and Society*, 6 (1): 81–106.

van Leeuwen, T. (1996) 'The representation of social actors', in C.R. Caldas-Coulthard and M. Coulthard (eds) *Texts and Practices: Readings in Critical Discourse Analysis,* London: Routledge.

Vygotsky, L.S. (1934) *Thought and Language,* Cambridge, MA: MIT Press.

Welsh Assembly Government (WAG) (2002) *Dyfodol Dwyieithog/Bilingual Future,* Cardiff: WAG.

Welsh Assembly Government (WAG) (2003) *Iaith Pawb/Everyone's Language,* Cardiff: WAG.

Welsh Assembly Government (WAG) (2007a) *Schools in Wales: General Statistics, 2006,* Cardiff: Welsh Assembly Government. Online (accessed July 2008).

Welsh Assembly Government (WAG) (2007b) *Welsh in Schools.* Cardiff: Welsh Assembly Government. Online (accessed July 2008).

Wenger, E. (1998) *Communities of Practice: Learning, Meaning and Identity,* Cambridge: Cambridge University Press.

Williams, C. (2000) 'Bilingual teaching and language distribution at 16+: Welsh-medium and bilingual teaching in the Further Education sector', *International Journal of Bilingual Education and Bilingualism,* 3 (2): 129–48.

Williams, G. and Morris, D. (2000) *Language Planning and Language Use: Welsh in a Global Age,* Cardiff: University of Wales Press.

Wyatt-Smith, C. and Cumming, J. (2003) 'Curriculum literacies: expanding domains of assessment', *Assessment in Education,* 10 (1): 47–59.

Index

Literacies for Learning in Further Education

Film and booklet
by Simon Pardoe and Roz Ivanič

This film communicates visually some of the core ideas and research findings described in this book. It offers an introduction to considering reading and writing as social and professional practices rather than just 'basic skills'.

Based on engaging interviews with the authors and some of the college lecturers who participated in the LfLFE research (England and Scotland), the film is designed for a wide audience of vocational and subject lecturers and others concerned with education across the college curriculum.

> ## Warning
> This film contains language and images which may change your understanding of reading and writing in life, work and study.

The film develops and explains the framework for understanding literacy practices that is reproduced on p. 50 of this book. It is explained visually and through examples of reading and writing in life and work. It is then used to analyse the small but significant changes made by two of the participating lecturers to the reading and writing on their courses.

A colour booklet offers a summary of the film, notes on issues of 'skills' and 'literacy practices', prompts for discussions in teacher education, and a usefully annotated version of the framework to copy and use in curriculum review.

Produced by PublicSpace Ltd. Research Communication in collaboration with the LfLFE research team. The film was one of the two outputs of the research (England and Scotland) submitted to the funding body, the ESRC TLRP.

Available from: www.publicspace.org.uk

'dynamic, engaging and innovative'
Professor Andrew Pollard, Director, ESRC Teaching and Learning Research Programme

'It is a joy to see FE lecturers doing the research . . . that may well change the way in which vocational subjects are taught in the future.'
Christine Tyler, Association of School and College Leaders; former Principal of Eccles College

'I was surprised at how I couldn't stop watching it and how engaging it is . . . as an explanation of social practice.'
David Barton, Professor of Language and Literacy, Lancaster University

'The design, layout and text is super. . . . will be so useful for teacher training.'
Ian Gibb, Lecturer, Perth College of Further Education

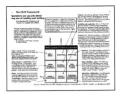

DVD: 47mins; SD PAL 4:3
Booklet: 38pp 48 images.
ISBN 978-1-86220-200-9
© Lancaster University 2007